Implementation of Strategic Planning

Peter Lorange
University of Pennsylvania

PRENTICE HALL, INC., Englewood Cliffs, NJ 07632

Library of Congress Cataloging in Publication Data
Main entry under title:

Implementation of Strategic Planning.

  Based on papers presented at a workshop held during the twenty-fourth international
meeting of the Institute of Management Sciences, June 18-23, 1979, Honolulu, Hawaii.

  Includes bibliographical references and index.
  1. Corporate planning—Congresses. I. Lorange, Peter.
HD30.28.I46   658.4'012   81-5854
ISBN 0-13-451815-2   AACR2

Editorial/production supervision and
   interior design by Richard C. Laveglia
Cover design by Jerry Pfeifer
Manufacturing buyer: Ed O'Dougherty

Printed in the United States of America

10   9   8   7   6   5   4   3   2

Prentice-Hall International, Inc., *London*
Prentice-Hall of Australia Pty. Limited, *Sydney*
Prentice-Hall of Canada, Ltd., *Toronto*
Prentice-Hall of India Private Limited, *New Delhi*
Prentice-Hall of Japan, Inc., *Tokyo*
Prentice-Hall of Southeast Asia Pte. Ltd., *Singapore*
Whitehall Books Limited, *Wellington, New Zealand*

Contents

iii

Preface

Considerable attention has been given to strategic planning over the last few decades. This is evidenced by the fact that many corporate managements believe in the planning approach and have been willing to put considerable resources behind this belief. As for all techniques and approaches, however, its effectiveness is normally not higher than that of its weakest element. Today the implementation tasks of strategic planning might be seen as the weakest links, whereas the conceptualization aspects seem to be better developed. In this regard, this book provides a broadly based discussion of strategic planning implementation issues developed by leading practitioners and academicians.

Although the general need for a systematic discussion of strategic planning implementation issues is founded on the beliefs expressed in the previous paragraph, a specific, practical impetus to this book came from a workshop held under the auspices of The Institute of Management Sciences at the XXIV International Meeting in Honolulu, Hawaii, on June 18–23, 1979. This editor chaired a workshop entitled "Strategic Planning: The State of the Art of Implementation." Initial versions of the chapters in this book were presented at this workshop. Significant progress was made in clarifying implementation issues and challenges through discussions with the chapter authors and contributions from a widely diversified audience of interested and knowledgeable individuals.

Thanks for making the publication of this book possible should go particularly to the authors who provided the chapters and contributed to the success of the Hawaii meeting. Melvin Shakun and Ambar Rao created a slot for strategic planning implementation within the broader, overall program activities of the Hawaii meeting. Theodore Jursek encouraged the idea of developing a book on the issue from early on. Pascal F. Tone provided superb and invaluable assistance with the editing and in keeping the project on track. My secretaries, Christine Hardiman and Eva Ferrari, did their usual impeccable jobs. Although the book has benefited greatly from all this help, the caveat must be added, however, that any shortcomings and errors that may have occurred in connection with the editing of this work are mine alone.

Peter Lorange

section one

Introduction

chapter one: The Task of Implementing Strategic Planning: An Overview and Introduction to the Book.

1

The Task of Implementing Strategic Planning: An Overview and Introduction to the Book

INTRODUCTION

Over the last few decades, considerable progress has been made in the development and use of strategic planning (corporate planning, long range planning) as a management tool. One indication of this development is corporations' current heavy emphasis on planning as a part of managing and searching for better ways of doing this job. Other indications are the proliferation of consulting services offered in this area, research efforts centered on planning within the academic community, and the emergence of an abundance of courses and seminars offered on planning. Despite our increased understanding of strategic planning, however, the issue of effective implementation remains critical. This is, of course, the key to achieving a satisfactory cost–benefit relationship when it comes to one's planning efforts.

This chapter* is designed to provide an overview of the key implementational issues in strategic planning. Given the evolution of the development of the state of the art of planning, one should always attempt to delineate the new, emerging implementational issues. With the emergence of today's turbulent environment, larger economic uncertainty and probably less stable growth, it

---

*This chapter is prepared by Peter Lorange, The Wharton School, University of Pennsylvania.

seems particularly important to reassess one's strategic planning implementational issues. Only then can the planning tool facilitate a corporation's handling of its more difficult and challenging strategic setting. The promise that the tool of planning has been making thus far, as an increasingly useful and indispensable decision-making vehicle, can only be proven by being able to handle the emerging implementational issues.

The following sections of this chapter present an overview of the major implementation issues related to strategic planning systems, as perceived by this author, from three points of view:

1. the major evolutionary steps of corporate planning, which will delineate the changes in the state of the art of planning and thereby provide an index for the changes in implementation focus,
2. the common body of knowledge of implementation of new managerial techniques and processes in general, which will delineate a set of critical elements of organizational acceptance of planning, based on experiences short of actually introducing planning, and
3. the key implementation issues for planning when this process is seen as part of a broader management process for the corporation as a whole.

The chapter concludes with a look at the structure of the book, outlining how its contents addresses the planning implementation issues raised in this introduction.

EVOLUTION OF STRATEGIC PLANNING: CHANGING IMPLEMENTATIONAL FOCUS

The three major evolutionary stages of strategic planning are labeled "extrapolative planning," "business planning," and "portfolio planning." We shall find this broad delineation useful in highlighting some of the major changes in planning and its corresponding shifts in implementation challenges.[1]

"Extrapolative planning" is generally seen as an outgrowth of the economic environment in the 1960s, which was characterized by generally stable, relatively rapid growth. At that time, planning focused on the constraints on a corporation's ability to pursue various growth opportunities. Usually these constraints were seen as financial, namely, how much funding might be available through internal resource generation and/or borrowing to achieve a specified high rate of growth. The execution of this type of planning activity was often built around the well-known discipline of preparing a budget. No wonder, then, that the strong evolutionary and task similarity with budgeting tended to influence this kind of planning, so as to make it highly extrapolative and heavily numbers oriented; hence, the extrapolative planning label we have given this type of planning.

Above all, until recently extrapolative planning tended to be one of bottom–up initiative, with primary responsibility for planning given to the various departments and divisions. These departmental estimates were then more or less mechanically consolidated, often via a relatively large corporate planning department staff. A true top–down/bottom–up dialogue, with inputs from senior line executives, was rare; instead, what little top–down feedback there was often came in the form of reactions from the corporate planning department. This often led to animosity between business line executives and the corporate planning staff. Moreover, because of its routineness and low involvement of corporate management, this type of planning lacked true decision orientation. It did, however, more or less explicitly emphasize some of the critical environmental constraints, thereby reflecting the limits to a firm's growth due to its own strategic resource availability.

It seems clear that extrapolative planning should no longer play a major role in its original form. However, realistic constraint identification should still be an aspect of all good planning practices. In a particular business, this would apply to dealing with such issues as competitors' moves, customer preference changes, new product innovations, and so on. It would also apply to the corporate level, dealing with such portfolio issues as the external financing climate, political risks, and sociopolitical changes with respect to business versus government, business versus labor, and other outsiders' relationships. The questions of who should scan and how this scanning actually might fit into the decision-making process is still a major challenge.[2]

The competitive climate for many businesses seemed to shift during the late 1960s and early 1970s due in part to increasing instability in patterns of social norms, changes in customer tastes and demands, new technological innovations, entries from foreign competition, new initiatives from old competitors, and so on. Many corporations experienced increasing uneasiness with the extrapolative, constraints-oriented, financially dominated planning activities; that is, it was often felt that this method of planning put too little emphasis on the specifics of a business's competitive setting and how the business could better position itself within this setting. As a response, a shift in the direction of planning emerged that might be labeled "business planning." This type of planning attempted to focus more closely on a better understanding of the properties of a firm's product and/or service in terms of its attractiveness as well as on the firm's own competitive strengths. In attempting to position its specific competitive setting, a firm might then develop plans for repositioning a product, if desired.

The planning process was often still bottom–up, with most actual planning done at the business level and corporate consolidation done without much de facto top–down feedback. Planning staffs were frequently much smaller than were those during the extrapolative planning heydays, and they often tended to act as catalysts. The approach, however, tended to become too focused on each business segment, without sufficiently pursuing the overall relationship among businesses. Another problem was the frequent difficulty in gaining organizational acceptance for its decision-making outcomes, particularly when this implied the "milking" of a business for its eventual shutdown. Despite these shortcomings, business planning added momentum to the overall strategic planning process by restoring the view that a firm needed to look at its competitive environment to develop a strategic plan.[3]

From the preceding discussion, we can deduce several challenges to business planning implementation. One deals with facilitating even better, tailor-made nonextrapolative business planning. This requires an open-ended reassessing of the opportunities in and threats to one's environment and then matching these to the strengths and weaknesses. In practice, however, the quality of business opportunity reassessment might be too low. The potential routine effect of having to replan every year might lead to a deterioration of business assessment over time, so that it could become a quick update of last year's assessment. The maintenance of vitality and creativity in planning thus seems to be a major implementation issue, because the entire process might degenerate unless high-quality inputs are injected continuously.

A second business planning implementation issue is the enhancing of a better linking of strategic programs to budgets. The goal is that each manager has more explicit, umambiguous responsibility for his or her part of the implementation of plans. This frequently requires a strengthening of cross-functional cooperation among operating groups in delineating the roles to be played by each in the strategic programs as well as the assessment of the resulting resource requirement on each group. This comes on top of the functions' operating roles. Thus, we might see an earmarking of strategic resource components as distinct from operating components, thereby ensuring that resources are set aside to actually implement the plans. Too often, time might pass with little de facto implementation of strategies as near-term pressures would tend to require almost all the resources and attention of management.[4]

The third stage of planning's evolution, "portfolio planning," stems primarily from further rising global instability. This has created a stronger need to see the various business positionings within a total corporate context, so as to assess the firm's overall exposure to risks. Emphasis is thus placed on an overall corporate or portfolio strategic resource balance, in terms of where the resources should be allocated and where they should come from. Further, strategic resources are often seen in a broader light than simply financial terms. They also include human resource considerations and technological and marketing expertise. It should also be stressed that a portfolio planning stage can only be reached by building a successful program based on sound business planning.[5]

The planning process may now have a more balanced, top–down/bottom–up emphasis, with the various business viewpoints being consolidated into the total corporate picture and each business receiving feedback contingent on its own fit within this portfolio. Both corporate and divisional levels can now bring important inputs to the process. There is a clear division of labor and a clear "value added" of each role. A frequent weakness, however, stems from the fact that the corporate level is not sufficiently able to play an explicit role in resource allocation decisions. Thus, corporate portfolio planning might degenerate into not much more than "adding" the various business inputs without reflecting sufficient priority setting among the businesses from an overall corporate point of view.

Several important portfolio planning implementation issues remain. One deals with improving the corporate-level mode of reviewing the inputs from the various businesses. It seems important that this mode of review is consistent with the requirements implicit in formulating a portfolio strategy, so that an overall picture of the fit among the business inputs can be developed in terms of resource generation versus utilization properties. Modifications of a particular business plan should also only be done within the context of its fit within the overall portfolio. This implies that no business planning input is "good" or "bad" per se. Instead, the issue is its fit (or lack thereof) within the overall portfolio. Thus, while one business might serve a useful role as part of one company's portfolio, it may not fit at all in another company's portfolio and might hence be a candidate for divestiture. To move from an incremental style of dealing with each business and toward an overall portfolio approach seems to be a key implementation challenge to many firms.

Another frequent challenge is to develop an improved monitoring and control system to ensure that signals of deviation are being analyzed and reacted to in a portfolio sense. For instance, a decline in expected cash flow from one business should not necessarily be seen as an isolated business problem but, rather, should be handled in terms of the resulting effect on the overall portfolio. It may or may not be necessary to modify other businesses' plans.

The task of maintaining an explicit overview of one's strategic resources seems to represent a continuous challenge for many companies. This applies not only to funds generation and utilization patterns but also to managerial resource imbalances and the body of technological and marketing know-how resources, as well as the developments in improving these. An implementation need for many companies is to manage the maintenance of these strategic resources, emphasizing that long-term success depends on the regeneration of all classes of resources, not only funds.

In terms of major implementation challenges emerging from our brief discussion of what broadly seem to be three major evolutionary stages of planning, let us summarize these as follows:

1. More effective implementation of corporatewide portfolio planning, implying a better ability to delineate how to get a more effective top–down/bottom–up communication process, how to strengthen a resource allocation decision-making emphasis that restores a stronger top–down corporate role, how to handle more realistically external and internal constraints on portfolio strategy changes, and so on.

2. Development of a better set of business plans, further emphasizing how to increase organizational acceptance of business plans, how to delineate a more focused strategic planning structure and to incorporate this with the more conventional operating structure, and so on.

3. The inheritance from extrapolative planning of understanding relevant constraints is still critical, be it external, such as competitive, sociopolitical, governmental, and so on, or internal, such as changing norms in attitudes toward growth, for example. Know-how constraints, technological as well as marketing based, also seem to become increasingly important.

Thus, we see an array of implementation issues, from extrapolative to business to overall corporate portfolio planning. Even though we have made important advances in each type of planning, important tasks remain. This "frontier" of implementational issues will of course continue to change as we build on our understanding of how to handle them effectively. However, we can always expect that new issues will emerge as time goes on.

LESSONS FOR EFFECTIVE IMPLEMENTATIONS

The subject of how to enhance the more successful implementations has been given much attention from practitioners and researchers alike for some time now. Thus, a relatively large body of knowledge is available on the implementation process in general. While most of these implementation challenges are necessarily quite different, several important conclusions can be drawn from within our own business settings. In this section we shall discuss nine such requirements for effective corporate planning implementation. Then we shall consider a set of implementational experiences that arise when we make use of outside resources, such as consultants, in enhancing planning.[6]

The first implementation challenge states that the benefits from adopting planning must be clear to the various "users." They must be able to understand explicitly what the answers are to such questions as, "What's in it for me?," "Why should we do this?," "Does this lead to a better decision-making process?," and so on.

For a division manager, the implementation process should emphasize possible answers to these questions as seen from his or her point of view. Useful planning should at least be able to provide some tentative indications that one is establishing a more legitimized vehicle for communication between divisions and corporate headquarters as well as for facilitating feedback to the division. A related benefit would be the delineation of a more explicit role for each business within an overall corporate portfolio. This might also imply an "earmarked" resource allocation to strategic tasks and operating tasks for each division, allowing them to pursue their specific opportunities. Also, a good planning process might open up a more flexible approach to management control emphasizing short as well as long-term performance. This may also allow for incentives to encourage a more balanced longer-term versus shorter-term performance mix basis. In total, an implementation issue is the creation of a planning framework that makes the perceived overall climate "more fun," that is, it engenders a professional management atmosphere.

For planning to be implementable, there must also be potential benefits from planning for the chief executive. The CEO might perceive planning as a means by which to undertake more explicit allocation and control of a firm's strategic resources. In fact, a CEO might end up seeing this as his or her only realistic opportunity to significantly affect the direction of a large and complex organization. If the CEO, as an alternative, attempts to impact the organization by involving himself or herself in the myriad of specific business decisions, he or she is likely to end up being spread "all over the map," thereby having little overall impact. In contrast, the planning process might give the CEO the means by which to impact the organization by putting on pressures, changing focus, and advancing and retracting in a much more uniform and cohesive manner.[7]

A second element of realistic implementation deals with explaining the concept in such a way that the relevant managers can understand it. This fairly broad issue might usefully be broken down as follows:

1. Have we been able to explain clearly the overall logic of the planning process to the various managers involved? Is a manager able to understand what he or she is supposed to do, thereby maintaining ambiguity at a reasonably tolerable level?

2. Is the division of tasks for doing planning sufficiently delineated among managers so that it is relatively clear who should do what? That is, who initiates planning? Who carries out the various steps? Who participates in the review? Who attempts to consolidate various subplans? Who gives feedback to whom?

3. Is the sequence of the various activities relatively clear? Can the planning approach point to when various activities are to take place (i.e., relatively explicit timing)?

In total, communicability in design implementation means developing time schedules, agendas for meetings, delineation of tasks and meeting attendances, and carefully planned and explained formats. An ad hoc, organically evolving process probably has less chance of becoming implemented effectively.[8]

A third aspect of planning for successful implementation deals with the extent to which the relatively complex overall planning task can be broken down into smaller elements. For instance, to what extent is the process divided among relatively self-contained stages, say, the setting of direction (objectives setting) as distinguished from strategic programming? A second example of this divisibility comes to one's approaching the control activity. Here it might be fruitful to monitor strategic progress separately from near-term budgetary process. If mixed, there is a danger that none of the monitoring tasks will receive sufficient attention.

It should be underscored, however, that divisibility should never be carried out to the extreme that one loses the broader picture. For instance, when it comes to assessing a division's performance, one cannot make a judgment on this by examining short-term profit results without also assessing whether the division has made satisfactory progress on its strategic programs as well as whether the business's strategic position has changed in a positive or negative direction (say, by building up or losing market share).

Another often critical implementation task is identification of what might be appropriate units of analysis in the planning process, that is, how do we come up with businesses that lend themselves to be planned for and managed in a strategic manner? Several sets of implementation issues might be brought to bear on how to divide the firm into a useful set of units of planning analysis:[9]

1. How can a potential planning unit be identified vis-à-vis its environment in such terms, for example, as distinctive growth rate, customers, market share, and quality advantages? If these questions cannot be answered with confidence, a further breakdown might be necessary.

2. Is a business unit of sufficient size and/or potential to merit management's spending its time and other resources on it? It is important not to segment into

such small business elements that they cannot be managed economically, say, by having at least a part-time manager assigned to them.

A fourth requirement for successful implementation seems to be the degree to which the proposed innovation breaks with past experience and tradition. For instance, a company should probably have had some experience with extrapolative planning before it attempts business planning and/or corporate portfolio planning. In addition, budget development and budgetary control are also probably both important bases of experiences in laying the ground for planning as well as for more strategically directed control.

In general, successful implementation generally occurs as a natural evolution of experience and understanding. Conversely, starting more or less from zero with elaborate, extensive new schemes and no benefit of established approaches, systems, and processes is less likely to succeed. Evolution, not quantum leaps, seems to be an important lesson for the implementation of planning.

As a fifth requirement, there should be a well-defined, readily identifiable sponsor for the implementation task in question; that is, it should be clear who is behind strategic planning. In fact, top management will probably be the only truly realistic sponsor for a corporate planning activity.

A related requirement is that the need should be clearly felt by the client. Top management must see the benefit of a better specified strategic planning system, as, for example, how corporate planning might facilitate a more explicit trade-off between emphasis on today's operational concerns versus "investments" to build up future positions.

A seventh requirement is that planning must be able to demonstrate some results relatively quickly. We should be careful to avoid too much background analysis and preparation to "get ready for planning," but instead attempt to actually *do* planning as early as possible. However, as an initial effort, aspirations should not be set too high.

An eighth implementation experience involves getting an early commitment by the user. This requires the endorsement of general line management vis-à-vis corporate management as well as the functional managers reporting to them. As is true for all new activities, planning needs to "force its way" into the agendas of managers so as to become part of their work habits. This kind of commitment is necessary and will have to be built up relatively early to make planning work. Conversely, if it is seen as a nonessential activity, planning most likely will be given "lip service."

A final requirement for successful implementation deals with the realistic assessment of resource needs. The firm must be willing to allocate the necessary resources, make the necessary staff support available, provide the necessary budgets for training, meetings, and so on. The time required by line managers is substantial and "has to come from somewhere." Implementational experiences indicate that corporations often underestimate their resource requirements. Thus it is crucial that the chief executive officer and his or her closest line associates adhere to realism in this matter.

The preceding general characteristics of successful implementation and their implications for planning systems design are just a few; the list could definitely be extended. However, the examples do indicate the types of challenges faced when designing realistic approaches to strategic planning; this, then, sets the groundwork for more realistic pursuance of implementation.

The discussion so far has emphasized some fairly common "do's" and "don'ts." However, we should also examine the roles of outside consultants and change agents in the strategic planning implementation process. That is, how might the way in which executives interact to achieve a consensus on the direction of the organization be impacted by outside agents?

Generally, a corporate plan is best achieved by internal decision making. It therefore seems as if the most useful role of an outside consultant should be as a catalyst to help the organization improve its own planning. The role of an outside consultant to actually develop and/or execute plans probably tends to have much less de facto value, despite the fact that it is not uncommon in practice.[10]

In elaborating the usefulness of a consultant in planning process implementation, let us build on an extensive body of knowledge based on planned change within organizations. Planned change is usually depicted as having three major stages: unfreezing, moving to institute the change, and refreezing.[11] This general framework may be developed further to, say, a total of seven stages. These stages are outlined in Exhibit 1-1. Let us now discuss this seven-step model within the context of the implementation of the strategic planning process.[12]

Scouting. This step often involves the determination with senior management of the purpose of strategic planning as well as the firm's needs for planning. Senior management should be encouraged to expand its understanding of what issues are at stake in planning, for example, by specifying priorities for the utilization of strategic resources. Also, senior management should have realistic expectations of how a planning process might meet the firm's needs. Inadequate attention to this implementation step might cause lack of realism to become a problem at later stages.

Entry. This stage is characterized by meetings with each of the various business managers and senior corporate line managers to discuss the business strategic settings as seen by each manager, thereby getting a feel for the overall portfolio setting. Existing processes and systems should also be discussed to see how the line managers view the functioning of these, be it the control process, the budgeting process, or the appropriateness of the present organizational structure. The entry stage is designed to develop a picture of the strategic settings, and any deficiencies that may exist in the present systems in terms of serving the strategic needs. This implementation challenge, however straightforward, might nevertheless be difficult to execute well.

Diagnosis. This step consists of formalizing the fact gathering from the entry stage to diagnose the strategic needs of each business as well as to determine overall portfolio strategic needs. Operationalizing the strategic requirements of

EXHIBIT 1-1

A Model for a Consultant's Intervention Process
in an Organization (from Kolb and Frohman)

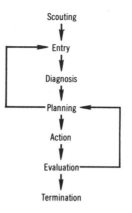

Scouting

Entry

Diagnosis

Planning

Action

Evaluation

Termination

each business should be expressed in terms of adaptive and integrative needs (i.e., the emphasis on pursuing relatively rapidly changing new business and growth opportunities versus the emphasis on strengthening the firm's internal efficiency measures).[13] A business that is just starting up, for instance, will generally have relatively high adaptive needs and relatively low integrative needs. Conversely, a mature business will tend to have relatively high integrative needs and low adaptive needs.

In terms of overall corporate portfolio strategy needs, diagnosis represents an assessment of the imbalances in the overall portfolio as well as an attempt to ameliorate these imbalances. One set of imbalances might stem from funds flow shortages or excesses. This might require a short-term integrative or a longer-term adaptive response. Another set of imbalances might relate to the mix of businesses, the risks, and/or the human and/or technological resources that are out of balance. This typically requires a longer-term adaptive repositioning of the over-all corporate business mix. Carrying out a good diagnosis continues to be a major part of planning implementation.

"Planning." This design task consists of such steps as developing a planning manual tailored to various businesses' needs, a planning calendar with firm time schedules, a set of agendas for planning review meetings, a realignment of the control process so as to monitor not only short-term but also strategic position changes, and a reassessment of the organizational implications so as to facilitate more appropriate organizational designs for each business given its strategic needs (for instance, a more autonomous project organization for a start-up business versus an efficiency-driven functional organization for a mature business).[14] A

second aspect of this stage might be to conduct workshops or discussion meetings with the line executives involved to induce self-analysis among these executives, the purpose being to develop a sense of agreement regarding their needs for planning as well as for the capabilities designed into the planning process. Unless a clear consensus emerges regarding needs and capabilities, the process may have to be restarted again by a second entry move. However, repeated restarts often cause strain and eventually lower the organization's tolerance for positively contributing to the implementation of the planning process.

Action. This step consists of the actual hands-on institution of the first round of planning among line managers. It is critical here that the line managers themselves, not the consultant, carry out the planning. However, the process consultant should be available for explanations and clarifications of the steps involved. Particularly, it seems important that the process consultant reiterate the criteria for the various decision-making meetings that will have to be held. For instance, at the corporate level the criteria for corporate portfolio analysis may have to be restated so that the top executives follow these without getting side-tracked.

Evaluation. This step, to be carried out *after* the first round of planning is completed, involves solicitation of the *users'* viewpoints. Each business manager should provide feedback regarding what he or she sees as valuable versus less valuable and what he or she considers to be useful steps of improvement. Similar information should be solicited from the corporate management but within the context of portfolio planning. The evaluation should then address the ways in which the design of the planning process might be modified to meet those perceived needs.

Termination. This step is surprisingly critical in two respects. First, by seeing an implementation task as having clear termination, both the process consultant as well as the organization will more likely be sensing the need to push for relatively rapid progress. Thus, the necessary and healthy accelerator built into the process moves it toward a useful closure. Second, the process consultant attempts to build up the role and competence of the corporate planner to allow him or her to gradually assume the process consultant's role as catalyst. Because no planning process will ever be completely finished, it will have to be managed so that the capabilities of the process meet the firm's changing strategic needs. An articulated set of steps, a "plan for planning," will have to be followed each year by the corporate planner. Although on a less dramatic scale than for the initial implementation, the planner will recurrently face the challenges of unfreezing, moving, and refreezing.[15]

The sequence of implementation steps just discussed seems to resemble Quinn's process of "logical incrementalism."[16] In a firm's goal-setting process, he points out the following set of stages:

sensing needs
building awareness

broadening support
creating pockets of commitment
crystallizing a developing focus
obtaining a real commitment

In any event, although it is helpful to delineate a set of steps and to attempt to develop further insight into critical issues of each step, we should be prepared to expect that the real-life evolution of implementation of planning systems and processes tends to be iterative and never ending rather than linear and finite.

To systematize our experiences regarding the introduction of planning within the context of its being a process of organizational change seems useful; however, many implementational issues remain regarding successful mastery of such massive organizational intervention processes as is represented by an introduction or major revamping of a strategic planning process.

STRATEGIC PLANNING AS PART OF A
CORPORATION'S MANAGEMENT PROCESS

Thus far we have discussed implementation of strategic planning from two angles: as a function of the evolving "frontier of knowledge" with regard to approaches to strategic planning processes and in terms of what seems to emerge as major remaining implementational issues after systematically reexamining our experiences regarding implementation "pitfalls," "start-ups," and evolution. We shall, however, need to address the planning implementation issue from a third angle, namely, the systemic issues that might arise within the firm that would impact its management systems and internal management style. We often deal with relatively "soft," although typically not insignificant, implementation issues. To remain relatively specific in our discussion, we shall relate these issues to various disciplinary bases: to systems theory, to organizational theory, and to the contingency theory of process design.

Let us first discuss some implementational issues that emerge when the strategic planning process is seen as an element of an overall comprehensive set of management systems. This calls for a management philosophy that sees the planning task as the epitome of a "whole system." The various strategic issues should be seen in total, as part of an overall strategy, not on a more incremental basis. Thus, a comprehensive management style that is more or less coincidental to the portfolio point of view seems critical.

Second, the process should be seen as part of an "open system"; the corporation is merely one element in an overall societal setting. This requires the planning process to help facilitate the positioning of the corporation within the larger societal system. Thus, strategic planning should address the question of what is good for the company in terms of positioning itself within the overall social system so that it also contributes positively to this broader system. An increasingly open systems approach will likely be required in the years ahead.

A related systemic aspect deals with assessing the elaborateness of a planning system. In isolation, an elaborate system cannot do much good. The issue is to arrive at a proper planning system approach, seen within the context of a firm's setting, environment, and infrastructure. Thus, successful implementation probably hinges on being able to see planning more properly within a broader overall systems context than has been true in the past.

Certainly we have come to accept the need to tailor the planning process specifically to the particular strategic needs at hand; however, this may be too narrow a view. A somewhat broader view calls for a more unified design of planning with organizational structure, control, and incentive systems.[17] Further, given the almost constant changes in a firm's strategic needs due to environmental turbulence as well as to its own decision making, there is a continuous need to update and manage the evolution of these broad, interrelated systems. Modifications of the planning process and organizational redesign, reemphasis of the control tasks, and refocusing of the incentive schemes should all be seen as aspects of the same overall task. Through such a unified view, use of available tools might dramatically improve the firm's ability to reinforce a strategic direction.

One important issue relates to coping with potential internal resistance to business and/or portfolio planning. For instance, managers of a mature business may feel that they are planning their own gradual liquidation through the firm's role as a cash cow. Further, the requirement to focus on each business element as a separate strategic entity might be seen by some as a threat to the existing organizational structure and hence to those involved. It may be seen as threatening to be requested to break oneself up into parts.

For handling issues of this kind, it is sometimes useful to group individual elements into "business families" of more than one business element. Whereas each element would continue to focus on its generic, competitive position and a clear business environment, several business elements combined might enjoy certain similarities or significant synergies in a "family" setting. Thus, "old" business elements might provide some of its resources for the internal development of "new" business elements within the family, thereby perhaps contributing to a better sense of organizational continuity. It might also encourage better use of selected growth opportunities that typically exist even within a mature business area.

Another call for a "softened" approach might occur when dealing with the de facto constraints on portfolio strategy decisions. Increasingly, corporations will be faced with limitations to their freedom when it comes to closing down or liquidating certain businesses, locating new businesses, and so on. Increasingly, therefore, portfolio positioning will have to be worked out with close observance of societal, labor and organizational, and governmental requirements.[18]

When it comes to internal constraints on portfolio changes, intentions to make strategic portfolio moves must be handled sensibly. For instance, a firm would normally not want to have its intention to divest announced and widely debated. Such decisions should be accepted as sensitive and should be handled accordingly. Moreover, every business activity within a corporation should feel that it is part of the portfolio, though this will not necessarily preclude a relatively quick move to get out of a particular business.

Let us now assess some management style considerations that may have to be recognized and dealt with to implement a strategic planning process. It is important to develop a flexible approach when executing the strategic decision making, keeping multiple targets, and not making premature commitments. It follows from this that the planning process should allow for the creation of a psychology and style that permits decision makers to accept ambiguity rather than force a premature reconciliation of issues. Too often, cultural pressures are exerted on a manager to resolve the issue, "play it conservatively," and commit the organization too early.[19]

Another aspect of flexibility deals with the timing of decision making. The plan and strategy should be used as a buffer against the pressure to overreact or to overcommit too early, on the one hand. When it comes to deciding too late, on the other hand, the strategic control process should be adjusted so as to cut down reaction time. In all circumstances, however, some sense of decisiveness must be maintained.

A business plan request seldom gets turned down out of hand. It gets delayed. Thus, reassessment of the priority of resource commitments to the businesses within the portfolio is a major aspect of successful portfolio implementation.

Another aspect of the flexible style allows the organization to do some trial-and-error testing, when possible. It also allows for "saving face," so that managers might lessen their fear of failure within the strategic management process. It is important to permit managers to modify their strategies themselves. We are, in short, calling for a heightened sense of "feel" on behalf of senior management.[20]

It is important to see the "style signals" from senior management as part of the development of a mode of interaction. Signals might include personal attendance in planning meetings, personal signing of memoranda, personal speeches on planning conferences, and so on. It is also important that a healthy bottom–up strategic thinking remains a vital input in the process. Senior management should not disallow the organization from "discovering" its strategic directions. The bottom–up process enhances broad organizational commitment to strategies; heavy-handed dictating from the top down does not. The interplay between bottom–up and top–down is of course an essential aspect of implementation.[21]

Several other aspects of management style and culture are involved in the implementation of strategic planning, and we are probably only now starting to understand these challenges. However, it seems clear that these less tangible issues are becoming more and more recognized as frequent and serious barriers to successful implementation.

EXAMINING THE IMPLEMENTATIONAL TASKS:
OUTLINE OF THIS BOOK

A major argument in this introductory discussion on implementation of strategic planning has been that these issues can be seen from several perspectives. Implementation can be considered from a planning process point of view. We have seen how the evolution of planning processes has created a number of implementational challenges. Implementation can also be thought of as a function of the lessons we have learned in the past when it comes to other experiences within organizations for introducing innovations and new processes and systems. This might lead to a list of "do's and "dont's" that in themselves represent implementational issues for practical behavior. Or, by reviewing the actual steps that organizations have taken in carrying out the introduction and evolution of strategic planning systems, we might identify several implementational challenges associated with effective interventions by outside and/or inside consultants.

A third perspective — looking at the broader management processes within a corporation — leads to an assessment of the implementation tasks that arise from attempting to make strategic planning a more integral element of the broader system, the overall management style, and the actual mode of working and value systems within a corporation.

All these viewpoints do, of course, have merit and lead to useful insights regarding how to do a more effective job in implementing strategic planning. An excessively one-sided approach would easily constrain and narrow the issue of implementation artificially.

What is called for is a broad, multiperspective, relatively open-ended examination of implementation of strategic planning. Such a view recognizes that we are dealing with some of the most challenging implementational tasks that an organization might face: focusing on essential strategic choices and raising organizational design alternatives, in short confronting the centers of a firm's power structure.

This book hopes to shed light on various aspects of the challenges to strategic planning implementation by having the issues addressed by leading experts in the field. Some of these are practitioners, others are academicians; however, all have actively experienced aspects of the challenges of implementing planning. It would probably be unnecessarily constraining for most of these authors to address implementation by adhering to an overly formal outline or framework, such as examining the issues strictly along one of the three major dimensions identified in this chapter. Instead, most of the chapters deal with a relatively broad range of issues that tend to touch upon aspects relating to two or more dimensions. Rather, the book falls into two parts according to another useful distinction. The first deals with implementation implications of methodological and systemic issues; the second deals with companywide, situational implementational issues.

In the systemic and methodological section, Christenson discusses strategic planning from a systems science point of view. He argues that strategic planning processes and systems can play an important role in evolving the pattern of coordination of actions of a cooperative system. He shows how concepts of systems science can be useful in thinking about strategic planning and demonstrates how strategic planning can be understood when seen in an organizational systems context.

In the next chapter Steiner addresses the issue of how to better evaluate a strategic planning system. He develops several criteria for useful performance, and provides a self-assessment methodology for checking a system's appropriateness, and discusses experiences with carrying out such systems' evaluations in practice.

Next, Kervern, Ponssard, and Sarrazin discuss how a strategic decision-making process is a function of the past but must also be positioned so as to be useful in the future. They look at operationalizing a concept of the future, linking the more futuristic plans with the nearer-term management tools and developing a sense of flexibility to deal with the ambiguous circumstances of the future. A general system's theory viewpoint is taken, but it is related to implementational experiences in one large, multinational corporation.

Anand and Merrifield then examine how to modify and extend resource allocation procedures so as to better facilitate investment priorities based on the attractiveness of the overall strategy of which the investment is an element. Traditional capital budgeting methods do not ensure such strategic fit considerations. A methodology for strategic ranking is developed and practical experiences in using this methodology are explained. The approach is based on research findings for multiattribute investment criteria rankings, also reported on in this chapter.

Nathanson, Kazanjian, and Galbraith discuss the important roles of organizational design as part of successful strategic planning implementation. A framework is developed for seeing a strategic situation, a corresponding operating organization structure, and a particular planning process approach as having to be mutually consistent. Several practical aspects of organizational adjustments are discussed from the point of view of restoring and/or maintaining such consistency.

Finally, Hurst discusses roles of strategic control as part of a strategic decision-making process, emphasizing data considerations and orientation toward more futuristic and frequently more external reference points than conventional budgets. The discussion includes several important differences between strategic control and conventional control as they relate to perceiving the strategic control task, and implementing such an extended control approach.

In the second part of the book, a number of corporatewide implementation issues are discussed that tend to touch upon what might be seen as typical real-life situational design issues and challenges. Aguilar discusses several issues relating to the maintenance of creativity and quality in the strategic thinking. Aspects of this challenge include conditions that tend to facilitate the creation of new strategic moves, ways in which to reduce barriers to the initiative of new strategic thinking, and resistance to risk taking. These issues are discussed from organizational, control systems, as well as behavioral, points of view.

Hax and Schulmeyer analyze the question of introducing a formal strategic planning system in a particular business firm. The company depicted, located in Europe, is a subsidiary of a larger corporation located on another continent. The introduction of strategic planning is seen as hinging on a delineation of useful ways of categorizing a company's strategic positions as they relate to the various other business elements and support systems that exist. The approach taken is partly a conceptual delineation of how to operationalize a firm's thinking when it comes to strategic segmentation and partly a description of the company's actual experiences in redefining its business focus and starting a planning process.

The chapter by Ball discusses the evolution of strategic planning in a large, integrated oil company. His emphasis is on how the strategies of the company changed over the years, which created corresponding changes in the needs for strategic planning. Evolving a design for the strategic planning processes consistent with developing needs is seen as a major requirement. The discussion also includes several difficulties encountered in achieving effective planning over time as they related to management processes, management style, management succession, and management communications.

The question of acceptance of strategic planning is discussed by Gage through addressing the basic problem of acceptance, seen by members of an organization, of the benefits of planning relative to costs. Various requirements to the planning process are then identified as axioms that have to be fulfilled to develop a positive argument of benefits from planning. One company's experiences with the acceptance of strategic planning are being analyzed throughout. This is a rapidly growing, highly diversified firm within the high technology field. Its particular situational setting is discussed in terms of the implications for what specific acceptance challenges one might have to deal with in this strategic climate.

The chapter by Collier deals with strategic planning as a tool for reinforcing changes in strategic emphasis due to overall shifts in a company's strategic position. At one evolutionary stage, strategic needs were primarily integrative (i.e., to "trim" the organization in terms of its focus so as to enhance the performance). At another stage of the organization's development, the issue was more adaptive (i.e., to enhance selected internal growth and extend the present portfolio of businesses with new acquisitions to get a better overall portfolio balance). It is demonstrated that the planning process, in terms of format as well as style and flavor of interaction, changes as a function of the changing strategic needs.

Finally, Springmier discusses the implementation of planning in a complex organizational setting, a so-called matrix structure. This discussion is based on planning experiences with a specialty chemical company that had been organized as a multidimensional structure for almost ten years. Several experiences and pitfalls are noted as the evolution of planning is analyzed within this highly demanding corporate setting.

In total, the chapters of this book give a variety of in-depth insights from leading practitioners and academicians and a number of useful recommendations that should be of value in other implementational settings. However, the diversity of approaches also reflects the fact that there are probably only at best relatively few general conclusions regarding effective implementation. This is no surprise when it comes to such a complex managerial issue as strategic planning. Instead, a careful situational analysis and corresponding design seems to be the only workable way. Only continued efforts among practitioners and researchers, reporting on trials and errors as well as interaction and discussion among ourselves regarding our experiences, will bring us further progress. It is in this spirit that this book should be interpreted.

NOTES

[1] For a more detailed discussion of evolutionary patterns of planning, see Peter Lorange, "Three Stages of Evolution of Planning in Coping with Environmental Turbulence," *Revue Économique et Sociale*, Vol. 38, No. 3/4 (September 1980), pp. 134-166.

[2] Francis J. Aguilar, *Scanning the Business Environment* (New York: Macmillan, 1967); Harold E. Klein, "Incorporating Environmental Examination into the Corporate Strategic Process" (unpublished Ph.D. thesis, Columbia University, N.Y., 1973); K. S. Radford, *Information Systems for Strategic Decisions* (Reston, Va.: Reston Publishing, 1978); and Peter Lorange, *Corporate Planning: An Executive Viewpoint* (Englewood Cliffs, N.J.: Prentice-Hall, 1980).

[3] Derek F. Abell and John S. Hammond, *Strategic Market Planning* (Englewood Cliffs, N.J.: Prentice-Hall, 1979).

[4] Richard F. Vancil, *Decentralization: Managing Ambiguity by Design* (Homewood, Ill.: Dow Jones-Irwin, 1979).

[5] George A. Steiner, *Strategic Planning: What Every Manager Must Know* (New York: Free Press, 1979), and Peter Lorange, *Corporate Planning: An Executive Viewpoint* (op. cit.).

[6] Michael J. Ginzberg, "A Process Approach to Management Science Implementation" (unpublished Ph.D., dissertation, Massachusetts Institute of Technology, Cambridge, Mass., 1975); Peter G. W. Keen, "Implementation Research in MIS and OR/MS: Description versus Prescription," (Stanford Business School Research Paper No. 390, Palo Alto, Calif., 1977); and Peter G. W. Keen and Michael S. Scott-Morton, *Decision Support Systems: An Organizational Perspective* (Reading, Mass.: Addison-Wesley, 1978).

[7] Peter Lorange, "Roles of the CEO in Strategic Planning and Control Processes," paper presented at the ESSEC Conference, Cergy, France, April 28–29, 1980.

[8] Richard F. Vancil and Peter Lorange, "Strategic Planning in Diversified Companies," *Harvard Business Review*, Vol. 53, No. 1 (January–February 1975), pp. 81–90.

[9] Arnoldo C. Hax and Nicholas S. Majluf, "Organizational Design," M.I.T. Operations Research Center Technical Report No. 163, Cambridge, Mass. 1979, and Peter Lorange, "Business Element Delineation: Implications for Organizational Design, Planning and Performance Measurement," IMEDE Working Paper, Lausanne, Switzerland, 1980.

[10] Peter Lorange, *Corporate Planning: An Executive Viewpoint* (op. cit.), pp. 275-277, and Edgar H. Schein, *Process Consultation: Its Role in Organization Development* (Reading, Mass.: Addison-Wesley, 1969).

[11] Edgar H. Schein, "Management Development as a Process of Influence," *Industrial Management Review*, Vol. 2, No. 4 (May 1961), pp. 59–77.

[12] David A. Kolb and Allan L. Frohman, "An Organization Development Approach to Consulting," *Sloan Management Review*, Vol. 12, No. 1 (Fall 1970), pp. 51–65.

[13] For a discussion of the adaptation and integration concepts, see Lorange, *Corporate Planning: An Executive Viewpoint* (op. cit.), pp. 4–8, 95–98, and Peter Lorange, Ilene S. Gordon, and Richard Smith, "The Management of Adaptation and Integration," *Journal of General Management*, Vol. 4, No. 4 (Summer 1979), pp. 31–41.

[14]H. Randolph Bobbitt, Jr., and Jeffrey D. Ford, "Decision-Making Choice as a Determinant for Organization Structure," *The Academy of Management Review*, Vol. 15, No. 1 (January 1980), pp. 13–23.

[15]Peter Lorange, "Designing a Strategic Planning System," in *A Handbook on Business Planning*, ed. Thomas Duodick (New York: Van Nostrand, 1981).

[16]James Brian Quinn, "Strategic Goals: Process and Politics," *Sloan Management Review*, Vol. 19, No. 1 (Fall 1977), pp. 21-37.

[17]For what seems to be a good example of this, see the case, "Texas Instruments Incorporated," in Peter Lorange and Richard F. Vancil, *Strategic Planning Systems* (Englewood Cliffs, N.J.: Prentice-Hall, 1977), pp. 338–361.

[18]Jay L. Bourgeois, III, "Strategy and Environment: A Conceptual Integration," *The Academy of Management Review*, Vol. 5, No. 1 (January 1980), pp. 25–39.

[19]Ralph G. H. Siu, "Management and the Art of Chinese Baseball," *Sloan Management Review*, Vol. 19, No. 3 (Spring 1978), pp. 83–89, and Richard Tanner Pascale, "Zen and the Art of Management," *Harvard Business Review*, Vol. 56, No. 2 (March–April 1978), pp. 153–162.

[20]Richard D. Arvey and John M. Ivancevich, "Punishment in Organizations: A Review, Propositions and Research Suggestions," *The Academy of Management Review*, Vol. 5, No. 1 (January 1980), pp. 123–132.

[21]Peter Lorange and Richard F. Vancil, "How to Design a Strategic Planning System," *Harvard Business Review*, Vol. 54, No. 5 (September–October 1976), pp. 75–81.

section two

Conceptual and Methodological Implementational Issues

2

Strategic Planning Systems From a Systems Science Point of View

According to many, "a system is more than the sum of its parts." What is the extra ingredient that turns a mere aggregate of parts into a system?

Several possibilities are hinted at by Churchman, who writes that, "although the word 'system' has been defined in many ways, all definers will agree that a system is a set of parts coordinated to accomplish a set of goals."[1] I would depart from the consensus by omitting reference to "a set of goals." Goals are characteristic of what Simon has called "artificial systems."[2] It is possible to understand "natural systems," such as the solar system, without reference to goals (although a similar concept, that of "function," is often useful in studying natural systems).

This leaves us with coordination as the extra ingredient in a system. To be more precise, it is *coordination of actions*, as it is in its behaving that a set of parts displays its systematic aspect.

This chapter explores the concept of coordination of actions as it relates to strategic planning. The discussion focuses on the relevance of this concept to an understanding of both the functions of strategic planning systems and to the problems encountered in implementing or changing them.

---

*This chapter is prepared by Charles Christenson, Harvard University, Graduate School of Business Administration.

THE NEW SYSTEMS SCIENCE AND THE OLD

Some authors who have written about corporate planning from a systems science point of view have stressed the novelty of contemporary systems science. Ackoff, for example, has said that "the currently emerging intellectual revolution is bringing with it a new era that can be called the Systems Age," replacing the machine age that was ushered in by the Renaissance.[3] Ackoff identifies two main components of this intellectual revolution: the supplementation of analytical thinking with synthetic thinking and the replacement of a closed-system perspective by an open-system perspective.

Synthetic versus Analytical Thinking

"Machine Age thinking was analytical and based on the doctrines of reductionism and mechanism," Ackoff writes. "Analytical thinking is the mental process by which anything to be explained, hence understood, is broken down into its parts."[4] In the systems age, "the doctrines of reductionism and mechanism are being supplemented by . . . a new synthetic (or systems) mode of thought."[5] "The Systems Age is more interested in putting things together than in taking them apart," Ackoff concludes. "In [the synthetic mode] a problem is not solved by taking it apart but by viewing it as part of a larger problem."[6]

Other authors have agreed with Ackoff that "a problem is not solved by taking it apart" and that analysis needs to be supplemented by synthesis. One such author, for example, has written that the thinkers "of the last age have very much improved analysis but stop there and think they have solved a problem when they have only resolved it, and by this means the method of synthesis is almost laid aside." The author quoted is Sir Isaac Newton (unpublished manuscript reproduced in Cohen), explaining why he had used the synthetic mode in composing his *Principia*—that Bible of the machine age.[7] Perhaps our systems age thinkers are not so revolutionary after all!

What did Newton mean by saying that the *Principia* was written in the synthetic mode? The answer will provide an important insight into a little-understood aspect of the methodology of machine age science.

Newton begins the paragraph cited by saying that "the Ancients had two methods in mathematics which they called synthesis and analysis, or composition and resolution." Newton's authority on the methods of "the Ancients" is, without a doubt, Pappus, a Greek mathematician of around A.D. 300 who wrote about the methods of analysis and synthesis in geometry. Because Newton's own remarks on the two methods (published as well as unpublished) are brief and cryptic, it is helpful in interpreting them to refer to Pappus. (Polya provides a paraphrase of Pappus, commenting that "the procedures described by Pappus are by no means restricted to geometric problems; they are, in fact, not even restricted to mathematical problems."[8] Newton's familiarity with Pappus is evidenced by the opening sentence of the preface to the first edition of the *Principia*.)

Pappus defines "synthesis" as "construction of the thing sought."[9] In this sense, Euclid's *Elements* is for the most part concerned with synthesis, in the form of geometrical constructions. A typical Euclidean theorem asserts the possibility of carrying out a specified geometrical construction ("the thing sought") and the corresponding proof shows how to carry it out. To use a somewhat old-fashioned term, the proof is a demonstration of the theorem. It is, of course, a logical demonstration—"in words at length," to quote Newton—rather than a physical one. This way of looking at Euclid emphasizes that (although "nonconstructive" proofs are sometimes used in mathematics) there is a substantial overlap between the concept of deductive proof, on the one hand, and those of demonstration, construction, and synthesis, on the other hand.

In the *Principia*, Newton imitates Euclid's deductive style. In the light of his remarks on synthesis, we can understand why. The concept of "mechanical explanation" espoused by Newton, apparently, is that something is to be "explained, hence understood" not by taking it apart but by demonstrating how it is put together. The method of demonstration used in the *Principia* is constructive logical proof.

It is also possible to demonstrate how something is put together by constructing a model of it. Post-Newtonian machine age scientists generally did not follow Newton in his imitation of Euclid, but they did follow him in his notion that explanation should be synthetic. Their characteristic approach was to construct a model of the thing to be explained. Typically it was a mathematical model, although for a good many years scientists were not satisfied with a mathematical model unless they could find a "mechanical interpretation" for it, that is, a representation in the form of a constructible material system. (Materialism, not reductionism, is what distinguishes machine age thinking most from that of contemporary science; see, for example, Whitehead.)[10]

If machine age explanation was synthetic, where did analysis come in? Newton, in the passage quoted, gives the answer: "By the method of analysis [the Ancients] found their inventions. . . . The propositions in the following book were invented by analysis." Analysis is a method of discovering explanations which, to be accepted, must be proved by synthesis. (Polya suggests that analysis might preferably be called "heuristic".)[11]

There is considerable common sense to this. You would not think you had "explained, hence understood" an automobile engine if you had succeeded only in reducing it (in Newton's words, resolving it) to a pile of castings, rods, nuts, and bolts. But, if you could put the parts back together again to make a functioning engine, then you have understanding.

What do you need, besides the parts, to reassemble the engine? You need to know how the actions of the parts are coordinated in carrying out the functions of the whole. It may be said, then, that the main objective of systems analysis is to discover the "extra ingredient" in a system, that is, its coordination of actions.

Closed versus Open Systems

In thermodynamics, a closed system is one that does not exchange energy with its environment. According to the Second Law of Thermodynamics, the entropy of a closed system cannot decrease. It is observed that entropy does decrease locally in space time in biological systems and in some physical systems (such as flames and whirlpools). Bertalanffy[12] pointed out that these systems were open to energy exchanges with the environment, so that their behavior did not refute the second law. He suggested the need for a general theory of open systems. (Note that the openness of a system is not sufficient to explain its entropy-defeating character.)

Bertalanffy's distinction has been adopted in a metaphorical way in the new systems science. That is, an open system is considered to be one that has any kind of interaction with its environment; a closed system is one that has none.

Ackoff expresses a point of view typical to the new systems science. In the machine age, he says, "the quest for causes was environment free. It employed what is now called 'closed-system' thinking. . . . Specifically designed nonenvironments, laboratories, were used to exclude environmental effects on phenomena under study." In the systems age, it is recognized that "a system's performance depends on how it relates to its environment—the larger system of which it is a part—and to the other systems in that environment." The behavior of a system is co-produced (using the terminology of Singer) by the system itself and by its environment.[13]

Another author says almost precisely the same thing: "The most superficial examination of what goes on around us shows that all natural phenomena result from the reaction of bodies one against another. There always comes under consideration the body, in which the phenomenon takes place, and the outward circumstance or the environment which determines or invites the body to exhibit its properties. The conjunction of these conditions is essential to the appearance of the phenomenon." The author attributes the view that phenomena are co-produced by body and environment to "ancient science," just as Newton attributed recognition of the need for both synthesis and analysis to "the Ancients."

The author just quoted is Claude Bernard, called by the *Encyclopedia Britanica* "one of the greatest of the great 19th-century physiologists." Bernard introduced the experimental method into physiology. "All the analytic sciences [sic] divide problems," he wrote, "in order to experiment better." The distinction between body and environment is itself the result of the analysis of phenomena. The experimenter controls phenomena by controlling the environment. A laboratory is not a nonenvironment but a controlled environment, that is, one for which the experimenter knows the conditions even if he or she cannot manipulate them.

Bernard makes clear that the double conditioning (or co-production) of phenomena by body and environment characterizes inorganic as well as living bodies. But he does argue for a difference between the two classes of phenomena: "We see that conditions of environment in all natural phenomena govern their phenomenal manifestation. The conditions of our cosmic environment generally govern the mineral phenomena occurring on the surface of the earth; but organized beings include within themselves the conditions peculiar to their vital manifestations. . . . To sum up, if we wish to find the exact conditions of vital manifestations in man and the higher animals, we must really look, not at the outer cosmic environment, but rather at the inner organic environment."[14]

According to Bernard, in other words, the behavior of every body, inorganic or living, is controlled by its environment(s). In the case of inorganic bodies, there is only the outer cosmic environment to take into account. In the case of living bodies, control is shared by the outer and inner environments. Control by the inner environment causes the actions of the body to be coordinated in such a way that disturbances in the outer environment are prevented from passing through to the inner environment, such that, as Bernard puts it, the "stability of the inner environment" is preserved. The greater the degree of control exercised by the inner environment, the more perfect the organism, in Bernard's terms, and the more autonomous the organism will be of external conditions.

By recognizing the existence of two environments, Bernard arrives at a conclusion regarding organic systems almost diametrically opposed to that reached by the new systems scientists who recognize only one. The new systems scientists emphasize the control of the organism by its (outer) environment; Bernard emphasizes its independence of that environment.

Barnard's Systems Theory of Organization

Bernard's book, with the distinction between outer and inner environments and the idea that higher organisms were controlled primarily by their inner environments, strongly influenced several biological scientists of the next generation. Among them was Walter B. Cannon of the Harvard Medical School, who coined the term "homeostasis" to refer to what Bernard had called "the stability of the inner environment." Norbert Wiener became aware of the analogy between Bernard's view of organisms and feedback-controlled machines through working with Cannon's research group.

Another biological scientist influenced by Bernard was Cannon's colleague L. J. Henderson, a theoretical physiologist and blood chemist. Henderson wrote the introduction to the English translation of Bernard. At that time, Henderson had already begun to collaborate with Professor Elton Mayo of the Harvard Business School on psychological problems of industrial personnel. Shortly thereafter, Henderson was the prime mover in the establishment at the Business School of the Harvard Fatigue Laboratory.[15]

Through Dean Wallace B. Donham of Harvard Business School, Henderson met Chester I. Barnard, president of the New Jersey Bell Telephone Company. Henderson arranged with Harvard President Lowell for Barnard to be invited to give the 1937 Lowell Institute Lectures on the subject "The Functions of the Executive."[16] He later encouraged Barnard to revise and extend his lectures into a book under the same title. Barnard's preface to the book acknowledges Henderson's "invaluable advice concerning many questions of method, and indispensable aid and encouragement regarding the exposition as a whole."

Under the circumstances, it is not surprising that Barnard emphasizes the internal processes of an organization in his statement of the main problem addressed by his book: "The survival of an organization depends upon the maintenance of an equilibrium of complex character in a continuously fluctuating environment of physical, biological, and social materials, elements, and forces, which calls for readjustment of processes internal to the organization. We shall be concerned with the nature of the external conditions to which adjustment must be made, but the center of our interest is the processes by which it is accomplished." According to Emery and Trist,[17] who are among those who have espoused the "revolutionary" status of the new systems science, Barnard's "otherwise invaluable contribution" suffers from "the limiting perspective of 'closed system' theorizing." In fact, Barnard's is a "two-environment" theory in which effective coordination blocks the passage of disturbance from the outer to the inner environment.

Cooperative Systems

"Cooperative action," according to Barnard, "is a synthesis of diverse factors, physical, biological, and social, and affects the total situation in which these factors are all present."

In general, cooperation is unstable and short lived. The problem is to explain the exceptions: to give necessary conditions for the persistence of cooperation. Barnard identifies two conditions: (1) effectiveness, which "relates to the accomplishment of cooperative purpose" and "is social and non-personal in character," and (2) efficiency, which "relates to the satisfaction of individual motives, and is personal in character." Barnard's use of "efficiency" is a bit unusual but not quite as unusual as it might seem. His "efficiency" is a vector rather than a scalar, with a component for each individual cooperator. The efficiency of cooperation to each individual is a function of that individual's contribution (or input) to the cooperative action and of the inducement (or output) received in exchange.

Barnard defines a "cooperative system" as "a complex of physical, biological, personal, and social components which are in a specific systematic relationship by reason of the cooperation of two or more persons for at least one definite end." He argues that, if there is anything common to all cooperative systems, it is not to be found in the physical, biological, personal, or social components. These are purely contingent factors of each concrete cooperative system, varying in details from system to system.

Formal Organization

The one common element that Barnard identifies in all cooperative systems is a subsystem he calls *formal organization*, defined as "a system of consciously coordinated activities or forces of two or more persons." By this definition, Barnard points out, the physical, biological, personal, and social components of each concrete cooperative system are relegated to the external environment of the formal organization, although they are still internal to the cooperative system itself.

Although Barnard's has been called "the most famous definition of organization,"[18] its most unusual feature does not seem to have been widely adopted by organization theorists. It is still customary to think of the ultimate constituents of organizations as persons, organization members, rather than as the activities of persons. Barnard's argument for his definition is, in my view, conclusive: (1) Most activities of persons who are conventionally considered as members of an organization are not subject to coordination by that organization; each of us has a personal life, even when we are physically "on the job," that we devote to family, self, or other systems. (2) Some activities of persons not conventionally considered as organization members are subject to coordination; customers, for example, may have to come to the place where a firm does business or otherwise conform to its requirements for placing orders. Treating members as the ultimate constituents blurs these points, but Barnard's definition focuses on the essential point: the activities that are coordinated, whether or not performed by persons conventionally considered as members.

Implicit in the definition are the necessary and sufficient conditions for a formal organization to come into existence: (1) communication (2) among persons who are willing to contribute actions (3) for a common purpose. Communication is implied by the coordination of actions (as will be argued in more detail in the next section); willingness to contribute by the fact that the actions are of persons who can choose; and common purpose by the fact that the coordination is conscious. For the continued existence of a formal organization, as Barnard reminds us, effectiveness and efficiency are also necessary.

Executive Functions

The functions of the executive are not to manage the organization but to maintain it. "The functions with which we are concerned," Barnard says, "are like those of the nervous system, including the brain, in relation to the rest of the body. It exists to maintain the bodily system by directing those actions which are necessary more effectively to adjust to the environment, but it can hardly be said to manage the body, a large part of whose functions are independent of it and upon which it in turn depends."

It follows from the conditions for the persistence of formal organization that the executive functions are (1) the maintenance of organizational communication, (2) the securing of essential efforts, and (3) the formulation and definition of purpose.

This brief summary hardly does justice to Barnard's theory of organization. In the context of this chapter, however, the focus now shifts more narrowly to a single aspect of the theory; the concept of "coordination of actions."

COORDINATION, STRUCTURAL STABILITY, AND STRATEGIC CHANGE

As an example of a "nonsystem," or "mere aggregate of parts," systems theorists often use a pile of stones. This same example can illustrate some points about coordination of actions.

First, note that the stones in the pile are spatially related to one another; the pile as a whole forms a geometrical configuration. Thus, mere relationship of the parts in a whole is not an essential aspect of a system, as relationships are to be found even among the parts of a nonsystem.

Next, suppose that one of the stones in the pile is disturbed, for example, by being pushed away from its original position. In general this disturbance will change the geometrical configuration of the pile. At a minimum, if a stone on the top of the pile is disturbed without affecting the others, the relationship of that stone to the others will be altered. At the other extreme, if a stone at the bottom of the pile is disturbed, a minor avalanche will result and the geometrical configuration of the entire pile may be altered substantially.

These phenomena may be described in either of two essentially equivalent ways: (1) the structure (geometrical configuration) of the stone pile is not stable with respect to the disturbances being considered; or (2) the actions (motions) of the parts are only weakly coordinated with respect to these disturbances. (Some coordination is provided by natural factors such as gravitational force.) The two ways of looking at the phenomena are linked through the concept of "position"; a geometrical configuration is a relation among positions and a motion is a transition from one position to another.

From this example of a nonsystem, we can conclude that the function of coordination in a system is to maintain the structural stability of the system in the face of disturbances from its environment(s).

Whether a given collection of parts is a system or not will depend, in general, on the nature of the disturbances. If, for example, I give an ash tray a push with my finger, it will move as a whole, maintaining its geometrical configuration, despite the fact that my initial disturbance of the ash tray affected directly only a small proportion of its ultimate components. If, on the other hand, I strike the ash tray sharply with a hammer, it will shatter. Its structure will be destroyed.

Structural Stability in General

In each of the two examples, the pile of stones and the ash tray, the actions of the parts that are (or are not) coordinated are motions, transitions of positions; and the structure that is (or is not) maintained is a geometrical configuration, a relation among positions. One of the most important intellectual contributions of the machine age was the generalization of this set of concepts to more abstract kinds of structures than those existing in ordinary geometric space.

One of the key developments was Galileo's conception of a "state of motion." The word "state" was originally synonymous with "position." Motion is, in this sense, a change of state. Galileo's insight was that it might be fruitful to conceive of a change of state as itself a state and to inquire how it changed. That is, environmental disturbance (force) was to be used to explain change of motion, not change of position as in earlier theories.

The line of thinking begun by Galileo's insight led to the concept of a dynamic system and culminated in Newton's theory of motion. More importantly, so far as the present chapter is concerned, by freeing the concept of state from its identification with geometrical positions, it made possible a generalized concept of structure.

Given a collection of parts, we can now think of each part as having a state. An action of each part is a transition from one state to another. The structure of the whole is a relation among the states of the parts. If the actions of the parts with respect to a class of disturbances is coordinated in such a way that the structure is maintained, then the collection of parts is a system with respect to that class of disturbances.

The scientist, it should be pointed out, does not usually begin with the knowledge of how to characterize the states of the parts of a system or even what the parts are. Galileo had to discover that motion could fruitfully be viewed as a state. The analytic method of science begins by treating an object of study as a "black box" and attempts to find a way of dividing it into parts with states such that the whole behaves as a system, that is, such that some relation among the states is maintained when the whole is subject to disturbance.[19]

In Barnard's theory, what must be maintained for a cooperative system to exist is efficiency and effectiveness, and the purpose of formal organization is to maintain these factors.

Strategic Planning and Evolutionary Planning

According to the well-known definition of Anthony,

> Strategic planning is the process of deciding on objectives of the organization, on changes in these objectives, on the resources used to attain these objectives, and on the policies that are to govern the acquisition, use, and disposition of these resources.[20]

Although "change" is mentioned only once in this definition, with reference to objectives, it could be argued that it is implicit even in the parts of the definition where it is not mentioned. An ongoing organization already has not only objectives but also resources and policies. Strategic planning must be concerned with changing policies and resources as well as with objectives.

In terms of the concepts discussed in this chapter, it could be argued that the purpose of strategic planning is to change the coordination of actions of a cooperative system—its formal organization, in Barnard's terms. (The purpose of management control, it could be argued, is to maintain the coordination of actions.)

There is something paradoxical about attempting to change the coordination of actions of a cooperative system, because the function of coordination is to resist change, that is, to maintain the structure of the system in the face of disturbance. In terms of a metaphor of Otto Neurath's, the strategic planner is in the position of a sailor who must rebuild his ship on the open sea without being able to pull into a drydock.

Barnard analyzes this problem in *The Functions of the Executive*[21] and in an article entitled "On Planning for World Government."[22] In the latter, he distinguishes among three kinds of planning: instrumental, functional, and evolutionary. Evolutionary planning is the type that appears most relevant to strategic change.

"Evolutionary planning," Barnard says, "is that involving attainment of a future situation or system through a series of intermediate states or systems." In this approach, the desired future state is analyzed to identify what Barnard calls the "limiting (strategic) factor . . . one whose control, in the right form, at the right place and time, will establish a new system or set of conditions which meets the purpose."[23] This then leads to a new situation that must again be analyzed to determine its limiting or strategic factors, and so on, until some actions that must be taken in the here and now are identified.

"This is the meaning of effective decision," Barnard says, "—the control of the changeable strategic factors, that is, the exercise of control at the right time, right place, right amount, and right form, so that purpose is properly redefined and accomplished."

SUMMARY

This chapter has tried to show how some concepts of systems science can be useful in thinking about strategic planning, particularly in the coordination of actions. In contrast to some new systems scientists, the emphasis has been on the importance of analytic thinking and reductionism, both in the understanding of organizational systems and in the planning process itself.

NOTES

[1]C. West Churchman, *The Systems Approach* (New York: Delacorte Press, 1968), p. 29.
[2]Herbert A. Simon, *The Science of the Artificial* (Cambridge, Mass.: M.I.T. Press, 1969).
[3]Russell L. Ackoff, *Redesigning the Future* (New York: Wiley-Interscience, 1974), p. 8.
[4]*Ibid.*, p. 9.
[5]*Ibid.*, p. 12.
[6]*Ibid.*, p. 14.
[7]I. Bernard Cohen, *An Introduction to Newton's Principia* (Cambridge, Mass.: Harvard University Press, 1971), 294.
[8]G. Polya, *How to Solve It* (Garden City, N.Y.: Doubleday & Co., 1957), p. 143.
[9]Jaako Hintikka and Unto Remes, *The Method of Analysis* (Boston: D. Reidel, 1974), p. 9.
[10]Alfred N. Whitehead, *Science and the Modern World* (Macmillan & Co., 1925), Chap. VI.
[11]G. Polya (1957), *How to Solve It* (op. cit.), p. 112.
[12]Ludwig von Bertalanffy, "The Theory of Open Systems in Physics and Biology," *Science*, Vol. 111, N.s., No. 3, (1950), pp. 23–29.
[13]E. A. Singer, Jr., *Experience and Reflection* (Philadelphia: University of Pennsylvania Press, 1959).
[14]Claude Bernard, *An Introduction to the Study of Experimental Medicine*, trans. H. C. Greene (New York: Macmillan, 1927), pp. 97, 98.
[15]Steven M. and Elizabeth C. Horvath, *The Harvard Fatigue Laboratory* (Englewood Cliffs, N.J.: Prentice-Hall, 1973).

[16]Chester I. Barnard, *The Functions of the Executive* (Cambridge, Mass.: Harvard University Press, 1938).

[17]Fred E. Emery and Eric L. Trist, "Socio-Technical Systems," in *Management Science, Models and Techniques*, eds. C. W. Churchman and M. Verhulst, Vol. 2 (London: Pergamon Press, 1960), pp. 83–97.

[18]J. Kenneth Galbraith, *The New Industrial State* (Boston: Houghton Mifflin, 1967).

[19]W. Ross Ashby, *An Introduction to Cybernetics* (New York: Wiley, 1956).

[20]Robert N. Anthony, *Planning and Control Systems: A Framework for Analysis* (Division of Research, the Harvard Business School, 1965), p. 16.

[21]Chester I. Barnard, *The Functions of the Executive*, (op. cit.), Chap. 14.

[22]Chester I. Barnard, *Organization and Management* (Cambridge: Mass.: Harvard University Press, 1949), Chap. 6.

[23]Chester I. Barnard, *The Functions of the Executive*, (op. cit.).

3

Evaluating Your
Strategic Planning System

Despite a quarter century of experience with formal strategic planning systems (FSPSs) in business, there still exists much dissatisfaction with the systems now being used. Of the many reasons cited, two in particular stand out: First, the systems are not designed or operated properly. They violate some of the major lessons of experience about what should and should not be done to achieve planning effectiveness. Second, dissatisfaction with FSPSs is often caused by blaming, quite improperly, the planning system for management and staff errors and shortcomings.

Appropriate evaluation of a company's FSPS should result in improving the system and reducing dissatisfaction with it. This chapter* seeks to help managers and planning staffs to make useful evaluations of their FSPS.

APPROPRIATE EVALUATION IS NOT A SIMPLE MATTER

Evaluating a company's FSPS is an extremely complex undertaking. This is so for many reasons. To begin with, a company's FSPS should be designed to fit the unique characteristics of the company. Because every company differs in some degree from every other, it follows that FSPSs will differ from one company to

---

*This chapter is prepared by George A. Steiner, Graduate School of Management, University of California at Los Angeles.

another. The design and operation of an FSPS will reflect such considerations as the readiness of managers and staffs to plan, managerial styles, company size and organization, problems facing the company, and many others.[1] Because continuous change is taking place in these areas, one can expect that the requirements for an effective FSPS in a company will also undergo constant modification.

Then, too, an FSPS in a company of any size is actually composed of a number of subsystems. Each of the subsystems can be evaluated as can the system as a whole. For instance, in a fairly large company, the strategic planning system can encompass posture and portfolio planning at the top management level, comprehensive formal planning at the divisional level, and corporate planning, which might combine elements of both, to name a few of the more prominent planning systems. The evaluation process of these systems will vary.

The best grade for FSPS probably should be given when it is perceived as aiding a company in achieving exceptional prosperity and vitality in a highly competitive and dangerous environment. But the success of a company is the result of good management, not the planning system per se. So, how does one disentangle the effectiveness of a planning system from the capabilities of managers and their staffs?

Furthermore, a company may have a textbook-perfect system, but an unexpected environmental change may bring unsatisfactory results. Does the system get a good grade? A company also may have an "ideal" system of planning but choose the wrong strategy. There is nothing inherent in a strategic planning system that guarantees that the "right" strategy will be chosen. If a wrong strategy is chosen but the planning system appears to be "ideal," does the system get a good or poor grade? Such considerations make it clear that there is no simple way to evaluate a company's FSPS.

APPROACHES TO EVALUATING FSPSs

Four approaches to FSPS evaluation are discussed as follows: (1) identifying the major purposes of the system and evaluating whether they have been achieved, (2) identifying the requirements for a successful system and evaluating whether they are being employed, (3) identifying an "ideal" system for a company and comparing it with the company's actual system, and (4) making a comprehensive survey of the most important characteristics of the system in terms of managerial need and design.

These approaches are not mutually exclusive. Each company must choose which approach is most appropriate to its situation. Also, the nature of the systems review and the final evaluation will differ depending upon who is looking at the system. That is, a chief executive officer will look at his or her strategic planning system differently from a corporate planner. And each of them is likely to view the system differently from the manager of a decentralized profit center, a management consultant, or a manager from another company.

Are the Purposes of the FSPS Achieved?

Managers should have in mind clear purposes for their strategic planning systems. If so, it is possible to determine whether the system is or is not achieving the purpose or purposes and how well. For example, some chief executive officers have a strategic planning system that feeds information to them upon which basis they make decisions. A planning system may be designed primarily to flush up strategic issues to top management. Other basic purposes of an FSPS may be to change the direction of the company, accelerate growth and improve profitability, weed out poor performers among divisions, strengthen the frame of reference for current budgets, improve internal coordination and communication among functional areas, train managers, and pick up the pace of a "tired" company. This does not exhaust the list of purposes.[2]

If top management has designed a system to accomplish one or more of these purposes, it is possible, of course, to determine whether the purposes have been achieved. If a chief executive officer designs a system solely to produce information for his or her decision making, he or she can easily decide whether the system is achieving the purpose sought. Such a system might be viewed as poor by a staff evaluator looking for textbook design perfection.

Evaluating the degree to which a system meets some of its stated purposes may be rather difficult. For example, if a system is designed primarily to train managers, an evaluation of whether or not the purpose has been met is not easy. When a system is designed to achieve a number of different purposes the evaluation process becomes complex. Then one of the following approaches may be used.

A company starting formal planning for the first time may attempt to accomplish one or a very few specific purposes. In such a case, the planning system is usually simple, and the objectives sought for the first cycle are generally very limited. Thus, a simple approach will be more fruitful than the other more complex approaches discussed in this chapter.

Are Requirements for Successful FSPSs Being Met?

There is an extensive literature that seeks to summarize the lessons of past experience about what is required in a successful FSPS.[3] An evaluator of an FSPS could, of course, review this literature and extract the major requirements of a successful planning system as perceived by the various writers. The system to be evaluated could then be measured against these standards. This would be a tedious task. To help managers in identifying requirements for effective planning, a number of writers have identified major pitfalls to be avoided or requirements to be met.[4]

For example, Walter B. Schaffir, an experienced practitioner of and consultant on strategic planning, says that violating one or more of the following ten areas will likely produce unsatisfactory results from a planning system.[5]

1. The primary purpose of any business plan must be to help its author to manage his/her own operations more effectively.
2. The second purpose of a business plan is to establish a mutually agreed upon commitment between the author of the plan and his/her boss.
3. A business plan must contain sufficient information to lend credibility to its promise.
4. A business plan must have strategic focus; that is, it must be part of an overall scheme to accomplish enduring objectives within the context of dynamic, interacting environmental forces.
5. A business plan must foster awareness of options and their likely consequence.
6. A business plan must boil up critical issues, choices, and priorities on which management attention must be focused.
7. A business plan must be linked firmly to the system for allocating and committing capital funds.
8. A business plan must keep paperwork manageable.
9. Business plans must accommodate a plurality of managerial and planning styles.
10. Planning must be woven into the fabric of the organization to become a natural part of getting the job done.

Some years ago this author sought to identify the major pitfalls that should be avoided if an effective FSPS were to be developed. A national and international survey among managers and staff planners produced a total of fifty pitfalls that should be avoided; of the total, ten were identified as the most lethal to effective formal strategic planning.[6] By and large, the pitfalls identified in the survey must be avoided if a company is to have an effective planning system. However, if a comparable survey were to be made today, the ten most important pitfalls to be avoided would probably not be the same.

A broad current survey of major pitfalls to be avoided in designing and operating FSPSs would very likely produce the following ten most important ones:

1. Failure to develop throughout the company an understanding of what strategic planning really is, how it is to be done in the company, and the degree of commitment of top management to doing it well.
2. Failure to accept and balance interrelationships among intuition, judgment, managerial values, and the formality of the planning system.
3. Failure to encourage managers to do effective strategic planning by basing performance appraisal and rewards solely on short-range performance measures.
4. Failure to tailor and design the strategic planning system to the unique characteristics of the company and its management.
5. Failure of top management to spend sufficient time on the strategic planning process so that the process becomes discredited among other managers and staff.
6. Failure to modify the strategic planning system as conditions within the company change.
7. Failure to mesh properly the process of management and strategic planning from the highest levels of management and planning through tactical planning and its complete implementation.

8. Failure to keep the planning system simple and to weigh constantly the cost–benefit balance.
9. Failure to secure within the company a climate for strategic planning that is necessary for its success.
10. Failure to balance and link appropriately the major elements of the strategic planning and implementation process.

There is some overlapping in these two lists, and they contain many of the pitfalls to avoid or requirements to be met in other listings. The reader can add to or eliminate from these lists other items, but it is thought that the two lists contain those areas of most significance in designing and operating an effective FSPS.

An evaluation based upon either of the lists given can be made in several ways. One may ask whether the system under review meets the requirements of Schaffir's list or avoids the pitfalls in this author's list. Both lists can be modified easily to pose questions by prefacing the items with "Does the system . . . ?" Answers can be based on personal observation or organized responses from many different people.

Details can readily be added to each of the items listed. Evaluators might well add details of particular concern to the company being evaluated. Care should be exercised in adding subquestions, for it is easy to make the resulting listing much too long. Indeed, these lists condense a very large part of the detailed lessons of experience incorporated in a number of the major references given. For example, many detailed questions can be added to Schaffir's area 1 or to the author's pitfall 10, to pick two at random.

Does the System Fit the Characteristics of the Company?

A major lesson of experience with FSPSs is that each system must be designed to fit the unique characteristics of each company. We do not know from experience those principles and practices that must be employed, or avoided, if a system is to be effective. Many of them are identified in the lists given. Unfortunately, however, we do not have off-the-shelf systems that can be installed without change to fit particular settings. We still must tailor each system to each situation.

An approach to evaluation, more theoretical than operational, is to identify the unique characteristics of a company that most influence the design of the planning system and then design the system to meet the particular needs of the company. Once this is done, the design can be compared with the system that is actually being used.

This approach may be interesting but very difficult to use. It is not likely to yield results as effective as the other approaches cited. For this reason, it is not recommended except as an intellectual exercise that a manager or planner may wish to undertake.

COMPREHENSIVE EVALUATION SURVEY

Exhibit 3-1 is a survey form that should yield useful insights about a company's FSPS.[7] The questionnaire is more appropriate for a company that has a comprehensive FSPS and has gone through several cycles. A quick glance at the questionnaire shows that it seeks to determine how much value managers attribute to the planning system, whether or not the system produces valuable substantive results, whether or not the system meets the most important standards for a good design, and whether or not the planning processes are effective.

EXHIBIT 3-1

How Effective Is Your Strategic Planning System?

	Not Effective (No)	Very Effective (Yes)

A. *Overall Managerial Perceived Value*

1. The chief executive officer believes the system helps him or her to discharge better his or her responsibilities.
2. Other major line managers think the system is useful to them.
3. Overall, the benefits of strategic planning are perceived to be greater than the costs by most managers.
4. Major changes are needed in our strategic planning system.

B. *Does Our Strategic Planning System Produce the "Right" Substantive Answers and Results?*

5. Developing basic company missions and lines of business.
6. Foreseeing future major opportunities.
7. Foreseeing future major threats.
8. Properly appraising company strengths.
9. Properly appraising company weaknesses.
10. Developing realistic current information about competitors.
11. Clarifying priorities.
12. Developing useful long-range objectives.
13. Developing useful long-range program strategies.
14. Developing creditable medium- and short-range plans to implement strategies so as to achieve goals.
15. Preventing unpleasant surprises.
16. Our major financial indicators have been better after introducing planning than before:
    Sales
    Profits
    Return on investment
    Earnings per share
17. Our company performance has been better than others in our industry not doing comprehensive managerial planning.

EXHIBIT 3-1 (cont.)

How Effective Is Your Strategic Planning System?

	Not Effective (No)				Very Effective (Yes)

C. *Does Our Planning System Yield Valuable Ancillary Benefits?*

18. The system has improved the quality of management.

19. The system is a unifying, coordinating force in company operations.

20. The system facilitates communications and collaboration throughout the company.

D. *The Design of the Planning System*

21. Top management has accepted the idea that strategic planning is its major responsibility.

22. Our system fits the management style of our company.

23. The system fits the reality of our strategic decision making processes.

24. The corporate planner is situated close to the top management of the company.

25. The corporate planner works well with the top management.

26. The corporate planner works well with other line managers and staff.

27. The planning committee structure is just right for us.

E. *Are the Planning Processes Effective?*

28. Top management spends an appropriate amount of time on strategic planning.

29. There is too much foot-dragging about planning. It is given lip service but too many line managers really do not accept it.

30. Line managers generally spend an appropriate amount of time with other line managers and/or staff in developing strategic plans.

31. The system proceeds on the basis of an acceptable set of procedures.

32. The planning procedures are well understood in the company.

33. The work requirement to complete the plans is acceptable to our managers and staff.

34. The process is effective in inducing in-depth thinking.

35. Too much attention is paid to putting numbers in boxes. The process is too proceduralized, too routine, too inflexible.

42

EXHIBIT 3-1 (cont.)

How Effective Is Your Strategic Planning System?

	Not Effective (No)				Very Effective (Yes)

36. New ideas are generally welcomed.

37. Managers really do face up to company weaknesses in devising plans.

38. Divisions do not get sufficient guidance from head-quarters for effective planning.

39. Divisions are encouraged and helped by headquar-ters to do effective planning.

40. The ability of managers to do effective strategic plan-ning is taken into consideration in a proper manner when they are measured for overall performance.

Survey forms such as this one are subject to many weaknesses. For example, different people will attribute different meanings to the questions. Also, different people will give the same result different evaluations. Also, questionnaires such as this are not effective in producing a single evaluation or grade. It is possible, of course, to grade a system by putting numbers on each evaluation, by giving weights to different questions, and then calculating the total result.

On the other hand, the great strength of this survey form is that it provides a format for evaluating a system in terms of accepted design standards and major results that ought to be achieved. This, in turn, provides a basis for dialogue among managers and staff about shortcomings that should be corrected in the system.

This survey form should be modified to suit the interests of different persons in an organization. For instance, top managers should be asked to evaluate all items in parts A, B, and C but only selected items in parts D and E. Here, again, some of the items may not be exactly appropriate for a company, and the survey should, therefore, be modified accordingly. For a particular company some of the items might be sharpened to pinpoint a specific issue in the company.

Overall, the purpose of this questionnaire is to organize thinking about an FSPS as a basis for informed and dispassionate discussion of its design and results, with a view toward improving it in terms of perceived managerial needs. The form in its present state, or modified to suit unique situations in a company, appears to do this.

The form certainly probes major requirements for an effective system. Space does not permit an extended analysis of the significance of each of the forty questions raised, but a few comments may be in order. For example, what a chief executive officer thinks about the system is of crucial importance. If he or she thinks the system is very valuable in making the "right" strategic decisions for the company, the system is fulfilling its highest purpose. If the CEO does not believe the system is helpful, it must receive a low grade no matter how it measures up against a textbook ideal.

In addition to the CEO, the views of other managers about the system are very important. There will be problems in a company in which the CEO believes the system is important in his or her decision making but a number of division managers view the system as excessively burdensome and/or a waste of time. Such a situation should be corrected.

A mature planning system must deal with questions 5 through 14 in part B. Some of them are more important than others and problems may arise in their evaluation. For instance, questions 13 and 14, which concern the development and implementation of strategies, are of very high significance. A top grade on these two questions can offset a lower grade on some of the others. On the other hand, high grades on some of the other questions will not offset a low grade on 13 and 14 because the main focus and purpose of most FSPSs is to help companies formulate and implement appropriate strategies to adapt to their changing environments.

A point made previously is worth reiterating, namely, that a perfect planning system will not guarantee that management will choose the "right" strategy. However, it can be said that, other things being equal, a company is more likely to develop the "right" strategy with an appropriate FSPS than without it. It might be added, too, that skilled managers are more likely to formulate better strategies than are unskilled managers and that skilled managers are more likely to develop an FSPS appropriate to their situation than are unskilled managers. Good management and effective strategic planning systems go together.

This observation applies also to questions 5, 6, 12, and 13. Evaluators may have some problems in rating these and other questions on the survey form. For instance, an evaluator may give the formal planning system a low grade on 5 (developing basic company missions and lines of business) simply because these strategies are formulated solely by the CEO and not developed in the FSPS. Generally speaking, however, weaknesses in any of the questions in part B should be matters of concern to a company.

An effective planning system should produce high marks for questions 15, 16, and 17. However, environmental circumstances can result in low grades on these questions even with a suitable planning system. So, here again, a system must be evaluated in relationship to other phenomenon that affect its operations and/or results.

An FSPS has value to a company aside from substantive results. An effective system should improve the quality of management (18), become a unifying, coordinating force in company operations (19), and facilitate communications and collaboration throughout the company (20). These are recognized as major assets of high importance and any system that does not develop them is truly deficient and in need of repair.

Questions in part D concern the organizational design of the system. Many more questions about organization could be asked, but those on the form are of major importance. A system is not likely to be effective when its organizational design is not appropriate. If top management assumes that the responsibility for strategic planning rests on someone else's shoulders (e.g., a planner) (21), troubles are inevitable. If the system does not fit the style of management in the company (22), it will not be effective. If the composition of a planning committee is inappropriate (27), its performance will surely suffer.

Finally, part E deals with the planning processes. Poor grades on any of the questions 28 through 40 identify serious problems. For example, if top management accepts the idea that the formulation and operation of the FSPS is its responsibility, the system is likely to be successful unless (28) top management does not spend an appropriate amount of time on this task. A system will not be successful if line managers give lip service to it and really do not accept it (29). Also, closely associated with this, poor results will follow when line managers do not spend an appropriate amount of time on strategic planning (30). Problems will result if managers believe the system requires too much of their time (33).

A system that is based on generally known and accepted procedures is more likely to succeed than one that does not (31). However, a system that is not flexible and too ritualistic is likely to be less effective than it should be (32 and 35).

A strategic planning system must stimulate managerial and staff in-depth thinking (34). This can mean many things. For example, managers and staff must become conceptualizers as distinct from operational day-to-day thinkers. A conceptualizer is more likely to see opportunities and devise strategies to exploit them than a person whose eyes are focused solely on narrow short-range problem solving. In an important sense, strategic planning is as much an intellectual process as a set of procedures, structures, and techniques.

Program strategies have failed because company managers have been unable and/or unwilling to face up to weaknesses in the company. A brilliant strategy can fail to be implemented if a critical company weakness in implementing it is not identified and corrected. In identifying, evaluating, and implementing strategy, it is imperative than managers forthrightly address weaknesses that bear on the formulation and implementation of strategy (37).

It is rare to find a company whose headquarters and divisions operate in perfect harmony. An FSPS may generate and exacerbate tensions and divisions between these two groups as well as resolve conflicts. Sometimes divisions want and do not receive what they consider to be proper guidance. (38). Or they may feel too restrained by company headquarters (39). In either event something needs to be done to improve the situation.

Finally, managers throughout an organization are not likely to try to produce first-rate long-range strategic plans if their performance is measured and their salaries and bonuses are based solely on short-term bottom-line figures, such as margin, ROI, or net profit. Such performance standards (40) will naturally lead managers to focus attention solely on the short run and may result in practices that enhance their short-run financial position at the expense of future profits. That, of course, is not good management.

CONCLUDING OBSERVATIONS

Comparatively little research has been done on, and not much attention has been paid in the planning literature to, the evaluation of FSPSs. Past experience with FSPSs does show rather clearly some of the most significant requirements for an effective FSPS. Applying these lessons to a particular company, however, is beset with complex and puzzling problems.

Four approaches to evaluating FSPSs have been described here. None of them is as perfected as might be desired. Nevertheless, whether used in the form presented here or modified to fit particular company conditions, several of the techniques are quite capable of identifying areas in which a planning system should be improved.

An FSPS cannot be evaluated without reference to various forces that affect its design, operation, and results. An effective FSPS results from a synthesis of management style, management intuition, planning knowledge, thought processes among managers and staff, and organizational culture, as well as from planning techniques, tools, and procedures.

Considering all these factors, FSPSs can be evaluated. If more companies systematically evaluate their FSPSs, it is more than likely that their effectiveness will improve and that dissatisfactions associated with them will decline.

NOTES

[1] George A. Steiner, *Strategic Planning: What Every Manager Must Know* (New York: Free Press, 1979).

[2] *Ibid.*, p. 58.

[3] For example, *ibid.*; Peter Lorange and Richard F. Vancil, *Strategic Planning Systems* (Englewood Cliffs, N.J.: Prentice-Hall, 1977); William E. Rothschild, *Putting It All Together: A Guide to Strategic Thinking* (New York: AMACOM, 1976); Merritt L. Kastens, *Long-Range Planning for Your Business* (New York: AMACOM, 1976); David Hussey, *Corporate Planning: Theory and Practice* (New York: Pergamon Press, 1974); Russell L. Ackoff, *A Concept of Corporate Planning* (New York: Wiley-Interscience, 1970); George A. Steiner, *Top Management Planning* (New York: Macmillan, 1969); and E. Kirby Warren, *Long-Range Planning: The Executive Viewpoint* (Englewood Cliffs, N.J.: Prentice-Hall, 1966). To this list must be added many articles appearing in such journals devoted to strategic planning as *Long Range Planning*, *Managerial Planning*, and *Planning Review*.

[4] For example, Harold W. Henry, "Formal Planning in Major U.S. Corporations," *Long Range Planning*, Vol. 10, No. 5 (October 1977), pp. 40–45; Walter B. Schaffir, *Strategic Business Planning: Some Questions for the Chief Executive* (New York: AMACOM, 1976); Malcolm W. Pennington, "Why Has Planning Failed and What Can You Do About It?" *Planning Review* (November 1975); Paul J. Stonich, "Formal Planning Pitfalls and How to Avoid Them," *Management Review*, Vol. 64, No. 5, 6 & 7 (June–July 1975), pp. 4–11, 29–34; George A. Steiner and Hans Schollhammer, "Pitfalls in Multi-National Long-Range Planning," *Long Range Planning*, Vol. 8, No. 2 (April 1975), pp. 2–12; Xavier Gilbert and Peter Lorange, "Five Pillars for Your Planning," *European Business*, No. 42 (Autumn 1974), pp. 57–63; Edward R. Bagley, "How to Avoid Glitches in Planning," *Management Review*, Vol. 61, No. 3 (March 1972), pp. 4–9; George A. Steiner, *Pitfalls in Comprehensive Long Range Planning* (Oxford, Ohio; Planning Executives Institute, 1972).

[5] Walter B. Schaffir, *Strategic Business Planning: Some Questions for the Chief Executive*, (op. cit.) pp. 15–16.

[6] George A. Steiner, *Pitfalls in Comprehensive Long-Range Planning*, (op. cit.); and George A. Steiner and Hans Schollhammer, *Pitfalls in Multi-National Long-Range Planning*, (op. cit.).

[7] George A. Steiner, *Strategic Planning: What Every Manager Must Know*, (op. cit.), pp. 301–303.

4

Proposition for a Relational Conception of Strategic Planning: Adaptation to the Past and Integration of the Future

INTRODUCTION

The last ten years have been characterized by an economic crisis that engendered a feeling that something radically different was to emerge. While this feeling seems to be widely spread and deeply rooted in peoples' minds, it is remarkable that nobody is able to define precisely what is changing and why. Everybody talks about the shock of the future; very few talk about the shock of the past. For a corporate planner, the most striking shock is the shock of the past.

The objective of this chapter* is to describe precisely, in the context of an industrial organization, what is meant by the "past," and how the process of planning has to adapt to it. Then, the question of the "future," as seen from 1980 onward, is introduced and its integration into the planning process is discussed within the framework of an industrial corporation operating on an international basis, including Europe and United States. The two concepts of adaptation and integration introduced by Lorange[1] are put to work, although they are not in the order that was expected by the theory.

---

*This chapter is prepared by Georges-Yves Kervern, The Pechiney Ugine Kuhlmann Group, Paris; J. P. Ponssard, Ecole Polytechnique, Centre de Recherche en Gestion, Paris; and Jacques Sarrazin, ESSEC, Paris.

PECHINEY UGINE KUHLMANN AND ITS STRATEGIC
PLANNING SYSTEM

The Pechiney Ugine Kuhlmann Group

The French group, Pechiney Ugine Kuhlmann, has a long-established international reputation for industrial expertise in the area of advanced metal-based and chemical materials and products. The group is dedicated to the development of high-performance aluminum-, carbon-, chromium-, copper-, molybdenum-, nickel-, titanium-, zirconium-, and plastics-based materials and products for advanced technology applications in the aerospace, automotive, building, electrical, engineering, and telecommunications industries. In general, its activities involve the production of materials requiring the latest technologies in terms of physics and solids, fine chemistry, and sophisticated metallurgy. Pechiney Ugine Kuhlmann has developed mastery of many aspects of energy applications and occupies a key position in the nuclear fuel cycle. The group has industrial or commercial facilities in sixty-five countries. Its principal establishments are located in France, the United States, Spain, Greece, and Africa.

The companies that form the Pechiney Ugine Kuhlmann group have an historical background of leadership in the development of original technologies based on scientific knowledge and experimentation. One employee out of sixteen is an engineer or a scientist.

The group has always been a leader in the use of advanced systems for promoting interrelationship and cooperation among the various stakeholders on which its future depends: its employees, shareholders, customers, and suppliers as well as the administrative and governmental authorities in the countries in which it operates. It was the first French industrial corporation to commit all its pollution abatement investments in a single contract agreement between the group and the French government. For many years, Pechiney Ugine Kuhlmann has pursued a policy of consultation in its plants in the form of shop workers' meetings.

Group sales in 1978 amounted to over $6 billion. The PUK workforce numbers nearly 100,000. Shares are owned by 300,000 shareholders. Over the last seven years (1972–1978), Pechiney Ugine Kuhlmann has invested $2.25 billion and has allocated nearly $500 million to research and development.

Since 1972, the Pechiney Ugine Kuhlmann group has progressively built up an international sales network consisting of marketing units that are wholly owned subsidiaries or companies in which it has controlling interests. The services of this sales network are available to numerous small- and medium-sized European companies anxious to expand their export trade rapidly. The group has made its advanced techniques available to a number of companies in North America, South America, Africa, and Asia.

The underlying philosophy of the Pechiney Ugine Kuhlmann group is based on the notion that the company is a living entity. This entity has an organization, but the organization is made for people; people are not made for the organization. Following this humanistic philosophy, the principal function of an industrial company is to adapt the organization to the customer, not the customer to the organization. More generally, the main focus of a modern industrial company is on the relations with the various stakeholders within its environment.

The firm is composed of six autonomous operational "branches": aluminum products, special steels and electrometallurgical products, chemical products, copper products, nuclear and new technologies applications, and the U.S. operations. Each branch is itself organized into divisions. Six major functional departments (labor relations, finance, R&D, corporate planning, control, and marketing) are located at the corporate level.

Against this background, a certain philosophy is taking shape—that of decentralization. It is exhibited by the exercising of real responsibility at each level of the organizational structure. In particular, a division is both a profit and an investment center, responsible for the development of its own product lines, having its own, independent R&D capabilities, and possessing independent marketing and distribution forces.

The Corporate Planning System Used up to 1976

The corporate planning system used up to 1976 was a formal, comprehensive, mostly bottom–up approach, based on the planning concepts and procedures often encountered in the literature early in the 1970s.

The process started with the C.E.O.s making general guidelines for the development of the company in the future. Each division was then asked to formulate a long-term plan composed of a strategic plan and long-term financial projections. For the main divisions only, these projections encompassed alternatives for various expansion rates and various strategic choices.

As far as the strategic plan was concerned, the divisions had to follow the well known, two step procedure suggested by Steiner:

1. Analysis of the situation of the unit in terms of served market and internal capabilities to pinpoint the major problems and opportunities for development.
2. Determination of the objectives of the division and of the strategies that would allow their achievement, followed by the building of the action programs to be undertaken in the short term.

It was the responsibility of the branch manager to approve the division plans or to ask for a change in their proposals. Then, each branch submitted a branch plan to the C.E.O., based on division plans. A branch plan was a general policy statement emphasizing the fundamental development decisions of the branch and their implications for the whole corporation in terms of risk and financing.

The discussions between the C.E.O. and each branch manager could lead to the modification of branch plans and, therefore, division plans. The corporate plan was made up of the approved plans.

A Diagnosis of the Functioning
of the Corporate Planning System

In 1976, a diagnosis of the functioning of the corporate planning system described was made both by the company and by an external consultant. The results of the diagnosis led to the following classical but pessimistic picture:

1. All hierarchical levels taking part in the planning procedure were often disappointed when they evaluated what they were actually getting from the planning process. The divisions did not have much feedback from the hierarchical levels above them on their proposals. As a result, they felt that they were producing a lot of paper and few decisions. On the other side, branch and corporate levels were quite frustrated with the content and the form of the proposals that were submitted for their approval by the divisions.

2. The product mixes and the market mixes of the divisions had not changed much from 1971 to 1976. Further, for most divisions, resource allocations by corporate headquarters did not differ significantly from their own cash generations. There were indications that the planning system failed to encourage significant strategic change.

When looking for the explanations to these facts, five major bottlenecks emerged from the diagnosis:

First, in Lorange's terminology,[3] adaptation was weak and integration strong. There was little attempt to balance the bottom–up planning procedure with top–down planning. The corporate level viewed itself more as reacting to branches' and divisions' proposals rather than as a manager of an overall corporate portfolio. As a matter of fact, a global diagnosis of the group's portfolio of activities was lacking, and planning discussions were bilateral (C.E.O. to branch managers one by one) rather than devoted to the corporate portfolio as a whole.

Second, when trying to define a relevant business segmentation, Pechiney Ugine Kuhlmann met particular difficulty with its organizational structure of activities, based heavily on legal considerations rather than on business strategy criteria.

Third, each hierarchical level did not spend enough time on planning. In particular, planning and budgeting staffs were spending most of their time on budget data gathering. Top managers were not concerned enough with the management of the group's portfolio of activities on a worldwide basis.

Fourth, divisions lacked the formal tools and methods for analyzing and assessing strategic opportunities.

And, fifth, planning procedures were the same for every division, whatever its specific characteristics and the degree of importance of its strategic opportunities and problems for itself and for the company as a whole.

General Conclusions that Emerge from the Planning
Experience up to 1976

Pechiney Ugine Kuhlmann was not the first company to be confronted with the planning difficulties listed. Most of these pitfalls were discussed in particular by

Ringbakk[4] in his well-known article "Why Planning Fails" as early as 1971. In that respect, the group's experiences was only new empirical evidence of Ringbakk's and other's findings. But what makes its experience original is its reaction in front of its planning difficulties.

In 1976, after the diagnosis of its planning system, three main courses of action were available to the company:

1. Dropping extensive formal strategic thinking, particularly at the corporate level, by letting each operational unit manage its own development according to the famous "muddling through" theory of Lindblom.[5]
2. "Trying harder" to remove most of the planning bottlenecks.
3. Using its own experience to shed some new insights on planning theory, by testing and studying some of the underlying assumptions and problems.

It was a strategic choice of the group's top management to maintain the idea of strategic planning in the firm. Accordingly, the existing Corporate Planning and Control Department was split into two distinct functional units. The new Corporate Planning Department was placed under the authority of a vice president of the company (who would also be in charge of one of the five operational branches). The split between Planning and Control was intended to open up for a less numbers-oriented, less "extrapolative" planning process.

The new Corporate Planning Department did not adopt the second course of action listed, that is, the improvement of the existing planning procedures by adding new rules and planning methods. The fundamental causes of the planning difficulties encountered up to that time were not entirely clear. For instance, why was top management in the group, as in other firms, apparently not much interested in an explicit strategic management of the overall corporate portfolio? Or, why didn't operational units spend enough time on planning? As a consequence, one could wonder if adjustments of the existing planning procedures would significantly improve performance or if the real problem was not the "fit" between the planning system and the whole management system and culture of the firm.

Pechiney Ugine Kuhlmann thus chose to use its own experience to try to shed some original light on planning theory, while maintaining a decentralized and flexible planning procedure within the enterprise along the lines of the three cycles corporate planning system proposed by Lorange and Vancil.[6] Up to now, its corporate planning department has been working on three main topics:

1. To facilitate the adaptation of the strategic decision-making process to the past of the company, by making explicit the systems of values and norms, the "business creeds," of the organization and by linking them to planning methodology.
2. To enhance the acceptance of the validity and use of portfolio analysis in strategic planning.
3. To develop a new conception of the interaction between the firm and its environment, based on the concepts of flexibility and negotiation and on some concepts of systems theory.

STRATEGIC PLANNING: ADAPTATION TO THE PAST AND INTEGRATION OF THE FUTURE

Strategic Planning and the Systems of Values in the Organization: Adaptation to the Past

A theoretical perspective. From the group's planning experience emerged the major hypothesis that a corporate planning system cannot be composed only of methods and procedures aimed at the production of strategic studies, action programs, and budgets. If it did, a feeling of frustration would spread throughout the corporation. Something would be missing in the planning system.

But what precisely would be missing and why?

We did not find any theoretical framework that provides a fully satisfying answer to such a question. However, two distinct approaches offer interesting insights into that problem.

First, Ozbekhan[7] tries to link planning and change, change and perception of the environment, and perception of the environment and a system of values in a logical manner. In Ozbekhan's terminology, a corporate planning system must then be viewed as a three-level system: (1) a normative planning level, where the system of dominant values in the enterprise is defined; (2) a strategic level of definition of the objectives of the organization, the system of values allowing the ranking of possible objectives; and (3) an operational or mechanistic level, where decisions are made to achieve corporate objectives. According to Ozbekhan, normative planning must be accomplished first, then strategic planning must be realized, and at last operational planning should be completed.

The other approach is one suggested by Argyris.[8] He introduces the concept of double-loop learning, that is, the process through which the organization is questioning the validity of underlying policies and objectives, the "rules of the game." This second approach is also encountered in the field of psychology. In particular, Bateson[9] and Watzlawick[10,11] of The Mental Research Institute at Palo Alto suggest that "double binds" appear in the relationships among people. The negative effects of these double binds can be cured only by acting at higher organizational, or logical, levels.

Both approaches emphasize the impossibility of designing and implementing any planning system or, more generally, any management system, without taking explicit account of the *raison d'être* of the organization in which the system is going to be implemented, of its rules of functioning, and of its system of norms and values. Very often, these notions are put together under the term "business creeds."

If one agrees with these two approaches, a central problem then is the choice of a methodology of developing explicit business creeds in an organization.

A methodology to make business creeds explicit. When the group tried to apply the previous theoretical approaches to its own situation, the problem immediately arose as to the manner by which the existing system or systems of values prevalent in the organization could be brought to light. As a matter of fact, in 1976 the company did not have any statement of its general policy. A survey of two hundred of its managers revealed their anxiety relative to the lack of explicit "rules of the game" within the enterprise.

When looking for a methodology to bring to light the group's business creeds, the company first analyzed the content of the business creeds already made explicit in numerous United States firms. The survey showed that, however disparate these business creeds seemed to be at a first glance, most of them dealt with the kind of relationships the organization wanted to have with social groups such as employees, stockholders, trade unions, the government, society, and so on (see Exhibit 4-1). But no rational methodological scheme emerged from the analysis which would provide answers to the group's main questions:

—Why business creeds?
—How to define them?
—How to support them?
—Where do "the rules of the game" existing in an enterprise come from and how do they change?

Consequently, Pechiney Ugine Kuhlmann then attempted to develop a methodological scheme by using the well-known analogical approach taken from the field of biology. Let us recall that biologists set forth the theory that living organisms behave as if their behavior followed four basic rules.

1. The main objective of living organisms is their own survival.
2. Living organisms are endlessly trying to expand themselves, to grow, or to increase their influence on their environment.
3. The growth of a living organism goes with the complexity of the organism, which arranges itself into specific subsets at different hierarchical levels. From this hierarchical structure emerges a *raison d'être* more and more developed as the living organism grows. Each hierarchical level has its original characteristics and properties that are not the result of the mere adding up of the characteristics and properties of the levels below it. Moreover, each level can be understood as an internally and externally oriented control device, aimed at the survival and the expansion of the whole organism.
4. At last, living organisms seem to behave according to the minimal energy principle: Their behavior is oriented toward the minimization of the energy and, more generally, of the means required for their evolution.

In biology, these four basic rules lead to patterns of behavior of living organisms such as reproduction, memorization, pedagogy, trial and error, feeding, selection, expansion, hierarchical organization, internal and external control, negotiation, and escaping.

In management, if we make the hypothesis that we can establish an analogy between the behavior of a living organism and that of an enterprise, it is in fact quite easy to link the previous biological patterns of behavior to the usual business functions: production, learning, research and development, purchasing, financing, selling, corporate planning, organizing, budgeting, management control, auditing, marketing, and legal affairs. Exhibit 4-2 shows these analogical relationships between both kinds of behavior patterns.

EXHIBIT 4-1

Principles / Corporations	Good relationships with	Suppliers	Unions	People	Government	Stockholders	Customers	Employees	Market leadership	Competition	No waste	Mutual respect (reciprocal) rights and obligations)	Internal	External	Innovation	Creativity	Products and services	Behavior in the society	Management methods	Precise field of activity	Fair remuneration — Stockholders	Fair remuneration — Employees	Customers (through prices)	Profitability	High standards of recruitment or careful selection	Development and formation of the employees	Financial independence	Information — Stockholders	Information — Employees	Customers	People	Productivity	No waste	Free enterprise	Integrity, probity	Growth	Quality	Progress	Decentralization	Marketing	Teamwork	Job conditions and tools	Freedom of thought, belief and political support for employees	Equal treatment in the promotion procedure for administration and technical employees	No discrimination according to race, color, sex, national origin, religion, or political beliefs	Growth in the fields of competence, management science, technic, finance, production, marketing	Take into account world sociopolitical trends	Optimism with regard to country's resources	To drop unworkable products and activities quickly	Diversity and pluralism (indeed inconsistency)	Awareness of critics	Flexibility
American Airlines				×	×	×	×		×	×	×		×				×			×	×	×	×	×																											
A.T. & T.							×	×							×				×	×	×	×	×	×	×	×																										
Armco						×	×	×	×								×	×	×		×			×	×		×			×		×	×												×							
Bemis			×	×	×	×	×	×				×	×				×		×	×	×	×		×		×			×	×				×																		
Blawknox		×		×	×	×	×	×									×				×	×		×	×																											
Clevite							×																																													
Calumet and Necia		×			×	×	×	×									×				×	×												×			×	×		×												
Donaldson		×		×	×	×	×														×	×							×								×	×														
General Electric				×	×	×	×	×					×		×		×	×	×	×	×	×	×	×	×	×								×	×		×	×	×	×	×	×	×				×					
General Mills					×	×	×	×													×	×	×	×											×	×	×	×		×												
General Motors				×	×	×	×	×					×				×				×	×	×	×											×	×	×																
General Telephone & Electronics		×			×	×		×	×								×			×	×	×	×	×	×			×	×						×	×	×		×	×			×	×	×	×	×					
Lawce				×	×	×	×	×	×				×							×	×	×		×	×						×				×																	
Monsanto				×	×	×		×					×							×	×	×		×							×			×									×			×	×		×			
North American Aviation					×								×			×																																×				
Standard Oil of Indiana				×	×	×	×	×	×				×	×		×	×	×		×									×					×	×	×																
Sunoco					×			×	×																	×								×	×												×				
Westinghouse		×	×	×	×	×	×	×					×	×	×	×	×	×			×	×	×	×	×	×									×							×									×	
Dow Chemical		×	×	×	×	×	×	×					×	×			×	×			×	×	×	×		×									×			×													×	
Union Carbide		×	×	×	×	×	×	×			×		×	×								×		×		×								×	×							×										×

EXHIBIT 4-2 Roles, Behavior, Functions

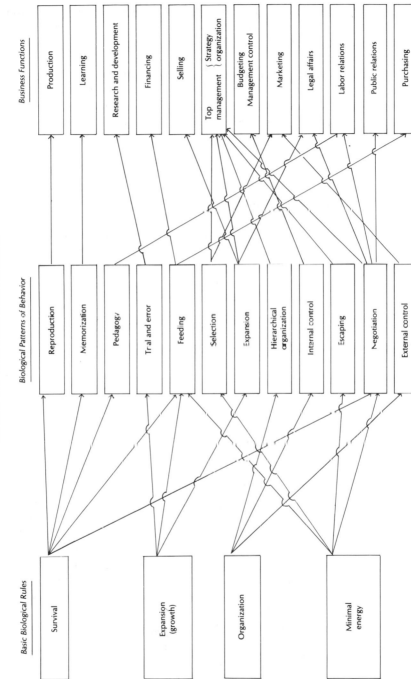

55

It was found worthwhile to go further with the analogy between industrial organizations and living organisms and to try to translate the four basic biological rules into the field of business. This led to a set of basic business "rules" analogous to the four basic biological rules. Exhibit 4-3 shows both sets of rules and their relationships.

This set of basic business rules has been submitted to a committee of the group's executives. They evaluated the rules and made choices, the intention being to end up with a set of "rules of the game" that take into account what an industrial organization is, in general, and specifically reflect the group's historical, cultural and sociological background.

That final set of rules has been called the "business creeds" of Pechiney Ugine Kuhlmann. It has been distributed throughout the entire enterprise. Observations do suggest that it is being used as a reference tool in strategic planning discussions in numerous divisions. One of the business creeds explicitly refers to the selection and appraisal of so-called business units as part of a so-called "portfolio" planning methodology. Since the publication of that rule, substantial progress has been made in the acceptance of that approach by the group's management.

But perhaps the greatest benefit from the group's effort in making its business creeds explicit has been the fact that the company has become more fully aware of the drastic importance of its relationships with various sets of external factors for its own development and, in fact, for its own survival. This last point is illustrated by the adoption by the group of several business creeds dealing with the exchanges between the group and its environment. For instance, a rule refers to the improvement of relationships at the local level between plant managers and local authorities. This rule is being followed by most plant managers and is becoming especially important, taking account of the more politically constrained setting experienced in most of Europe.

Strategic Planning and Management Tools

A second topic currently under investigation at Pechiney Ugine Kuhlmann deals with further operationalization of management tools commonly used in strategic planning. This task is not completed yet but is already yielding challenging results particularly when making the portfolio approach more practically useful. In this section, we shall show the necessity of taking explicitly into account the "past" when applying the portfolio methodology. In the next section of this chapter, we will suggest that the portfolio approach also is a means of incorporating the "future." We shall do this through the analysis of negotiation relationships among various sets of actors.

Management Tools: A Life-Span Hypothesis. Management is not a science. A lot of accumulated experience plays a significant role in practice, but it cannot always be communicated to others. Mintzberg[12] emphasizes this in his work. This may partly explain the feeling that many management tools exhibit the life span

EXHIBIT 4-3

Business Rules Drawn from the Biological Analogy

Basic Biological Rules and Biological Patterns of Behavior	Business Functions: Rough Statements of Rules
Rule 1: Survival	The firm lives maximizing its life over time.
—Memorization	The firm lives accumulating its learning over time.
—Pedagogy	The firm lives spreading and transmitting its experience over time.
—Life and death of the models	The firm lives managing a set of models that emerge, grow, reach maturity, and die.
Rule 2: Expansion (Growth)	The firm lives maximizing the scope of validity of its models.
—Trial and error	The firm lives renewing its models through trial and error, risk taking, and exploitation of the failures. ures.
—Selection	The firm lives choosing the models the most adapted to the internal and external characteristics of its operations.
Rule 3: Organization	The firm lives organizing itself through differentiation into specialized units and specific hierarchical levels.
—Maximal exchange	The firm lives maximizing internal and external informational exchanges.
—internal and external control	The firm lives setting up internal and external detection and control devices at all the organizational levels.
—Negotiation, mutual respect, reciprocal balance of rights and duties	The firms lives maintaining joint responsibility among the elements existing in its internal and external environments, through a set of negotiations, maintained in balance through the mutual respect of the characteristics of the existing elements and leading to the making explicit of the conflicts among the elements, then to shared objectives in terms of rights and obligations of the existing elements during the period of time considered in the negotiation.
Rule 4: Minimal energy	The firm lives minimizing the amount of resources that it takes from the external environment.

of a new product (emergence, maturity, decline) but seem hardly able to contribute to a more comprehensive analysis of some real phenomenon. Examples include operations research and management information systems, as extensive "families" of techniques, return on assets analysis, return on investment analysis, and portfolio analysis, as more specific approaches.

Clearly many such tools are useful, given certain circumstances. The trouble, however, is that they might easily develop a life of their own within the organization, become part of its culture. For instance, proposals for decisions may have to be proposed in accordance with the restrictive format of a given tool; otherwise they might not even be considered. It follows that tools may be studied not from the point of view of their intrinsic validity but as mechanisms that constrain the behavior of an organization (see, on that point, Berry et al.).[13] The danger is that the manager might be pursuing a never-ending synthetic approach to his or her global problems and is continually confronted by different, possibly incoherent tools unfit to deal with a moving reality.

Such descriptions seem to characterize many planning activities in Pechiney Ugine Kuhlmann as in other French corporations. The uses of such management tools as portfolio analysis or return on investment analysis in these firms tend to follow the life-span hypothesis. In its mature stage, the management tool is, thus, as much a required communication device, a "ritualistic" language, as a pragmatic decision analysis tool. There is an increasing risk that the original purpose of the tool, to help the decision maker, might become of minor relevance relative to the communication purpose.

The Portfolio Analysis Approach. Pechiney Ugine Kuhlmann experienced the previously described phenomenon with portfolio analysis, i.e., that it became ritualistic in use rather than maintaining a useful decision-making focus. That management tool was first introduced in a division of the company by the Boston Consulting Group. Let us recall that this model is based on the experience curve hypothesis and leads to three well-known inferences:[14]

1. Market share dominance explains differential profitability for competitors on the same product.
2. It is important to fight for market share whenever the growth rate is high because then one is more fluid with respect to time and the outcome of the battle will have long-range profitability consequences.
3. A corporation's long-term profitability requires an appropriately balanced mix of products with different cash flow characteristics.

According to many criteria, the Boston Consulting Group study was a success. Two years later most of the group's managers talked in terms of "cash cows," "stars," and so on, and their strategic plans exhibited share–growth matrices for the positioning of their business activities. However, the methodology used by divisions to exhibiting these matrices of strategic positions often appeared questionable in the following ways:

1. Segmentation into business activities was done without in-depth analysis of the value added at each intermediary production stage.
2. No attempt was made to quantify the magnitude of the experience curve effect.
3. The four quadrants of the matrix were positioned without explicit reference to the growth rate effect. For instance, the borderline between "star" and "cash cow" may be set at 3.75 percent on the growth rate scale because the French GNP was growing at that rate (many activities presently grow at 2 or 3 percent when they do not decline; in that case, much of the potential value added by the tool seems to be lost by the more or less arbitrary setting of the borderline).
4. Inferences on profitability that may be drawn from the strategic position of the activities were not satisfied in practice (i.e., the expected increases in profitability as market share increased did not occur).

Two years after its introduction in some division plans, the portfolio tool disappeared with the reintroduction of a return of investment emphasis.

What emerges from these observations is that many managers do not take enough time to get a full understanding of the underlying assumptions behind the portfolio tool. Consequently, they either take for granted or simply reject its final implications. That behavior may come from time pressures, from the feeling of the "enormous" empirical evidence that seems to support portfolio matrix conclusions, or from the appealing character of the analysis to any experienced manager. In any event, the group soon recognized that the conclusions from a product portfolio analysis could sometimes be grossly misleading if managers are not fully aware of the conditions for use of the approach.

These conclusions coincide with findings already drawn by several researchers. In particular, Day[15] stressed that the three major inferences of the share–growth matrix model may not always be true, and exhibited quite a few counter-examples encountered in the real world. However, Day's normative prescriptions are based on the empirical observation of pitfalls in the implementation of the approach, rather than on a logical analysis of the underlying hypotheses of the model. In general, most research has been oriented toward in-depth empirical analysis of the share–growth matrix. However, several interesting results can easily be obtained by letting the simple mathematics of the experience curve hypothesis work on its own.

The Simple Mathematics of the Experience Curve Hypothesis

Let us recall the experience curve hypothesis: The unit cost* (c) of a "product"[†] is reduced by a constant factor (K) each time its rank in the cumulative production (Q) is doubled:

$$c\,(Q) = c_1 Q^{\log K/\log 2} \implies c(2Q) = Kc(Q)$$

*cost is expressed in constant terms, such as units of labor or constant money.
†the problem of defining what is meant by a product has to be solved in practice by the so-called art of segmentation.

Corollary 1. Suppose that firms A and B have market shares σ_A and σ_B, respectively, and that these market shares remain constant over time; then the ratio of their unit costs remain unchanged:

$$Q_A = \sigma_A Q \qquad Q_B = \sigma_B Q$$

Application: $\implies C_A / C_B = (\sigma_A/\sigma_B)\log K/\log 2$

$$\sigma_A/\sigma_B = 2^n \implies C_A / C_B = K^n$$

Corollary 2. Suppose that the production grows at a constant rate ρ; then cost declines exponentially at a rate $\rho \log K/\log 2$.

Application. Let $T = 2/\rho$ (T is the time period required for doubling cumulative annual production); then annual unit cost declines at an approximate rate of $(1 = K)/T$.

It is clear that, if the experience curve hypothesis is not satisfied ($K = 1$), the first two portfolio analysis rules need not be true; market share dominance might not imply differential profitability and it might not necessarily be interesting to fight for high market share whenever the growth rate is high. This is in accordance with Day's empirical findings.

What is interesting here is that the simple considerations given suggest that the practical relevance of the first two portfolio analysis rules vary according to the numerical value of K, that is, to the slope of the experience curve. For instance, let us consider two of the group's products P_1 and P_2.

$$P_1 \quad \text{with } K_1 = 0.7$$

$$P_2 \quad \text{with } K_2 = 0.9$$

Let us suppose that the group's management wants to obtain a cost advantage of 20 percent over a competitor (who is supposed not to modify his or her level of cost) within a five years period. The two corollaries set forth previously then show that this requirement can only be satisfied with a market growth rate of greater than 9 percent for P_1 and greater than 22 percent for P_2.

More generally, two products that are located in the same position on the share–growth matrix can differ significantly in terms of profitability or strategic opportunities, depending on the value of the experience effects. Portfolio approach can thus be grossly misleading when applied to a set of products with various experience effects K. Thus, in its portfolio analysis, the strategic decision maker musk take explicit account of the possible variety of technological experiences. These may partly be a result of the different characteristics of the products and partly be due to the strategies followed in the past.

These conclusions suggest that in a large, diversified corporation strategic analysis based on taking advantage of experience curve effects seems to be far more applicable at the division levels, that is, at strategic business units levels, than at the corporate level. Thus, this presentation of the portfolio tool leads to an emphasis of an integration need for the experience effects stemming from different parts of the operation. Such an integration is now strongly recommended by the group's corporate level when evaluating the portfolio analysis of the different divisions.[16]

Let us conclude by making some general comments on some broader implications from the experience curve hypothesis. Its mathematical formulation provides a mechanical picture of the role of technological progress that would lead directly to monopolistic dominance based on known technologies and mature products and arms length competition for long-term innovation. In this respect, it is interesting to compare this picture with the classical economic analysis that rarely recognizes the profitability differential as originating from this dynamic change in the production function, but focuses on market structure instead. Of course, there is the major exception of Schumpeter's work on the theory of development.[17,18] In this latter framework (which scope embraces an analysis of the civilization of capitalism and thus is far more general than is our present discussion), technical progress is also seen as implying monopolistic practices on current production. However, then, competition becomes extremely harsh and creating an uncertain climate for forthcoming innovations (in market, supply, technology, and organization). Pursuing the idea of innovation in an uncertain dynamic environment in which the actors have incomplete information certainly appears as a more difficult task than just considering a mechanistic experience effect on the one hand, or a sophisticated competition on static models on the other hand, but that is what we should be talking about.

The Integration of the Future Through the Concepts of Negotiation and Flexibility

The Environment in the Future and the Future in the Environment. The last topic to be discussed deals with how to better integrate an emphasis on the future in corporate planning methodology. By "future" one usually means either the future characteristics of the organization's environment or the future states of the whole economic, social, and cultural system to which the enterprise belongs.

The environment is often presented as an outside force that is the cause of all the problems confronting the organization. The environment is "turbulent," "aggressive," "adverse to industrial rationality," "endlessly changing," "elusive," "unforeseeable." The enterprise frequently experiences a sense of adverseness vis-à-vis its environment; the enterprise does not understand its environment, or worse, it pollutes it.

The future, on the other hand, is usually defined as a set of hidden data that could be known if the organization had the "right person in the right job," that is, a corporate planner with a crystal ball that supplies him or her with a set of scenarios among which providence will have the good taste to choose. But the worldwide economic crisis of the 1970s exemplifies how hazardous guessing the future can be. Extrapolation does not work well: The sophisticated computerized forecasting models become ends by themselves, and technological forecasting is an art more than a science.

Then, how can we integrate the future into corporate planning methodology? Our effort in that field is oriented currently along two dimensions: Negotiation and flexibility.

A New Definition for Environment and for Future. The environment of an organization can be described in three ways: (1) a set of state variables—market growth, for instance, (2) a set of phenomena and general laws of functioning—product life cycle, for example, and (3) a set of social groups of actors—consumers, stockholders, suppliers, government, competitors, and mass media, to name a few.

From some recent work on that subject, we have adopted the third definition of the environment listed. In that perspective, the future can be understood as the potential outcome of negotiation relationships among various social groups. A critical question to be asked is thus whether these stakeholders are inside the organization or outside, or both. Strategic planning can be defined as the analysis of the consequences of these negotiation settings for the enterprise, attempting to keep viable links between the corporation and the various social groups.

A New Interpretation of the Portfolio Approach. The portfolio approach may be seen as a way to analyze the interactions among competitors in terms of strength in some kind of indefinitely repeated stochastic game. (For a precise game theoretical approach to "strength" in another context, see Levine and Ponssard).[19] A specific definition of strength has to be worked out in each context, but it seems that it could proceed in two steps.

The first step would be to analyze the dimensions of present strength, such as relative market shares, amount of excess capacities, financial postures, and so on. The second step would be to analyze the determinants of future strength, such as relative cost structures, market growth, technological barriers, and so on. To use an analogy with physics, such an analysis of strength might focus on the current positions as well as the speed of change associated with these positions in absolute terms. Current positions particularly determine short-term strategy sets, and speed of change analysis may help to define the evolution of these strategy sets. Such an interpretation is consistent with the usual portfolio matrix, which appears as the ultimate way in which to explore the analysis along one dimension (i.e., experience curve effect), as well as with General Electric's nine-block matrix described by Allen, which encompasses many more dimensions but then has to face the classical aggregation problem.[20]

A Generalization: The Relational Conception of Strategic Planning

Whenever one takes a scientific standpoint to analyze decision processes in business corporations, one has to start with some modesty.[21,22] Many more research studies need to be done to fully understand what a strategic decision is. Above all, new directions presently followed in the fields of communications and biology might play the role of lighting the way for the group's evolving concept of strategic planning. These directions appear to converge on the idea of relationships among actors or social groups that are inside or outside the corporation. Just like a human being, to understand its own meaning a corporation has to be understood by other groups. To be understood by other groups, it needs to understand them as well. As a consequence, the only valid approach is one that is built explicitly on the understanding of its internal and external relationships.

The corporation is building its own reality through the perception of messages.[23] These messages are coming through the communication network that the corporation has established with different social groups. Only the reality of communication can assure the communication of reality.[24,25] This follows the lines of Watzlawick and the Palo Alto research group. The latter have shown the great importance of the rules of the game (metacommunication) to maintain the "good health" and quality of communication.

The business executive uses a cognitive approach that, in fact, leads to building and introducing change in an organization. At the heart of this cognitive approach one finds the ideas of distinction and indication, that is, of segmentation.[26] Here one finds Varela's research[27,28] as well as Simon's.[29,30] The cognitive process of segmentation leads to the development of graphs and hierarchies that have been enhanced especially by the works of the recent Nobel laureate. As a matter of fact, an explicit link appears in a corporation between the mode of strategic segmentation and the pattern of organization at different hierarchical levels.

Recent advances in biology are quite useful to better analyze the links that exist between organization and autonomy. The notion of autopoiesis formulated by Varela and Maturana[31] has provided a better understanding of the process through which a living organism can structure itself to more effectively resist external perturbations.

Following the principle of order from noise studied by Von Voerster[32] and Atlan,[33,34] it may even be seen how external perturbations coming from the environment can be integrated by an organism to improve its own organization. The antagonisms and conflicts that arise through the relationship between two social groups may be understood as part of a game of an ego-antagonistic couple. Bernard-Weill's research,[35,36] to some extent, allows the anticipation of the evolution of such a couple. The notion of interaction as used in cybernetics may then be humanized. But, rather than talking about the interations between the enterprise and its environment, which is quite abstract, it is better to focus on series of interactions between two actors or two groups of actors, either internal or external.

The psychological aspects of the relationship between two actors appears to be a source of renewed interest. These studies may cast some new light on the impressive capacity of industrial civilization to create consuming modes and behaviors that suddenly appear as essential needs for billions of people, whereas their very existence tended to be ignored by everybody earlier. A very stimulating approach to this phenomenon of social mimetism has been undertaken by Girard.[37-39] His work has been received quite well by scientists who seek to understand the meaning of this mixture of well-being or unhappiness flowing over us every day without reason.[40] Each group of actors tends to react to a representation of another group of actors. Even completely wrong representations show considerable power. This explains the curious process of self-fulfilling prophecies and the strength of "double bind" in many human conflicts.[41]

This research suggests that one may anticipate a complete reformulation of both the concepts of strategic planning and organization when emphasizing the concept of relationships. The set of relationships between internal and external actors may be seen as the very organization of the corporation. The analysis of these relationships, and the preparation of the negotiations that need to be done because of these relationships, would be understood as the task of strategic planning. The future of the corporation is being created through the process generated by these relationships. The future of the corporation, therefore, appears to be strongly dependent on a triangle, the points of which are strategic planning, organization, and negotiation.

Integration of the Future in Terms of Flexibility

The second dimension of the integration of the future which is currently studied in Pechiney Ugine Kuhlmann's setting is that of flexibility. That concern emerges from the pragmatic observation of the reality, which suggests that uncertainty is not a bottleneck that can be eliminated by rational methods, however sophisticated they might be, but a given feature of most decision situations, only partially removable. Therefore decision-making modes must adapt themselves to environmental uncertainty—that is, the environment cannot be oversimplified—to be taken into account by rational existing decision-making models. (See Sarrazin on that subject.)[42]

In that perspective, flexibility in corporate development appears to be a possible way in which to integrate the uncertainty, or the ambiguity, of the future. The approach to flexibility currently studied in the group tries to maintain a balance between realism and formalism. The realism point of view leads to a decision-making mode where decisions are broken down into successive, coordinated short-term steps rather than made "once for ever." The formalism point of view is expressed in the taking account of long-term corporate objectives and constraints, however ill-defined or "fuzzy" they might be. To this end, dynamic short-term corporate objectives are defined, the role of which being the reintroduction of long-term considerations in the determination of the short-term decisions, that is, the necessity of achieving long-term uncertain objectives and of respecting long-term uncertain constraints.

The concept of short-term objectives calls for several major comments:

1. They are set up for the point in time up to which enough reliable information still exists to allowing a deterministic or probabilistic evaluation of the state of development of the firm at that time.

2. They are defined as the minimal level of organizational performance most likely to be required at that time for the later achievement of the long-term objectives. In other words, they represent a quasi-necessary condition for the attainment of the long-term objectives, but this condition might not be sufficient.

3. They will be used as criteria of choice in the short-term steps decision-making mode. They will define "the track" toward the long-term objectives.
4. As the degree of ambiguity evolves and new long-term uncertain objectives emerge, the short-term objectives might also be modified. As a consequence, flexibility can be viewed as a dynamic process of adjustment of a stream of decisions to a stream of short-term certain objectives.

The dynamic set of short-term objectives can be illustrated as a dynamic "window" that evolves as time flows and to which the enterprise has to adjust its corporate development. At any time, this window splits the space of future development of the firm into two subspaces, a short-term certain one and a long-term uncertain, ambiguous one.

In the long-term uncertain space of corporate development, the bounds on the system "enterprise" and the system itself is likely to be defined ambiguously. The main concern of the firm must be to preserve maximal flexibility in corporate development, without neglecting the achievement of its long-term corporate goals. The determination of the short-term window has to conciliate these two preoccupations.

In Pechincy Ugine Kuhlmann's planning process, "short-term" space is explored by the budgets as well as by three-year strategic programs. Considerable efforts have been made to transform budget from the classical financial conception to more of a strategy-oriented concept of action plans. In the same manner, strategic milestones and "abort flags" are progressively introduced in three-year programs.

SUMMARY AND CONCLUSION: PROPOSITION FOR A RELATIONAL STRATEGY

Taking the example of a diversified industrial group in Europe, this chapter has set forth a series of empirical observations and theoretical propositions. Many of them seem not to be dependent upon the specific setting of Pechiney Ugine Kuhlmann, but can be considered valid for other industrial groups. These general observations and theoretical propositions can be recapitulated as follows:

1. The relative insufficiency of many planning processes and the insufficient time devoted by management to these processes and to their improvement.
2. The necessity of industrial organizations to make more explicit their values and "rules of the game." This need for explicitness is the first step of a good relational process of communication with the "environment."
3. The possibility of improvement of the portfolio approach through a broadened interpretation and analysis of the relationships and negotiations among competitors.
4. The definition of the environment as a set of actors and the definition of the future as an output of the relationships and negotiations among these actors and the firm.
5. The logic of flexibility justifying an emphasis on strategic characteristics of the budgeting and programming phases of the planning process.

In conclusion, the notion of relationships may be considered as the key that unites the three concepts of strategy, organization and negotiation. These concepts can sometimes be merged to create a unique entrepreneurial approach: the preparing of a decision followed by the action itself. Some works even use neologisms such as "organizaction."[43] We may propose as well "negotiaction," "relaction," and "communicaction," all of them presently mixed together with the term "interaction."

The future will hopefully bring a new understanding to enlighten the practice of strategic decision making. It is believed that this new understanding will be enhanced through advanced research on subjects such as organization, negotiation, communications, biology, and systems theory.

NOTES

[1]Peter Lorange, *Corporate Planning: An Executive Viewpoint* (Englewood Cliffs, N.J.: Prentice-Hall, 1979), pp. 4–12.

[2]George A. Steiner, *Top Management Planning* (New York: Macmillan, 1969), pp. 286–294.

[3]Peter Lorange, *Corporate Planning: An Executive Viewpoint, op. cit.*, p. 4.

[4]Kjell A. Ringbakk, "Why Planning Fails," *European Business*, No. 29 (Spring 1971), pp. 15–27.

[5]Charles E. Lindblom, "The Science of Muddling Through," *Public Administration Review*, Vol. 19, No. 2 (Spring 1959), pp. 79–88.

[6]Peter Lorange and Richard F. Vancil, *Strategic Planning Systems* (Englewood Cliffs, N.J.: Prentice-Hall, 1977), pp. 139–151.

[7]Hasan Ozbekhan, "Towards a Central Theory of Planning," in Erich Jantsch ed., *Perspectives on Planning* (Washington, D.C.: OECD, 1969).

[8]Chris Argyris, "Double-Loop Learning in Organizations," *Harvard Business Review*, Vol. 55, No. 5 (September–October 1977), pp. 115–125.

[9]George Bateson, *Steps to an Ecology of Mind* (San Francisco: Chandler Publishing, 1972).

[10]P. Watzlawick, *How Real Is Real?* (New York: Random House, 1976).

[11]P. Watzlawick et al., *Pragmatics of Human Communication* (New York: W. W. Norton, 1967).

[12]Henry Mintzberg, Duru Raisinghani, and A. Theoret, "The Structure of 'Unstructured' Decision Processes," *Administrative Science Quarterly*, Vol. 21, No. 2 (June 1976), pp. 246–275.

[13]M. Berry, J. C. Moisdon, and C. Riveline, "Qu'est-ce que la recherche en Gestion," Working Paper 78-15, Centre de Recherche en Gestion, (Paris: Ecole Polytechnique, September 1978).

[14]Patrick Conley, "Experience Curve as a Planning Tool," *Chemical Marketing Research Association*, (Houston, Texas, February 23–24, 1970).

[15]George Day, "Diagnosing the Product Portfolio," *Journal of Marketing*, Vol. 41, No. 2 (April 1977), pp. 29–38.

[16]Jacques Sarrazin, and J.-P. Ponssard, "Profitability and Strategic Posture," Working Paper, (Paris: Ecole Polytechnique, 1979).

[17]Joseph S. Schumpeter, *The Theory of Economic Development* (New York: Oxford University Press, 1934; originally published, 1911).

[18]Joseph S. Schumpeter, *Capitalisme, Socialisme, Democratie* (Paris: Payot, 1961; originally published, 1942).

[19]P. Levine and J.-P. Ponssard, "Power and Negotiation," in A. Brams *et. al.*, eds., *Applied Game Theory*, (Vienna: Physical Verlag, 1979) pp. 13–31.

[20]Michael G. Allen, "Diagramming GE's Planning for What's What," *Planning Review* (September 1977).

[21] Henry Mintzberg, Duru Raisinghani, and A. Théoret, "The Structure of the 'Unstructured' Decision Process," *op. cit.* p. 274.

[22]Henry Mintzberg, "The Manager's Job: Folklore and Fact," *Harvard Business Review* Vol. 53, No. 4, (July–August 1975).

[23]H. Von Voerster, "On Constructing Areality," No. 234 (Urbana: Biological Computer Laboratory, University of Illinois, 1978).

[24]P. Watzlawick, *How Real Is Real? op. cit.*

[25]P. Watzlawick et al., *Pragmatics of Human Communication. op. cit.*

[26]G. Brown Spencer, *Laws of Form* (London: Allen and Unwin, 1979).

[27]F. J. Varela, H. R. Maturana, and R. Uribe, *Autopoiesis: The Organization of Living Systems, Its Characterization and a Model of Bio Systems* (Amsterdam: North-Holland, 1974).

[28]F. J. Varela, "A Calculus for Self-reference," *International Journal of General Systems*, Vol. 2, No. 1 (1975), pp. 5–24.

[29]Herbert Simon and James March, *Organizations* (New York: Wiley-Interscience, 1958).

[30]Herbert Simon, *The Science of the Artificial* (Cambridge, Mass.: M.I.T. Press, 1969).

[31]F. J. Varela, H. R. Maturana, and R. Uribe, *Autopoiesis: The Organization of Living Systems, Its Characterization and a Model of Bio Systems, op. cit.*

[32]H. Von Voerster, "On Constructing Areality," *op. cit.*

[33]H. Atlan, *L'Organisation biologique et la Théorie de l'information* (Paris: Herman, 1972).

[34]H. Atlan, "On a Formal Definition of Organization," *Journal of Theoretical Biology*, Vol. 45 (March 1974), pp. 295–304.

[35]E. Bernard-Weill, *L'Arc et la Corde. Un Modèle d'Antagonismes dialectiques en biologie et Sciences Humaines* (Paris: Maloine Doin, 1975).

[36]E. Bernard-Weill et al., "Computer Analog Simulation of a Model for Regulation of Ego-Antagonistic Couples," *International Journal of Bio-Medical Computer.*

[37]R. Girard, *Mensonage romantique et Vérité romanesque* (Paris: Bernard Grasset, 1978).

[38]R. Girard, *La Violence et le Sacré* (Paris: Bernard Grasset, 1972).

[39]R. Girard, *De Choses cachées depuis la Fondation du Monde* (Paris: Bernard Grasset, 1978).

[40]J.P. Dupuy, "Le Signe et l'Envie—Variations sur les figures de René Girard," Working Paper (Paris: Cerebe, October 1978).

[41]P. Watzlawick et al., *Pragmatics of Human Communication op. cit.*

[42]Jacques Sarrazin, "Strategic Control as a Normative Theory of Corporate Development Under Ambiguous Circumstances," unpublished Ph.D. thesis (Austin: University of Texas Graduate School of Business, 1978).

[43]E. Morin, *La Méthode* (Paris: Le Seuil, 1977).

5

Strategic Resource Allocation Procedures

INTRODUCTION

This chapter* is concerned with the design of systems to help large manufacturing firms in allocating resources. The heart of the resource allocation process manifests itself in the investment decisions made by a firm. A system for supporting these investment decisions is described. This system is being used currently by the Continental Group, Inc. (CGI) for making investments in new businesses, but it is not in use for other types of investments.

Many such systems have been proposed and tried in firms over the past decade. The failure rate in these trials has been high. In many cases the customers for the services of the system (i.e., managers at the corporate level of the firm who make the final investment decisions) do not use the system. We believe that a major cause of these failures is that the systems do not provide outputs that communicate to its clients in terms that are meaningful to them. We also believe that there is probably no one system that would be universally useful for all firms. The following pages describe a methodology that might be used for designing a system specific to the needs of any given firm.

There are some indications that the design of a system should be tailored to

---

*This chapter is prepared by Sudeep Anand, Business Applications Analyst, The Continental Group, Inc., and D. Bruce Merrifield, vice President, Technology, The Continental Group, Inc.

the situational setting of the firm. The paper also discusses preliminary data on the impact of the situational setting of a firm on the design of a system for it.

CONTEXT AND BACKGROUND

Although the strategy of a firm is often stated in terms of a number of different elements, it is implemented through the allocation of resources. These allocation decisions are expressed in operating and capital budgets, the main tangible outputs of a firm's strategic planning process. Capital investments tend to reflect major strategy decisions (implicit or explicit); operating budgets outline the follow-on use of resources required for the day-to-day execution of the business strategy. For the most part, the management of a firm has real options in deciding on the investments it makes. The operating budget then follows more or less directly from these choices. We shall focus on systems for making these investment decisions.

We define investments in a broad sense to include all current expenditures that are not projected to give rise to profits until subsequent years. This includes not only capital expenditures required for the maintenance and expansion of the current businesses of a firm but also expenditures required for the development and introduction to market of new products and businesses. We have excluded one class of investment, namely, very large acquisitions that are usually handled outside the normal planning and budgeting activities of the firm. They are infrequent occurrences in most firms and are often handled by the temporary formation of a small ad hoc group or by a specialized acquisition task force.

Although most large firms today decentralize some of their decision making, the final choice of investment is still usually made at the corporate level of the firm. Decentralization results from the inability of a small group of managers to remain familiar enough with the products and markets of a firm to manage it effectively. This decentralization is normally implemented through a divisional structure with at least three distinct hierarchical levels: corporate, divisional, and functional. Chandler[1] traces this development for a number of large firms. In a decentralized organization, managers at the corporate level of the firm must be supported by information from, and the activities of, managers at other levels of the firm to make good investment decisions. A formal system is often used to facilitate this interaction.

In a wider context, good investment decisions are a key objective of the planning process of a firm. Vancil and Lorange[2] provide a useful framework for looking at this process. This framework, shown in Exhibit 5-1, gives an overview of the chronological order of planning activities in terms of three stages of identifying and narrowing a firm's strategic options, called cycles, and three organization levels of the firm, corporate, divisional, and functional. We believe that the heart of the planning process lies in the choice of programs and projects by corporate-level managers in Cycles 2 and 3. The remaining elements of the system shown should effectively support these decisions. These investment decisions also

EXHIBIT 5-1

Vancil and Lorange Framework for the Strategic Planning Process

Organization Levels	Formal Planning Cycles	Cycle 1 (objective setting)	Cycle 2 (program evaluation)	Cycle 3 (budgeting)
Corporate	State corporate objectives	Call for division plans → ... Approve division objective and strategy → State corporate strategy and tentative corporate and division goals	Call for division programs → Set corporate and division goals ← ... Make tentative resource allocations to division programs	Call for division budgets → Approve budgets; one-year resource allocation
Divisional		Define division charter, objectives, and strategy → Propose division goals and resource requirements	State division objectives and strategy → Recommend program and resource requirements	State division goals → Submit budgets for approval → Coordinate, review, and approve budgets
Functional			Call for program alternatives → Identify program alternatives → Analyze programs and recommend best ones → Select best mix of programs	Call for department budgets → Develop budgets → Submit budgets for approval

Source: Vancil and Lorange (1975)

70

provide the basis for the control system of a firm. This system should be designed to track many of the same variables used in making the investment decisions.

Cycle 2 concerns the evaluation of broad programs. These programs are general strategies for a product line or business. These strategies are formulated as a description of the present and (projected) future characteristics of the business. Cycle 3 concerns the evaluation of investment projects. Many projects may be part of one overall program. For example, an oil company program may involve a retail gasoline marketing plan for the United States. Within this program, each gasoline station would be an individual project. Generally, it is difficult to separate the evaluation of a project from the evaluation of the program of which it is a part.

It should be pointed out that corporate finance theory suggests the use of some summary measure of discounted cash flow for the evaluation of projects. These measures are inappropriate for the evaluation of programs because data are often not available at a detailed enough level to make reasonable cash flow projections.

Since the mid-1950s there has been a growing awareness of the severe limitations imposed upon rational decision making by human cognitive abilities. Simon[3] and March and Simon[4] suggest that decision makers do exhibit rationality, but only within the constraints of their perceptions of a decision problem. Typically, these constraints are quite narrow as compared with the complexities of managerial decision problems. This bounded rationality is often attributed to a psychological phenomenon that is labeled "cognitive strain." This breakdown of a decision maker's cognitive processes occurs when he or she is subjected to demands that exceed his or her information processing capacity. Taylor[5] summarizes the determinants of bounded rationality and suggests ways in which to open constraints imposed by cognitive limitations and increase the bounds of rational decision making and problem solving. One important technique for doing this is to present the decision maker with information in a way that matches his or her own special background and experience.

Specifically, a manager at the corporate level of a firm has usually developed a set of variables or yardsticks with which to differentiate among the investment programs being considered. A preference for an investment depends upon the manager's evaluation of it along each of these variables and his or her weighting of the variables. The manager's task in selecting among investments can be made easier if information is provided in terms of the variables that are important to him or her. Thus, the time and resources spent in different parts of an organization in developing the information required by corporate-level managers to evaluate investments should be focused on these key variables used by these managers. Some of the key variables may change over time, and a firm's planning system should evolve to remain consistent with these.

OUTLINE OF CGI SYSTEM

The system used a CGI to evaluate new businesses first evaluates broad programs through a "constraint analysis." If a program appears attractive, individual proj-

EXHIBIT 5-2

Logic Sequence of Constraint Analysis

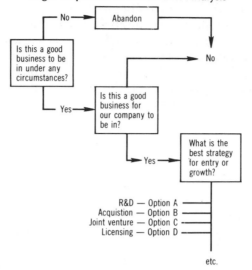

etc.

ects within it are evaluated using a "sensitivity analysis." The first part of this section describes the constraint analysis and the latter part looks at project evaluation.

The overall logic of the constraint analysis is shown in Exhibit 5-2. It is a decision tree that asks three questions:

1. Is this a good business for anyone to be in?
2. If 1. is affirmative, is this a good business for CGI to be in?
3. If the answers to 1. and 2. are yes, what is the best strategy for this business?

Each of these questions has an expanded list of critical factors. Exhibit 5-3 shows a "score card" that uses these factors. Twelve factors are rated on 10-point scales, giving a maximum score of 120, 60 for "business attractiveness" and 60 for "company fit." Experience indicates that programs with scores of 80 or above have a success rate of about 80 percent. Below 70 points, the probability of success drops rapidly. Although all factors are shown as having equal weighting, low scores on some of them can automatically disqualify a program, for example lack of Food and Drug Administration approval. Merrifield[6] discusses the twelve factors in detail. They are briefly described as follows.

Business Attractiveness Factors

Sales and Profit Potential. A program achieves a rating of 10 if, within five years of commercial operation, it can generate an additional 10 percent of sales for the company or profit center and its projects have a projected pretax internal rate of return of 40 percent. In other words, it should be sufficiently large to have a major impact on the firm or targeted profit center together with an adequate rate of return.

72

EXHIBIT 5-3

Score Card for Expanded Constraint Analysis

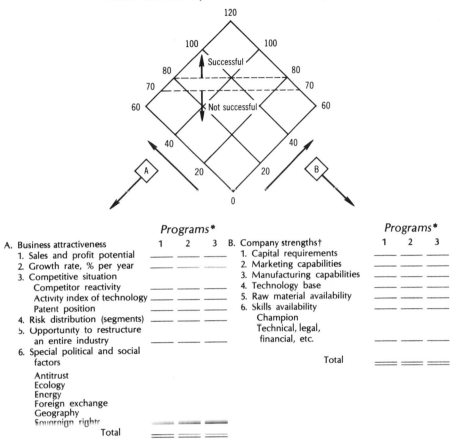

A. Business attractiveness	Programs*			B. Company strengths†	Programs*		
	1	2	3		1	2	3
1. Sales and profit potential	—	—	—	1. Capital requirements	—	—	—
2. Growth rate, % per year	—	—	—	2. Marketing capabilities	—	—	—
3. Competitive situation				3. Manufacturing capabilities	—	—	—
Competitor reactivity	—	—	—	4. Technology base	—	—	—
Activity index of technology	—	—	—	5. Raw material availability	—	—	—
Patent position	—	—	—	6. Skills availability	—	—	—
4. Risk distribution (segments)	—	—	—	Champion			
5. Opportunity to restructure				Technical, legal,			
an entire industry	—	—	—	financial, etc.	—	—	—
6. Special political and social							
factors				Total	=	=	=
Antitrust							
Ecology							
Energy							
Foreign exchange							
Geography							
Sovereign rights	—	—	—				
Total	=	=	=				

*Each factor rated on a scale of 1 to 10.
†Fit factors.

Growth rate. To achieve a score of 10, the expected growth rate should be at least 10 percent per year in unit volume or in sales adjusted for inflation.

Competitor analysis. Key considerations here are (1) the ability of competitors to react. (2) the strength of the patent protection, and (3) the technological activity in the industry, that is, the possibility that new developments will obsolete current products in a short period. A maximum of four points is assigned to 1 and three points each to 2 and 3 for a total of ten points.

Risk distribution. Ten points are assigned if at least four or five significant market segments are addressed by this program. This measures the potential negative impact of a significant new development by a competitor on the program or business.

Industry restructure opportunity. This factor can be illustrated by a case of significant technical development with strong patent protection in a technically stagnant industry that is fragmented among a number of small competitors but has an attractive total potential. An opportunity to "restructure" such an industry is particularly attractive because the need is already established. Ten points are assigned for a major restructuring opportunity.

Special factors. Political, social, geographical, and broad economic influences are considered. Included are government regulatory actions and subsidies. Five points are assigned if there are neither negative nor positive influences. Fewer are assigned if there are strong negative forces and more if these are positive.

Company Strength Factors

Capital requirements. In inflationary periods, capital-intensive businesses rarely make an adequate "real" return on investment. The point score declines with increasing capital intensity. This trend is moderated by the availability of capital to the firm to fund adequately the requirements for the program.

In-house marketing capability. If the program fits directly into a strong in-house marketing, distribution, and service capability, the probability of success is enhanced significantly. This marketing capability is evaluated relative to the competition. Ten points are assigned for a strong in-house capability and fewer points for a weaker situation.

In-house manufacturing capability. If production facilities exist in house, time to commercialization is shortened and capital expenditures can be minimized until a high probability of commercial success is established and risks are reduced substantially. Ten points are assigned for an existing full-scale manufacturing capability requiring little modification. Five points are assigned for an "interim" manufacturing capability.

Strength of the technology base. The technology base of a firm in a product area spans five functions, which range from basic scientific support to market support and customer service. Exhibit 5-4 assesses the technological strength in functional terms. For each function two points are assigned if the amount of effort required approximates the amount of effort allocated. The amount of effort required at each level depends upon the position of the business in the maturity cycle. An embryonic business usually requires a greater total effort and a greater percentage allocated to the new product development functions. A declining business tends to require most of its effort in product maintenance areas.

Raw material availability. Important ways of assuring raw material availability include integrating backward, engaging several suppliers, working on long-term contracts, and using "politically insensitive" materials. A score is assigned according to raw material accessibility, with a maximum of ten points.

Management and other skills. In-house availability of critical management, legal, and financial skills is essential to an effective program. Most impor-

EXHIBIT 5-4

Strength of the Technology Base

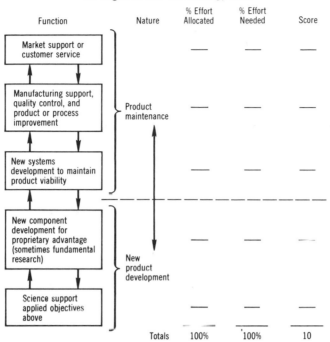

Function	Nature	% Effort Allocated	% Effort Needed	Score
Market support or customer service	} Product maintenance	—	—	—
Manufacturing support, quality control, and product or process improvement		—	—	—
New systems development to maintain product viability		—	—	—
New component development for proprietary advantage (sometimes fundamental research)	} New product development	—	—	—
Science support applied objectives above		—	—	—
Totals		100%	100%	10

tant is the availability of a manager who believes deeply in the program and persistently pushes it to completion. More potentially successful programs have probably failed for lack of a champion than for any other single reason. Availability of skills will vary for different programs and needs to be analyzed in terms of functions to be performed. For top-notch talent, ten points are assigned.

Use of Constraint Analysis: An Example

Use of this constraint analysis allows direct comparison of dissimilar opportunities vying for limited resources. Also, weaknesses that show up in the constraint analysis point out areas in which selective acquisitions, joint ventures, or licensing strategies may "rescue" an otherwise attractive program or offer a low-risk method of entry into a new business area.

An example of this is shown in Exhibit 5-5, in which company X developed a breakthrough in technology with exceptional business potential that could restructure two or three major industries—each with sales of $300 million and all of which were mature and badly fragmented among small competitors. Rapid penetration based on a solid proprietary position was envisaged. However, company X, recognizing its weaknesses in capital availability and manufacturing and marketing, licensed the technology to company Y. This added capital availability

75

EXHIBIT 5-5

How Constraint Analysis Can Lead to Licensing Strategy

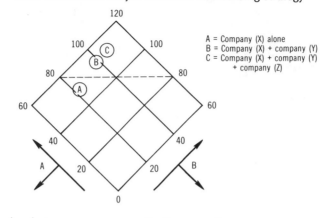

A = Company (X) alone
B = Company (X) + company (Y)
C = Company (X) + company (Y)
        + company (Z)

A. Business value factors	Score	B. Company fit or strength factors	A	B	C
1. Sales and profit potential	10	1. Capital needs	[0]*	10	10
2. Growth rate	10	2. Marketing	[0]	[2]	8
3. Competitor analysis	8	3. Manufacturing	[3]	[5]	7
4. Risk distribution	6	4. Technology base	[5]	6	6
5. Industry restructure	8	5. Raw materials	10	10	10
6. Ecology, etc.	7	6. Management	[4]	6	8
Total	49	Total	22	39	49

*Boxes indicate weaknesses requiring additional strength.

and some technical and management strengths but little manufacturing and marketing capabilities. A third firm, company Z, with marketing and manufacturing capability, was brought into the picture as an exclusive sublicensee in one segment of the business on a very attractive basis for all parties. The probability of commercial success for the program was enhanced substantially by this strategy.

Once the attractiveness of a program is established, a detailed financial analysis is done of each of the projects within it. This analysis simulates the cash flows and internal rate of return for the project. The simulation automatically shows the sensitivity of the IRR to the major assumptions. The output of the simulation is shown in Appendix 5-1. The sensitivity analysis is shown in Exhibit 5-6. This analysis describes concisely the assumptions critical to the success of the project.

EXHIBIT 5-6

Sample Sensitivity Analysis

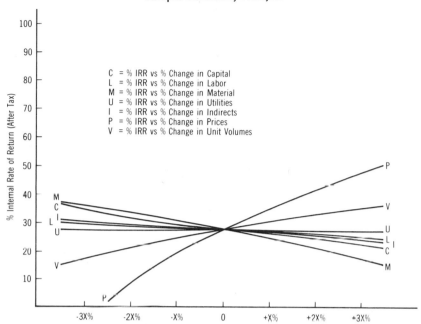

C = % IRR vs % Change in Capital
L = % IRR vs % Change in Labor
M = % IRR vs % Change in Material
U = % IRR vs % Change in Utilities
I = % IRR vs % Change in Indirects
P = % IRR vs % Change in Prices
V = % IRR vs % Change in Unit Volumes

FACTORS FOR FIRMS OTHER THAN CGI

As noted, most firms use some form of discounted cash flow analysis to evaluate investment projects. Thus the sensitivity analysis described in the previous section can probably be used with only minor modifications in other firms. The heart of the constraint analysis is the choice of the twelve factors. They reflect one manager's view of factors that he has found important to the success of investment programs that encompass a wide variety of business areas. This "view of the world" is conditioned by his own past experience. Any system that is designed to support him in his own investment evaluation must provide him with data about the twelve factors that are important to him. Other managers may have a different "view of the world," and a system to support them should provide data in terms of those factors that are important to them.

These factors used by a manager to describe investment programs are part of his or her "conceptual structure." An individual's "conceptual structure" is what he or she uses to process and organize stimuli and information. Riesing[7] provides a good summary of the literature dealing with this subject. An individual uses his or her conceptual or cognitive structure to organize and differentiate his or her perceptions, so that it determines what information will be perceived, how it will be related to various other pieces of information, how judgments are formed, and how problems are solved. This conceptual structure is the individual's "model" of the world. An individual's conceptual structure has many facets, each being associated with a particular domain. Thus, for example, the part of an individual's structure used to evaluate his or her subordinates may be quite different from the facet used to think about his or her social acquaintances. We are interested in how managers at the corporate level of a firm evaluate investments and would like to describe the part of their conceptual structure associated with the domain of investments.

As was pointed out by Riesing,[8] a cognitive structure is hierarchical. At the lowest level, the part of a structure associated with a domain is a conceptual space defined by a set of attributes that allows an individual to differentiate various objects or stimuli from the domain. This conceptual space can be spanned by a set of "independent attributes" called dimensions. The rank of the space is the number of such dimensions required to span it. Generally, there is overlap between the attributes defining the conceptual space. Hence, the number of dimensions required to span it is less than the number of attributes. Thus, the conceptual space can be described more parsimoniously in terms of the dimensions than of the attributes. However, it is often difficult to obtain these dimensions directly, and they have to be inferred through information about the attributes and the overlap between them.

A person's cognitive structure changes over time. Kelly[9] suggests that these changes are a result of learning and experience. Faletti,[10] in a laboratory setting, found that the dimensionality of his subjects' cognitive structures increased as they became aware of new things in their task environment. This dependence of a person's cognitive structure on experience has important implications for the design of systems for the support of investment evaluation. If the managers (at the corporate level of a firm) who make the investment decisions have been with the same firm for some length of time, they are likely to have had similar experiences and will have similar cognitive structures. Thus the cognitive structure of only one manager is required for the design of the system to support investment evaluation. However, this "common" structure may change over time, and the system should evolve to reflect this change.

This discussion of cognitive structures can be formalized into the following paradigm:

$$P_j = f(a_{j1}, a_{j2}, \ldots, a_{jk}, \ldots)$$

where P_j = the manager's perception for the jth investment

a_{jk} = the manager's perception of the rating of investment j on dimension k

$f(\ )$ = some function relating the manager's perceptions of an investment to his or her preferences

Within this framework, the following are some commonly used terms:

Attributes: Adjectival scales or constructs used by the manager to describe investments. If these attributes are not independent, the space defined by them can be described more parsimoniously by a set of independent dimensions.

Semantic structure: The number and definition (or labeling) of the independent dimensions derived from the attributes. These are the a_j.

Perceptual structure: The positions of the investments on the dimensions of the semantic structure. These are the a_{jk}.

Preference function: The form of the relationship between the manager's perceptual structure and his or her preference. This is the $f(\cdot \cdot \cdot)$.

In general, the cognitive structure of managers may differ in the attributes, semantic structures, perceptual structures, and preference functions. Appendix 5-2 shows the attributes used by the managers at the corporate level of thirteen different firms. The attributes are combined heuristically into broad groupings and the data are summarized in Exhibit 5-7. This illustrates the real differences in the attributes and dimensions used across firms. Our main thesis is that the resource allocation process should aid the managers at the corporate level of the firm in making better investment decisions. This can be done by providing information about investments to the manager in terms of the key variables that are important to him or her. Because these key variables differ across firms, to design better systems we need to obtain the semantic structure of the manager and the attributes that are markers for the dimensions of this structure.

EXHIBIT 5-7

Groups of Attributes Looked at by Managers in Sample Firms

Attribute Groups	Firms												
	1	2	3	4	5	6	7	8	9	10	11	12	13
Project profitability	√	√	√	√	√	√	√	√	√	√	√	√*	√
Project risk		√		√		√	√		√				
Size of market	√	√	√	√	√	√	√	√	√	√	√	√	√
Product strength in market	√	√	√	√	√	√	√	√	√	√	√	√	√
Market situation (competition)		√	√	√	√	√	√	√				√	√
Manager and business track record	√	√	√	√	√			√	√		√	√	√
Management knowledge of business							√	√		√		√	
Marketing strength			√	√	√			√				√	
Production strength	√	√	√	√	√	√					√	√	
Program risk	√							√	√	√		√	√
Government control			√		√								
Miscellaneous			√								√	√	

*Not actually used by manager.

METHODS FOR OBTAINING SEMANTIC STRUCTURES

In the previous section, it was indicated that the dimension used for the system to support investment evaluation in a firm should be based upon the semantic structure of its managers. In this section we look at how this semantic structure is obtained.

The twelve factors used in the CGI system describe Merrifield's semantic structure. The steps he used to obtain these factors are briefly as follows:

1. An initial list of attributes was developed from a number of different sources.
2. This list was refined by trying to determine the reasons why specific investments with which he had been involved in the past had succeeded or failed.
3. The "factors" were obtained by heuristically grouping attributes based upon the similarities of their meaning.
4. The factors were tested by rating a number of investments with which he was familiar on the factors and trying to explain the success of the investments based upon these ratings.

A similar procedure can be followed by managers at the corporate level of other firms if they are highly analytical and are willing to spend the time. If a manager invests the time in this approach, he or she is likely to be highly committed to the resulting system. Often, managers at the corporate level of firms are not willing to commit the time required and would rather have their planner design the system. The designer then needs a methodology for efficiently obtaining the semantic structure of the manager while having access to only short spells of the manager's time. Anand[11] has synthesized such a methodology and has used it successfully with managers in a number of different firms. The following is a brief outline of the steps in the methodology:

1. A list of attributes used by the manager is obtained. This is done through an interview with the manager and a study of the firm's old investment reports. The manager should aid the designer in understanding the meaning and definition of each attribute.
2. A list of about twenty investments familiar to the manager is obtained from him or her. One easy way to do this is to ask the manager to name an investment (evaluated by him or her in a recent budget) that satisfies each of a set of roles from him or her. One such list is shown in Appendix 5-3.
3. A five-point scale with both ends labeled is set up for each attribute obtained in step 1. Then the manager is asked to rate each investment obtained in step 2 on each labeled scale.
4. The manager is also asked to rate each investment on a preference scale.
5. The dimensions are obtained by factor analyzing the ratings of investments on the attributes. Each dimension is interpreted by the attributes that load highly on it.
6. The dimensions are validated by attempting to explain the manager's preferences for investments by their ratings on the dimensions, the factor scores.

Exhibit 5-8 shows the attributes and dimensions obtained for one firm by the use of this methodology.

Both methods described are quite similar. In designing a system for a firm, some combination of the two methods would probably provide the best results.

EXHIBIT 5-8

Attributes and Dimensions for One Firm

Attributes	Dimensions
1. Market size	Market potential
2. Market growth	
3. Market share	
4. Market share change	Product strength in market
5. Ability to provide base for future growth	
6. Promotion effectiveness	Strength of marketing organization
7. Distribution strength	
8. Life-cycle lags in international markets	Profit potential, international movement of assets
9. Return on investment	
10. Variable profit margin	
11. Divisional profitability	*Profitability–risk trade-off
12. Payback	
13. Risk	
14. Brand loyalty	
15. Quality–price ratio	
16. Effect on other products	*
17. Management familiarity with product line	

*Showed no power of discrimination among investments.

Once the important dimensions have been identified, they can be used to "put together" a system similar to the one described in the third section of this chapter.

The following are some desirable features that a system should incorporate:

1. It is difficult for a person to deal with more than three or four key variables simultaneously. As the number of variables used increases, some logical way to group them should be found. The combining of attributes into dimensions is the first step in this direction. It may be desirable to further group dimensions (an example is the grouping of factors into business attractiveness and fit factors in the CGI system).

2. The factors used should have functional significance. They should suggest strategies for improving the chances of success for the programs evaluated.

3. The factors used should be quantifiable so that a "scoring" method can be used for comparing dissimilar programs.

IMPACT OF SITUATIONAL SETTING ON DIMENSIONS

The thrust of the foregoing has been that a system to support the evaluation of investment programs by corporate-level managers in a firm should be designed around the dimensions that are important to these managers. Further, these dimensions may vary from firm to firm. There are indications that these dimensions are strongly influenced by the situational setting of the firm in which a manager works.

Anand[12] looked at a cross-section of firms and found that the number of dimensions in a manager's semantic structure increases with increases in the uncertainty in his or her firm's environment. Merrifield has also increased the number of factors he would like to use as the uncertainty of his environment has increased over time. Thus, a system for a firm in an uncertain environment would require more dimensions than one for a firm in a stable environment.

A key element in the design of a planning system is the tightness of the linkage between long-range planning and budgeting. In the terminology used here, this is the linkage between the evaluation of programs and the evaluation of projects. Anand[13] found evidence that managers in diversified firms found it difficult to make judgments about the impact of the characteristics of a program on the profitability of projects that are a part of it. In relatively homogeneous firms, corporate-level managers seem to have a deep enough understanding of the firm's businesses to make these judgments. Thus, the planning system for a diversified firm should have a much tighter linkage between program and project evaluation than is required in a homogeneous firm. Shank et al.[14] outline ways to impact this linkage.

In using the system described in the foregoing material, we have found that all investment programs in CGI's traditional businesses score equally high on the six "fit factors." Thus, these fit factors do not discriminate among such investments, and they do not provide any useful information for the evaluation of such investments. A firm whose managers plan to keep making investments only in the traditional businesses of the firm will probably not need any dimensions that measure the firm's strengths in the business area of the investment.

The impact of three situational variables has been crudely described. Further work is required to refine the description of the effects of these variables. There are undoubtedly other situational variables that are important, and, over time, data will accumulate on their effects on the dimensions that should be used for system design. It is hoped that a time will come when it will be possible to design a successful system to support investment evaluation in a firm based upon a description of its situational setting.

SUMMARY

The heart of the resource allocation process in the selection of investments to be made by a firm and the process should support the managers at the corporate level of a firm in making these investment decisions. It can do this by providing data about investments focused around key variables that are important to them. Thus, any system should be designed around the semantic structures of the managers whose decisions it seeks to support.

NOTES

[1]Alfred D. Chandler, *Strategy and Structure: Chapters in the History of the American Industrial Enterprise* (Cambridge, Mass.: M.I.T. Press, 1962).

[2]Richard F. Vancil and Peter Lorange, "Strategic Planning in Diversified Companies," *Harvard Business Review* (January–February 1975), pp 81–90.

[3]Herbert A. Simon, *Administrative Behavior* (New York: Macmillan, 1947).

[4]James G. March and Herbert A. Simon, *Organizations* (New York: Wiley, 1958).

[5]R. N. Taylor, "Psychological Determinants of Bounded Rationality: Implications for Decision-Making Strategies," *Decision Sciences*, Vol. 6, No. 3 (July, 1975), pp. 409–429.

[6]D. Bruce Merrifield, *Strategic Analysis, Selection, and Management of R&D Projects* (New York: AMACOM, 1977).

[7]Thomas F. Riesing, "Managerial Conceptual Structures and Managerial Performance" (unpublished Ph.D. dissertation, Massachusetts Institute of Technology, Cambridge, Mass., 1972).

[8]*Ibid.*

[9]G. A. Kelly, *The Psychology of Personal Constructs*, Vol. 1, (New York: W. W. Norton, 1955).

[10]M. V. Faletti, "An Experimental Validation of Some Measures of Cognitive Complexity" (unpublished senior thesis, Princeton University, Princeton, N.J., 1968).

[11]Sudeep Anand, "Resource Allocation at the Corporate Level of the Firm: A Methodological and Empirical Investigation of the Dimensions Used by Managers for Evaluation of Investments" (unpublished Ph.D. dissertation, Massachusetts Institute of Technology, Cambridge, Mass., 1977).

[12]*Ibid.*

[13]*Ibid.*

[14]John K. Shank, Edward G. Niblock, and William T. Sandalls, Jr., "Balance 'Creativity' and 'Practicality' in Formal Planning," *Harvard Business Review* (January–February 1975), pp 87–95.

APPENDIX 5-1   SAMPLE OF FINANCIAL SIMULATION FOR A PROJECT

Simulated Economic Analysis for Sample Product

	Res. and Dev.			Capital & Interest	Operations					% of Total in
	Year –3	Year –2	Year –1	Costs	Year 1	Year 2	Year 3	Year 4	Year 5	Year 5
					(000 Omitted)					
Capital Investments										
Land				—	—	—	—	—	—	—
Bldg. Investment										
New				—	—	—	—	—	—	—
Existing				—	—	—	—	—	—	—
Plant Investment										
New				1,036	1,036	1,036	1,036	1,036	1,036	46.0
Existing				—	—	—	—	—	—	—
All Other				196	196	196	196	196	196	8.7
Total Fixed Capital				1,232	1,232	1,232	1,232	1,232	1,232	54.7
Construction Interest				97	97	97	97	97	97	4.3
Total Working Capital				—	252	422	568	623	623	27.7
Research and Devel.	100	100	100	300	300	300	300	300	300	13.3
Total Capital Investment	100	100	100	1,629	1,881	2,051	2,197	2,252	2,252	100.0
Other Investment Related Items										
Investment Expenses				116						
Investment Tax Credit				85						
						OPERATIONS				
Production Capacity (Max.)					7,000	7,000	7,000	7,000	7,000	100.0
Annual Production (Plan)					3,000	5,000	6,500	7,000	7,000	100.0
Capital Intensivity Index (Dollars of Capital Required per One Dollar of Sales)					1.168	0.742	0.593	0.548	0.532	—

Simulated Economic Analysis for Sample Product

	Res. and Dev.			Capital & Interest Costs	Operations					% of Total in Year 5
	Year –3	Year –2	Year –1		Year 1	Year 2	Year 3	Year 4	Year 5	
					(COSTS IN $/UNIT)					
Direct Production Costs										
Labor										
Operating Labor					0.115	0.069	0.053	0.049	0.049	8.099
Maintenance Labor	3.300				0.011	0.007	0.005	0.005	0.005	0.807
	% of Plant Investment									
Control Laboratory					0.011	0.007	0.005	0.005	0.005	0.826
Total Labor					0.137	0.083	0.063	0.059	0.059	9.733
Lab. as % of Price					25.6%	15.0%	11.1%	10.0%	9.7%	–
Material										
Raw Materials										
Material 1					0.174	0.174	0.174	0.174	0.174	28.760
Material 2					0.056	0.056	0.056	0.056	0.056	9.256
Material 3					–	–	–	–	–	–
Material 4					–	–	–	–	–	–
Maintenance Materials	2.300				0.008	0.005	0.004	0.003	0.003	0.563
	% of Plant Investment									
Operating Materials					0.011	0.007	0.005	0.005	0.005	0.826
Total Materials					0.249	0.242	0.239	0.238	0.238	39.406
Mat. as % of Price					46.4%	43.7%	41.9%	40.6%	39.4%	–
Utilities										
Electricity					0.009	0.009	0.009	0.009	0.009	1.488
Steam					0.002	0.002	0.002	0.002	0.002	0.330
Fuel					0.003	0.003	0.003	0.003	0.003	0.509
Cooling water					0.002	0.002	0.002	0.002	0.002	0.331

Utility pricing notes:

- Electricity: 1.500 C/KWH — 0.600 KWH/unit; 1.750
- Steam: $/1000 LB — 1.140 LB/unit; 1.100, 2.800
- Fuel: $/MM BTU — 2.800 MBTU/unit
- Cooling water: 2.500 C/1000 GAL — 80.000 GAL/unit

APPENDIX 5-1 SAMPLE OF FINANCIAL SIMULATION FOR A PROJECT

Simulated Economic Analysis for Sample Product (continued)

	****** Res. and Dev. ******			Capital & Interest	****** Operations ******					% of Total in
	Year –3	Year –2	Year –1	Costs	Year 1	Year 2	Year 3	Year 4	Year 5	Year 5
Other					—	—	—	—	—	—
Total Utilities					0.016	0.016	0.016	0.016	0.016	2.657
Utl. as % of price					3.0%	2.9%	2.8%	2.7%	2.7%	—
Total Direct Production Costs					0.402	0.341	0.318	0.313	0.313	51.796
Dir. Cost as % of Price					74.9%	61.6%	55.8%	53.4%	51.8%	—
Indirect Costs										
Plant Overhead					0.022	0.013	0.010	0.009	0.009	1.488
Real Estate Taxes/Insurance				2.600 % of Fixed Capital	0.011	0.006	0.005	0.005	0.005	0.756
Selling Expenses					0.020	0.022	0.024	0.026	0.026	4.298
General and Administrative					0.042	0.035	0.032	0.030	0.030	4.959
Continuing Tech. Dev.					—	—	—	—	—	—
Depreciation					0.078	0.047	0.036	0.034	0.034	5.554
Start-up Expenses					0.009	—	—	—	—	—
Interest					0.061	0.032	0.012	0.007	—	—
Other Indirect Costs					—	—	—	—	—	—
Total Indirect Costs					0.243	0.155	0.119	0.110	0.103	17.054
Indirect Cost as % of Price					45.3%	28.1%	20.9%	18.8%	17.1%	—
Total Indirect & Direct Costs					0.645	0.496	0.437	0.424	0.417	68.849
Total Cost as % of Price					120.2%	89.7%	76.7%	72.2%	68.8%	—
Estimated Selling Price					0.537	0.553	0.570	0.587	0.605	100.000

Simulated Economic Analysis for Sample Product (continued)

	Res. and Dev.			Capital & Interest	Operations					Total in 6-15 Based on
	Year -3	Year -2	Year -1	Costs	Year 1	Year 2	Year 3	Year 4	Year 5	Year 5
					(000 Omitted)					
Cash Flow Analysis										
Based on Estimated Price:										
Revenue	–	–	–	–	1,611	2,765	3,705	4,109	4,235	42,350
Operating Costs	–	–	–	–	(1,936)	(2,481)	(2,841)	(2,965)	(2,916)	(28,743)
Investment Expenses	–	–	–	(116)	–	–	–	–	–	–
R & D Expense	(100)	(100)	(100)	–	–	–	–	–	–	–
Pretax Income	(100)	(100)	(100)	(116)	(325)	284	864	1,144	1,319	13,607
Book Taxes	50	50	50	58	163	(142)	(432)	(572)	(660)	(6,803)
Investmemt Tax Credit	–	–	–	85	–	–	–	–	–	–
After Tax Income	(50)	(50)	(50)	27	(163)	142	432	572	660	6,803
Book Depreciation	–	–	–	–	235	235	235	235	235	56
Dep. Tax Adjustment	–	–	–	–	80	42	4	(35)	(73)	(18)
Operating Cash Flow	(50)	(50)	(50)	27	152	419	671	773	822	6,842
Investment	–	–	–	(1,329)	(252)	(170)	(146)	(35)	–	–
Net Cash Flow	(50)	(50)	(50)	(1,302)	(100)	249	525	718	822	6,842
Cumulative Cash Flow	(50)	(100)	(150)	(1,452)	(1,552)	(1,303)	(778)	(61)	762	7,603

A.T. IRR (5 Years) 10.45%
A.T. IRR (15 Years) 27.41%

Sensitivity Index

(Per unit cost in Year 5 for indicated category as a fraction of per unit investment)

Labor	0.18
Materials	0.74
Utilities	0.05
Total Direct Costs	0.97
Total Indirect Costs	0.32
Total Costs	1.29

Attributes \\ Firms	1	2	3	4	5	6	7	8	9	10	11	12	13
Project profitability													
Discounted cash flow return	✓	✓		✓	✓				✓			✓*	✓
Return on assets	✓					✓	✓	✓		✓			
Payback period	✓	✓	✓	✓	✓		✓	✓	✓	✓	✓	✓*	✓
Return on sales							✓						
Cash contribution											✓		
Present worth											✓		
Profitability index											✓		
Size of market (present versus future)													
Size	✓	✓	✓	✓	✓	✓	✓	✓	✓	✓	✓		✓
Growth	✓	✓	✓	✓	✓	✓	✓	✓	✓	✓	✓	✓	✓
Maturity					✓								
Potential size										✓			
Market situation (competitively)													
Price elasticity		✓											
Projected supply–demand balance			✓		✓						✓		
Fraction captive demand		✓											
Degree of monopoly in market				✓		✓							
Number of large firms in market							✓						
New product threat									✓				
Importance of market to major competitors				✓									
Cost structure of industry					✓								
"Orderliness" of market											✓		
Track record of managers of business													
Earnings variability	✓												
Management's track record	✓			✓									
Business profitability record	✓	✓									✓		✓
Dividend performance history					✓				✓			✓	✓
Margins		✓	✓	✓				✓	✓		✓		
Returns				✓							✓		
Management knowledge of business													
Closeness to existing (core) business							✓						
Compatability with existing business							✓						
New talent required							✓						

*These attributes are not used by the manager for investment evaluation.

APPENDIX 5-2 (cont.)

	Firms												
Attribute Groups	1	2	3	4	5	6	7	8	9	10	11	12	13
Management familiarity with business								✓					
Management experience with business												✓	
Within basic competence area										✓			
Meeting present criteria										✓			
Risk of project or program													
Maximum cash exposure		✓		✓		✓	✓						
Impact of failure on income						✓			✓				
Program risk								✓				✓	✓
Risk protection provided									✓				
Patent situation									✓				
Probability of success										✓			
Cyclical vulnerability	✓												
Government control													
Impact of government control		✓		✓									
Nationalization risk		✓											
Miscellaneous													
Effect of program on firm's image		✓											
Effect on firm's portfolio balance												✓	
Long-term strategic importance of program												✓	
Effect on logistic balance										✓			
Lag in life cycle across international markets								✓					

APPENDIX 5-3   SAMPLE OF ROLES FOR OBTAINING LIST OF INVESTMENTS

1. An investment that you liked but was not undertaken by the firm.
2. An investment that you did not like but was undertaken by the firm.
3. An investment required to increase output of a product your firm was already producing.
4. An investment required to take your firm into a new business area.
5. An investment required to take advantage of market opportunities.
6. An investment required to improve the quality of one of your firm's products.
7. An investment required to reduce product costs.
8. An investment that was forced upon the firm by the actions of competitors.
9. An investment that was forced upon the firm by changing economic conditions.
10. An investment whose outcome was very uncertain at the time of evaluation.
11. An investment whose outcome was almost certain at the time of evaluation.
12. An investment with a long payback period.
13. An investment with a short payoff time.
14. An investment whose success depended upon factors within the firm's control.
15. An investment whose success depended upon factors to a large extent outside the firm's control.
16. An investment that had many intangible and nonquantifiable benefits.
17. An investment that promised to have a great strategic impact upon the firm.
18. An investment that was undertaken without considering all the relevant factors.
19. An investment that would have been accepted but for funds shortage.
20. An investment whose evaluation caused disagreement among different people in the firm.

6

Effective Strategic Planning and the Role of Organization Design

INTRODUCTION

The first section of this chapter* is a conceptual and definitional overview that introduces the concept of strategy as including both the organization's scope or domain and its "distinctive competencies" and pattern of resources. Similarly, strategic planning is viewed as a process that serves to aid in decisions not only of scope but also of allocation of scarce resources and other internal organization issues such as integration of strengths. This first section also introduces "organization design" as a decision process to bring about a coherence between the goals or purposes for which the organization exists.

In the second section, emphasis is placed on the fact that organization design is an important influence not only on strategy implementation but also on strategy formulation, selection, and adaptation to the environment. Some theoretical and empirical evidence is presented that illustrates the importance of the firm's existing organization design in strategic planning. Included here is a discussion of the political nature of the planning process and an illustration of the factors associated with the success and failure of the planning system. These factors are seen to be primarily organizational.

The first two sections, then, deal with the concepts of strategic planning and

---

*This chapter is prepared by Daniel A. Nathanson, Robert K. Kazanjian, and Jay R. Galbraith, The Wharton School, University of Pennsylvania.

organization design in a universalistic and generalized manner. The third section focuses on the contingency approach to the design of the planning process. Although the contingency literature is as yet relatively unrefined and untested, it provides us with some indication of the important variables and lends support to the theory that the planning process needs to be designed to meet the needs of the particular organization.

The main variable and interaction thereof are put into greater perspective in the final section in which some case examples are presented. These cases include firms with the new type of planning organizations, namely, the SBU (strategic business unit) system. The examples serve to integrate the concepts discussed in the previous sections while emphasizing the contingency concept. It becomes particularly apparent that strategic planning and organization design are complementary and interdependent mechanisms for dealing with the strategic situation of the firm.

In the final section, we present a contingency model that is, in actuality, a typological framework linking together some of the most important contextual variables with structural and planning process responses. It is hypothesized that planning organizations are created and place emphasis on various factors. The emphasis will depend upon the fit or, more appropriately, on the lack of fit between the strategic situation and organization structure. In other words, planning processes, as well as other information and decision mechanisms, act as intervening variables between the strategic situation and operating structure and serve to moderate the effects of an operating structure that cannot stand alone in dealing with the complexity and diversity of the environment.

CONCEPTUAL AND DEFINITIONAL OVERVIEW

Strategy

Strategy, strategic planning, and the strategy formulation process have been defined in various ways in the academic literature. Hence, we begin by defining these concepts, in terms of goals, purposes, and components, before developing our framework.

A useful and current definition that we shall employ is that of Hofer and Schendel, who define strategy as the[1] "fundamental pattern of present and planned resource deployments and environmental interactions that indicate how the organization will achieve its objectives." They further suggest that[2] "A critical aspect of top management's work today involves matching organizational competencies with the opportunities and risks created by environmental change in ways that will be both effective and efficient over the time such resources will be deployed. The basic characteristics of the match an organization achieves with its environment is called its strategy."

This definition of strategy conspicuously and explicitly includes the organization design. Hofer and Schendel state that they have included the organization components in their definition of strategy because "it is clear that no actions or goal achievements can take place unless some basic skills are created and resources obtained and deployed in ways that cannot be duplicated easily by others." Further, citing Hofer in 1973, they state that these organization variables may be more important than scope (domain):[3] "He found that when confronted with a major strategic challenge, the most successful firms were: first, those that changed both their scope and their distinctive competences; second, those that changed only their distinctive competences; and third, those that changed only the scope of their operations. The least successful were those that changed none of these." As Normann states;[4] "We want a concept which includes not only ideas about the market and the role of the company in the external environment (i.e., what is to be dominated), but also what is to be done to transform these ideas into concrete arrangements. It is not enough to say we are in the transportation business; there is no business idea until a formula for "earning money in the transport business" has been found, and until a formula has been translated into organizational and other arrangements." This broad concept of strategy, encompassing the organization's pattern of resources, its scope, domain or product–market strategy, and the interactions thereof, corresponds to our notion of strategic planning.

Strategic Planning

A predominant view of strategic planning[5] is that of a continuous, analytical, comprehensive process that encompasses both the formulation and implementation of strategy. Lorange states that[6] "the widely accepted theory of corporate strategic planning is simple: using a time horizon of several years, top management reassesses its current strategy by looking for opportunities and threats in the environment and by analyzing the company's resources to identify its strengths and weaknesses. Management may draw up several alternative strategic scenarios and appraise them against the long term objective of the organization. To begin implementing the selected strategy (or continue a revalidated one), management fleshes it out in terms of the actions to be taken in the near future."

Further, Lorange proposes that strategic planning has two principal purposes for an organization.[7] "First, it serves as the link between the organization and its environment, ensuring that the firm's outputs and its activities are consistent with the external milieu in which the enterprise operates. The second purpose is that of integration, through which the organization helps to ensure that those activities necessary for establishing and achieving goals are undertaken in a coordinated manner."

Organization Design

Organization design is conceived to be a decision process to bring about a coherence between the goals or purposes for which the organization exists, the pattern of division of labor and interunit coordination and the people who will do the work. The notion of strategic choice suggests that these are choices of goals and purposes, choices of processes for integrating individuals into the organization; and finally a choice as to whether goals, organizations, individuals, or some combination of them should be changed in order to adapt to changes in the environment.[8]

Based upon research of a range of organizational variables, a conceptual framework, shown in Exhibit 6-1, was developed by Galbraith. This framework outlines five areas of choice: task, structure, information and decision processes, reward systems, and people. Top management has the ability to vary and control each element to some degree.

We have introduced the concept of strategy as including both the organization scope or domain and its distinctive competencies and pattern of resources. Similarly, strategic planning is viewed as a process that serves to aid in decisions not only of scope but also of allocation of scarce resources, the adaptation to opportunities and threats, the integration of strengths and choosing appropriate options, and the organization's learning about itself.

EFFECTIVE STRATEGIC PLANNING AND THE ROLE OF ORGANIZATION DESIGN

It is the opinion of the authors that, although progress has been made toward recognizing organization design as an important variable, its role in determining the design of the strategy formulation or planning process, in influencing the selection of a particular strategy, and in coping with environmental contingencies and diversity is still largely overlooked and misunderstood. Instead, it tends to be emphasized mostly as the critical operational link for purposes of strategy implementation. This limited recognition of the role of organization design in effective strategic planning is responsible for many failures of strategic planning processes, particularly when planning is viewed as a rational and analytic process rather than as a political and behavioral one.

Steiner's widely referenced study of the pitfalls encountered in the design of formal planning systems highlights a prevailing view that planning can somehow be conceptually and operationally separated from the organization's ongoing structure and process.[9] (See Chapter 3.) These findings suggest strongly that formal planning, at the firms surveyed, was not integrated adequately with those firms' reward and information systems. Managers were neither involved fully in the formulation of strategy nor briefed fully on the nature of final long-run plans. Further, decision processes outside the formal planning system were commonly elected. In sum, the pitfalls can be attributed to a limited recognition of the role of organizational structure and process in strategic planning.

Recent research indicates that the existing organization design of a firm can heavily influence the strategic planning process as well as the determination of specific strategies. Because the current structure and process of the firm reflects a specific power balance, strategy formulation and selection becomes essentially a

EXHIBIT 6-1

Organizational Variables

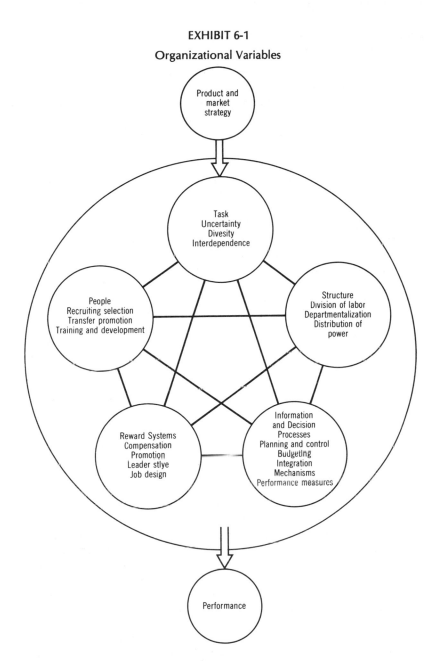

political interaction among coalitions. In addition, the organization design process and variables determine the design of the strategic planning process itself. Finally, the organization, including both structure and process, must be designed to "fit" the product–market strategy or scope.

Strategy Formulation as a Social and Political Process:
The Influence of the Existing Organization Design

A mounting body of theory and empirical evidence suggests the importance of the firm's existing organizational design in strategy formulation. We will focus here on summarizing some of these findings as well as on discussing the political nature of the strategy formulation process. It will be shown the factors associated with success and failure of the planning system are primarily organizationally determined.[10]

> The classical view of the role of organization design in strategic planning is that, after reviewing the company's situation, management designs strategies and then maneuvers the structure to fit, thereby making possible the realization of the strategies. In reality, however, the process is far more complicated than this. For instance, the company's power structure has considerable influence on the ideas that are able to catch on and vice versa. The organizational structure—in the shape of routines, resources, channels of communication, etc.—is also in many ways a determinant of which ideas and notions can take shape at all.
>
> Recently, a stream of research has appeared which suggests that effective long-range planning should be viewed as a strategic decision making process, involving the line managers of the organization, and reflecting the fact that a relatively large number of managers will be involved in it; thus, the process more closely resembles behavioral/political modes of organization decision making than rational/analytical ones.[11]

Cyert and March's *Behavioral Theory of the Firm*,[12] which predates much of the strategic planning literature, was one of the first statements of this position. According to the behavioral model, the dominant coalition establishes the goals of the enterprise through bargaining. The formation and composition of the coalitions, as well as this bargaining process are a direct reflection of the established structure and processes of the firm. This was reinforced by Cohen and Cyert.[13]

> The nature of the strategic search process in organizations often prevents an objective evaluation of proposed actions. When a potential action is advocated by a coalition member, he thereby becomes identified with the action. When this identification becomes close, the coalition member may view the ultimate adoption or rejection of the proposed action as a measure of his personal power position within the coalition. The strategic planning process would be far more effective if the proposed actions could be divorced from individual sponsorship. Typically, however, this is difficult to accomplish because proposed strategic actions are brought to the attention of the coalition through a chain of successive sponsorships within the organizations. In this chain, each manager in the hierarchy attempts to convince his immediate superior of the merits of the proposed action and sponsorship of the proposal passes upward with acceptance.
>
> The difficulty of the coalition's making an objective evaluation of the proposed actions is further complicated by the loss of information as proposals filter upward through the organizational hierarchy. So many details concerning proposals are eliminated in "the selling process" that it becomes virtually impossible for

coalition members to analyze interaction effects even if they so desired. Thus, each coalition member sponsoring a proposal becomes an "uncertainty absorber" with respect to the proposed actions that he advocates. This situation effectively forces the coalition into the necessity of making personal judgments concerning the competence of its members in the guise of selecting a strategic plan. In order to minimize personal conflict among coalition members, the coalition frequently adopts rules of thumb to allocate strategic resources among organizational subunits in some objective but nonoptimal manner, for example, budgeting research and development expenditures in proportion to sales and authorizing automatic reinvestment of depreciation charges.

Given this view of coalition-based decision making, it can be seen that the strategic search process depends heavily upon the existing organization design: the distribution of power and the shape of the firm (structure), the competence and type of personnel (people), and the quality and availability of information for decision making (information and decision processes).

Subsequent research in this area attempted to operationalize the behavioral model. Bower, Berg, and Carter each investigated decision-making processes for investment or acquisition decision.[14] These studies, although based predominantly on case studies, demonstrate some of the effects of the current structure and design of the organization in decision making.

Carter's findings point to a political and social coalition-based decision-making process within the firm.[15] Some of his hypotheses, representative of those of other authors studying this topic, were that "projects with the best chance of acceptance get proposed; projects with the least chance of acceptance get held back; staff will attempt to provide the specific data perceived as desired by top management; and, the acceptance-gaining effort of an individual or a department is determined by the importance of the decision to the individual or group, the probability of gaining approval, and the accuracy of supporting evidence."

These hypotheses of Carter and the behavioral model underscore the necessity of integrating strategic planning with organization design. First, and most broadly, they suggest that organization decision processes generally and strategy formulation specifically are affected by the existing organization design—the existing structure and processes. That is, through coalitions and political behavior, individuals attempt to protect or better their own position. In organizational terms, the existing organization design attempts to perpetuate itself.

More specifically, strategy formulation is essentially a decision-making process. In our view, the firm's information and decision processes are a key variable of organization design. Further, studies such as Carter's indicate that all the other organization design variables discussed here influence the final decisions. The project proposals submitted for consideration reflect the existing distribution of power. The associated information generated by staff and examined by management for project appraisal and evaluation and the final decision reflect the individuals' competence and style and the reward systems. The nature of the task will determine the relative dominance of specific functions. Finally, the effort generated by individuals or groups seems to be determined by individual and group motivation that are reflected by task and rewards. In this way, the existing organization design can be seen to play a significant role in strategic planning by its effect on strategy formulation and the final selection of specific strategies.

Fitting the Organization to the Product–Market Strategy: The Influence of Organization Design on Strategy Implementation

As stated, organization design is conceived to be a decision process to bring about a coherence among the goals or purposes for which the organization exists, the pattern of division of labor and interunit coordination, and the people who will do the work.[16] "It is at once apparent that the accomplishment of strategic purpose requires organization. If a consciously formulated strategy is to be effective, organizational development should be planned rather than left to evolve for itself."

Once the organization scope has been defined, the organization design process can be seen as the link to operational plans and implementation. According to Exhibit 6-1, the critical variables of organization design are task, structure, information and decision processes, reward systems, and people. All these variables must constitute an internally consistent organizational form as well as attain the appropriate "fit" or congruence with the firm's strategy. In other words, in organizations, everything is connected to everything else.

The notion of "fit," based upon the research of Lorsch, Scott, Leavitt, Khandwalla, and Child, is elaborated in Galbraith and Nathanson.[17]

> The product-market strategy chosen by the firm determines to a large extent the task diversity and uncertainty with which the organization must cope. The organization must then match the people with task through selection, recruitment, and training and development practices. The people must also match the structure. The structure, also chosen to fit the task, is specified by choices of the division of labor (amount of role differentiation), the departmental structure, the shape (number of levels, spans of control), and the distribution of power (both horizontal and vertical). Across the structure, processes are overlaid to allocate resources and coordinate activities not handled by the departmental structure. These information and decision processes are planning and control systems, budgeting processes, integration mechanisms, and performance measurements. And finally, the reward system must be matched with the task and structure through choices of compensation practices, career paths, leader behavior, and the design of work. In total, all these choices must create an internal consistent design. If one of the practices is changed, the other dimensions must be altered to maintain fit. Similarly, if the strategy is changed, then all the dimensions may need to be altered so that the form of organization remains consistent with the product-market strategy.

Therefore, we are developing the notion that strategic planning and organization design, although separated for conceptual purposes, are interrelated completely and must be considered, in some sense, part of the larger "strategic management process."

A CONTINGENCY APPROACH TO THE DESIGN OF PLANNING PROCESSES

As with so many other aspects of organizational design, there seems to be no one best way to structure the strategic planning process.[18] The earliest research on strategic planning clearly implied that "there is no single organizational planning pattern that fits all companies."[19]

Steiner suggested this notion by identifying types of planning organizations that ranged from no formal planning at all, with planning done by each executive individually and informally, to having a planning executive and staff at both the headquarters and the major divisions.

The explicit development of broader organization design contingency theories by Child,[20] and Lawrence and Lorsch,[21] in particular have influenced theories of the design of specific organization processes as well. Research by Wrapp, Warren, Ringbakk, Litschert, Miller, Lorange, Schendel, and others[22] have firmly established a contingency-based approach for the design of planning processes. These authors have identified, and in some cases tested, the influence of a range of factors and variables on the design and performance of planning processes.

Rather than review the specific theories and findings of many of these authors (as has been done elsewhere—see Hofer, Lorange),[23] we will attempt to summarize several representative studies before structuring our own contingency model.

Litschert examined the influence that industry, technology, organizational size, structure, and planning experience might have on planning group structure in twenty-seven firms in the electronics, chemical, oil refining, and heat and power utility industries.[24] Litschert found "that planning groups are normally responsible directly to the chief executive, have relatively few personnel, exist at both corporate and division levels, and use full-time staff planners." He further concluded that "the degree of organization structure, the nature of subunits, the use of special coordinating mechanisms, supplemental communication links, and venture teams are now also important structural characteristics."

Litschert's study also uncovered some interesting contingency-related findings:[25]

> First, it appears that technology has an impact on the structure of planning groups. Groups operating in environments characterized by rapid technological change were less structured—i.e., were not differentiated into formal subunits—than those operating in more stable technological environments.

Second, group differentiated into subunits were in all cases functionally oriented.

Third, the character of company departmentalization seemed to influence organization for long range planning as exemplified by variations discovered in groups found in companies organized on a product, functional or major market basis.

Finally, the study at least implied that the amount of experience with both long range planning and organization for this activity further contributed to the character of planning organization.

In a more recent study, Lorange concluded that[26] "it seems as if a contingency based approach toward the design of formal planning systems is necessary in order to achieve more effective systems. Thus, one probably should not expect to arrive at a general theory of planning systems design."

One of the earliest discussants of contingency based designs, Lorange further outlined his contingency views by identifying the institutional factors important for assessing a firm's planning system needs, to include demographic factors such as size and maturity of the planning system, the strategic posture as determined by the diversity of the portfolio and the nature of the product–market setting, and the management style or the perceived need for planning.

Lorange also links these contingency factors to a specific and appropriate design by presenting several system design factors. Such factors include[27]

1. top–down versus bottom–up
2. relative emphasis on longer-term objectives setting versus near-term action programs
3. element linking devices of the planning process: timing, plan content, organizational linkages
4. role of the corporate planner as well as other staff and line executives in the planning process

In a much more detailed presentation, Schendel "developed design parameters for a strategic planning system and the factors or variables which influence these parameters."[28] Schendel proposes that "it is the relationship between planning components, as defined by the design parameters, and organizational and environmental characteristics, that must be understood if a workable strategic planning process is to be developed." Propositions or working hypotheses that relate the three factors were then generated. The variables were identified as shown in Exhibit 6-2. For each environmental or organizational contingency, Schendel outlines working hypotheses regarding the design of the planning process.

Schendel concludes with a recognition that "the contingent linkage of components, design parameters, and organizational and environmental variables provides a starting point for designing and using strategic planning systems, and for further study of planning system design itself."

Lorange clearly concurs that a contingency approach to the design of planning processes is yet in its earliest stages, certainly for purposes of theoretical

EXHIBIT 6-2

Characteristics, Parameters, and Basic Planning Components

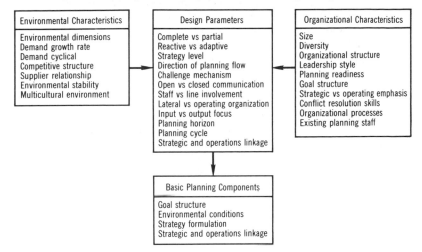

Environmental Characteristics	Design Parameters	Organizational Characteristics
Environmental dimensions Demand growth rate Demand cyclical Competitive structure Supplier relationship Environmental stability Multicultural environment	Complete vs partial Reactive vs adaptive Strategy level Direction of planning flow Challenge mechanism Open vs closed communication Staff vs line involvement Lateral vs operating organization Input vs output focus Planning horizon Planning cycle Strategic and operations linkage	Size Diversity Organizational structure Leadership style Planning readiness Goal structure Strategic vs operating emphasis Conflict resolution skills Organizational processes Existing planning staff

Basic Planning Components
Goal structure Environmental conditions Strategy formulation Strategic and operations linkage

consideration, and that far more testing and refinement is needed. He emphasized this point, with the following statement.[29]

> Admittedly, however, nothing more than a few rudiments of a contingency based approach of formal planning systems design seems yet to have emerged. Largely, this is what one would expect; it is a formidable research task to explore relatively exhaustive sets of situational and design variables in various types of settings. Even more monumental is the task of increasing our understanding about the specific nature of the interrelationship among the variables. Thus, our present findings should be considered a new start-up.

In sum, the literature indicates some of the contingency variables and provides us with only a loose theoretical framework that needs refinement and testing.

In the next section we present some brief cases that will both illustrate the interaction among the many variables discussed thus far and serve to introduce our contingency framework.

The cases represent recent developments in planning organizations, namely, the strategic business unit (SBU) concept. This new planning organization, often distinct from the operating organization, clarifies some issues and helps us to explain our conceptual framework. That is, from the literature reviewed thus far and the cases to be presented, we believe that the planning process needs to be designed to meet the needs of the particular organization. The importance of the planning process to the particular organization will vary depending upon

1. Size.
2. Product–market strategy, scope or domain—that is, the diversity or relatedness of

the products being manufactured and sold by the organization in terms of product diversity, market diversity and/or geographic diversity.

3. Crucial contingencies—here we are talking about the pressure points, that is, the most crucial aspects of the environment for the particular organization in terms of survival and success.

4. Technology—the level of scientific specialization needed.

5. The rate of change and the predictability of that change in the preceding four areas.

6. The degree to which the traditional operating structure and associated processes can cope with the strategic situation of the firm, that is, with the five areas outlined. This represents our major thesis. Organization structure is seen to be effective if it fits with the variable areas discussed. Associated processes help to ensure this fit. Included in the associated processes category is the planning process. However, the most recent response to today's complex environment is the planning organization. This response is a result of the inability of the organization structure and its processes to effectively handle the diversity, and so on, in the environment. In this way, the planning process and organization design are seen to be complementary and interactive mechanisms for coping with the strategic situation.

NEW PLANNING ORGANIZATIONS: CASE EXAMPLES

Recent developments within organizations have highlighted the fact that planning processes can be used as a response to diversity. Planning processes and planning organizations, distinctly different from the organization for execution, have taken form and are generally referred to as strategic business units, after the GE organization.

A recent study by Allen shows that the adoption of sophisticated planning, reward, and evaluation systems are the latest organizational innovations being created and adopted by American enterprise.[30] Using a sample of forty American corporations, Allen followed changes in structure and process from 1970 to 1974. He found little change in structure, but extensive changes are probably attributable to the adoption of some form of the SBU structure.

Therefore, as has been indicated and will be shown, the planning organization is an alternative mechanism for coping with diversity and is simultaneously interdependent with the organization's structure. To explain this new planning organization, we will describe the OST (objectives, strategies, and tactics) system used at Texas Instruments (TI). Then, other variations will be described. The following section is adapted from Galbraith and Nathanson.[31]

The OST System and Texas Instruments

The objectives, strategies, and tactics system at TI is one of the oldest of the new generation of planning systems. It was started in 1962 and was felt to be fully operational in 1967. Until that time, TI operated as did most United States enterprises with the standard divisionalized structure shown in Exhibit 6-3. This

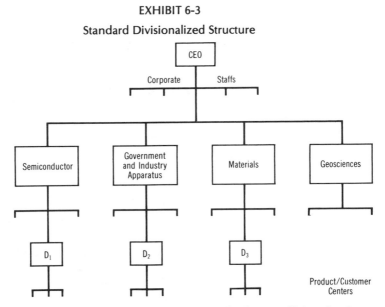

EXHIBIT 6-3

Standard Divisionalized Structure

CEO

Corporate   Staffs

Semiconductor | Government and Industry Apparatus | Materials | Geosciences

D_1 D_2 D_3

Product/Customer
Centers

structure was successful in generating TI's growth by decentralizing the short-run operations to Product/Customer Centers (PCCs). These units were $1- to $80-million businesses and were the basic profit centers. Long-range activity was concentrated in the top management, with the group and division managers serving as translators. In the early 1960s, however, a shaking out of the semiconductor industry and the loss of some government contracts caused a reexamination of the TI structure and process.

Several problems were found. Typical problems inherent in a divisionalized organization structure began to surface. The PCCs or divisions tended to duplicate expensive specialist resources with little sharing.

Each PPC was operating for its own benefit. Although this focused short-run thinking was a strength, it was also a liability. It generated small thinking in that new product ideas were keyed to existing capabilities or to incremental expansions. There was no way to call upon the resources of the entire corporation when several PCCs were operating in Europe or in the same market. There was interdependence across the PCCs for many long-range programs. The OST system was created to tap this source of interdependence by focusing on the strategic long-range goals of the company. Hence, the creation of such a planning system represented both a response or reaction to environmental diversity relatedness and an integration and realignment of the organization's internal resources to create a "fit" among structure, process, and product–market strategy. Notice also that the decline in economic performance needed to stimulate such a move toward a better "fit."

The OST system was created to supplement, not replace, the PCC structure. In essence, the PCC structure remains as it is shown in Exhibit 6-3 and is the structure for the execution and achievement of this year's budget. The OST system is used for planning and resource allocation. The people are the same, however, and must handle a short-run operating responsibility and a long-run strategic responsibility. The next paragraphs will describe the OST structure and how it operates.

The OST structure, shown in Exhibit 6-4, is similar to the divisionalized structure. Notice that the three planning levels—objectives, strategies, and tactics—correspond, respectively, to corporate-, business-, and functional-level planning. This case, then, also provides some greater insight into the different levels of planning and their interactions thereof.

At the top is the overall corporate objective that is to be achieved by nine business objectives. The business objectives are relatively stable businesses in which TI will operate. They are chosen and defined by the top management and the corporate development function. Each is a fairly self-contained business, and the objective states its character and sales, profit, ROI, and market penetration targets for a ten- to fifteen-year period. Objectives may be for the auto industry or for Europe. Quite often, they cut across the group and division shown in Exhibit 6-4.

For each objective, there is an objective manager. The objective manager for the automotive objective might be the group executive for semiconductors, as most of the sales will come from that area. Therefore, that executive is responsible for the strategic direction and coordination of the automotive objective and, simultaneously, for the short-run profit performance of the semiconductor group.

Each objective consists of several strategies. Strategies are also stated in terms

EXHIBIT 6-4

The OST Structure

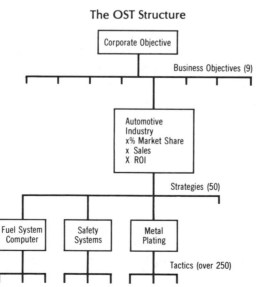

of five- to ten-year goals, with a time dimension and milestones to measure accomplishments. For example, one strategy for the automotive objective is to provide microprocessor computers for fuel systems.

The strategy manager is the division manager (D_1 shown in Exhibit 6-3) in the semiconductor group. He reports to the group executive for both short-run profit performance and long-run strategic performance. Second and third strategies are to provide safety systems and metal plating products. These strategies are implemented and developed by strategy managers in groups other than the semiconductor group managed by the objective manager. In 25 percent of the cases, there are cross-groups and cross-divisional objectives and strategies. The role of the objective manager is to identify strategies across the company and pull them together into a strategic plan for that objective. The strategy manager plays the same role for the next level in which there are tactics and tactic managers who report to the strategy managers.

Strategies consist of several tactics that are six- to eighteen-month checkpoints and are assigned to a PCC. Progress against them is reported monthly. The year in a tactical action plan becomes this year's budget. In this way, resource allocation is tied to strategic thinking and to execution organization. The planning and the doing are linked, as the same people operate in both modes.

In many instances the planning system will be aligned perfectly with the operating organization. Such is the case with most conventional planning organizations. This "overlayed" planning system serves as a response to the interdependency in the environment and need for a longer-term orientation than the operating structure could provide. Hence, once again, we see that structure and process work as complementary mechanisms for coping with the various sources of diversity in the environment or from the product–market strategy.

One of the points that has been stressed in this chapter is that one cannot make a substantial change in structure without making compensating and reinforcing changes in processes, reward systems, and people. Such is the case at TI. A couple of problems are created by the OST system. One is the matrix organization that is created in the OST structure. Strategy managers have multiple bosses, and there is the potential for conflict. Second, the managers have simultaneous short-run and long-run responsibilities. The conventional wisdom has always said that one cannot mix short- and long-run responsibilities in the same role, as the short-run drives out the long run. The changes in processes, rewards, and people are aimed at solving those problems.

The planning process itself is designed to channel conflict into the planning activity where it is resolved. The strategy managers then operate against a single set of agreed upon numbers. The process starts with some four hundred managers meeting for a week in March. At the meeting, each objective is presented by the objective manager and selected strategy managers. Guidelines for objectives come from the objectives and policy committee of the board of directors. This committee meets three times per year for two days to establish overall direction. Then, final approval of the objectives is negotiated with the corporate development committee, which consists of the top operating managers; the directors of corporate development, marketing, and research and development; and the patent attorney. This committee meets for one day about twice each month to review the OST system. The objectives are negotiated by objective managers after the annual planning conference. After final approval, the objective is reviewed throughout the year by the objective manager. Implementation falls to the strategy managers, and tactics are reviewed monthly. In this way, the budget for growth goals is allocated and managed. The budget for current operations, on the other hand, goes through the PCC system. The two budgets are integrated at the top through the operating committee, which consists only of group executives, corporate staff executives, and the office of the chief executive. It is in these forums with interlocking memberships that conflicts are raised and worked through.

Control over the strategic milestone is as extensive as that over the short-run operations. There is an OST information and reporting system as well as a PCC system. Tactic managers are responsible for over and under spending on OST milestones. Both the short- and long-run are integrated into an operating statement, which includes revenue, operating expense, operating profit, strategic expense, and organization profit.

Managers are held jointly accountable and are rewarded for short- and long-run performance goals. The strategic goals are kept visible and are measured along with the short-run goals. Both short- and long-run perspectives are part of the reward system. Thus, the information system and the reward system reinforce the OST system.

Another supporting process is the career movement of managers. Some attempt is made to have managers experience a line responsibility, then a staff job, then a line job, a staff job, and so on. In this way, the manager is exposed first to a task in which he or she must meet short-run operating numbers and exercise direct authority over subordinates. Then, the manager experiences an ambiguous staff job with longer-run responsibilities, in which, to implement policies, the cooperation of those who do not work directly for the manager must be secured. Those that are successful will be able to operate simultaneously in the line, in the short-run PCC structures, and in the long-range matrix OST system. By this process, people are prepared for the dual roles.

Thus, TI has created a resource allocation process to develop products for diverse businesses and markets. It has another structure—the PCC—for managing diverse products and technologies. The same managers operate in both modes. Resources are allocated through the OST system. Then, once the numbers are agreed upon, the managers shift to an operating mode in the PCC structure. They have one organization for planning and one for operations. There are reinforcing planning meetings, information systems, reward systems, and career movements that complete the fit among strategy, structure, and process. The general management work for strategically managing multiple sources of diversity is shared throughout the hierarchy.

Effective organizations, then, seem to be ones that have developed complementary mechanisms to deal with diversity.

Other variations are being adopted by other companies. GE adopted an SBU structure in 1968.[32] The numbers vary, but GE operates approximately forty-five SBUs, which are similar to strategies at TI. The SBU structure is for planning, and the standard multidivisional structure is for control and operations. At the moment, four SBUs are managed by group executives, twenty by division managers, and nineteen by department managers. This is equivalent to a PCC manager at TI. The level is indicated by whether the SBU is cross-departmental or cross-divisional and by the size of the business.

An SBU is subject to definition by a top management group that must continually define the SBU boundaries. An SBU is to be a relatively independent business mission (i.e., independent of other SBUs) with a clearly defined set of competitors and the capacity to measure profit and loss. The criteria are fuzzy and require continual updating of the SBU's charter.

What are the criteria and why do they require updating?

In TI's case, updating was a response to a need to retain the product specialists required by the technological and competitive nature of the particular industry and yet deal with the interdependency in the markets by reducing suboptimization and by forcing a long-term perspective. In short, they had a need to compensate for the dysfunctionalities brought on by a divisionalized organization structure. In TI's case, the short-term, splintered, goal orientation needed to be tempered by an integration device—a complementary planning process.

GE established the SBU for a number of reasons: (1) It served as a span of control reducer. (2) It served to highlight smaller pieces of the business that had large growth potential but would go unnoticed otherwise. (3) It served as a career path. (4) It served to control and assign and formulate goals.

Still other organizations define SBUs around markets. General Foods has a divisionalized structure that organizes different products produced by different technologies into divisions and groups. However, it has come to be recognized that the consumer thinks in terms of meals rather than products. He or she plans a main meal or breakfast and then purchases Birds Eye frozen foods, Good Seasons salad dressings, and Jello desserts. Therefore, some strategic coordination between the divisions on marketing and product development can lead to a more consistent offering. Therefore, a breakfast SBU, main meal SBU, and so forth were created for this strategic direction. In this case, however, the organization created a separate role of SBU manager instead of using the existing line organization managers. Each SBU manager has a market development manager and a controller reporting to him or her. The purpose is to guide long-run product development by market and to achieve cross-divisional coordinational coordination. Once the planning is accomplished, however, execution falls to the divisional structure. The technologies for manufacturing and distributing frozen foods are quite different from those for puddings and salad dressings. Divisions should be organized for production on a product basis; only the market positioning and product development require cross-division planning coordination.

These brief examples are representative of the various planning process structures currently evolving to handle business, market, or geographic diversity that is being experienced primarily by the product divisionalized companies. The separate organizations for planning and execution enable them to respond to multiple sources for diversity and cross-divisional interdependencies. As such, these planning organizations are the newest source of organizational innovation, the new type structures that some authors claim them to be. The reason is the extensive power-sharing, conflict-resolving mechanisms that are created as well as the new information systems, reward systems, and career movements that go with the innovation.

These new planning organizations are also found within firms with functional structures. Many functional organizations are either too small to divisionalize or the economies of scale are too great to make the divisionalized structure feasible. Other functional organizations remain as such because of an overpowering need for functional specialists. If these functional organizations simultaneously operate in diverse markets, an SBU or planning organization should be overlayed on the operating structure.

An example of a relatively small, functional, related product organization with multiple business markets is AXY. AXY manufacturers blades for both the consumer and industrial market. Each of these markets, in turn, has various submarkets that have their own unique potentials, opportunities, and risks. This rather small, functionally organized company has operated in a traditional manner. The functional organization is necessary because of the high degree of product relatedness. The raw material, manufacturing process, and technology are similar across products. In addition, the small size of the organization prohibits a divisionalized structure based upon markets because such duplication of resources would be much too costly.

Problems started to occur. Not close enough attention was being paid to the individual markets. The focus of attention would shift from one market to another based upon some current contingency. Resources would shift correspondingly, leaving other markets unattended.

The current structure was unable to handle the market diversity. An SBU structure was set up to maintain a continuing focus on all-important business markets, be they small and growing or large and stable. This was done by establishing dual responsibilities, both functional and product–market, and thereby providing a "champion" for the particular area. Hence, the functional organization can also benefit by these new planning organizations.

A CONCEPTUAL FRAMEWORK: STRATEGIC SITUATION, ORGANIZATION STRUCTURE, PLANNING PROCESS

As was stated previously, the organization literature, the planning literature, and the case studies indicate that the planning process needs to be designed to meet the needs of the particular organization. In addition, the planning process may act as a complementary information and decision-making mechanism to the organization structure. The planning process may be either aligned with the existing operating structure or distinctly separate, serving as a "planning organization." In either case, the planning process, other information and decision-making processes, and the organization structure must act in an interdependent and complementary manner in dealing with the strategic situation of the firm.

At the risk of being overly simplistic, we have developed a typology of strategic situations in which we believe many organizations today find themselves operating. We then describe the probable nature of the organization structure and the type of planning organization that would be required to complement the organization structure so as to deal with the strategic situation effectively. See Exhibit 6-5 for a summary of these fit relationships.

The framework we are developing has its roots in the so-called strategy–structure literature. Chandler stimulated much empirical and theoretical work in this area by studying seventy of America's largest firms. His main thesis states that[33]

> Organization structure follows from the growth strategy pursued by the firm. If a structural adjustment does not take place, the strategy will not be completely effective and economic inefficiency will result.

For the most part theorists have confirmed Chandler's hypothesis. That is, by refining his concept of strategy (specifying product–market strategy classifications[34] and structure, studies have shown that, in the presence of a competitive environment, structure does follow product–market strategy. Some theorists have also argued and shown empirical evidence to suggest that the relationship is often reversed, that is, structure influences strategy. We believe that both are true.

Another important finding is that most firms today have achieved this fit between product–market strategy and organization structure. A simplified version of these "fit relationships" is shown here:

Single business — Functional structure
Related products business — Multidivisional structure
Unrelated products business — Holding company structure

Why should these relationships hold? First of all, a firm's product-market strategy is seen as an important characteristic not only because it affects structure but also because each different strategy type is hypothesized to place a firm in a unique position with respect to its environment. Differences in product-market strategy reflect differences in the environmental diversity and complexity that top management faces. Therefore, each product-market strategy type is hypothesized to place a different degree, and perhaps a different kind of information processing requirement on the organization.

The literature indicates that a structure or a fit between a strategy and a structure should yield high performance because each structural type is assumed to have certain underlying structured processes and systems associated with it that will aid in coping with other diversity presented to it by the particular product–market strategy.

EXHIBIT 6-5

Fit Relationships

Strategic Situation Product–Market Strategy	Operating Organization Structure	Planning Process
1. High product relatedness with high market relatedness	Functional structure: necessary because of product market and geographic relatedness. No need to divisionalize.	Business-level planning focus on: competition, competitive advantage, distinctive competences product–market segmentation, stage of product–market evolution. Synergy-integration of different functional areas. Market share, production efficiencies, technological innovation.
2. High product relatedness with low market relatedness	Functional structure: necessary because of product relatedness.	SBUs to deal with the market or geographic diversity, to focus attention on each market and allocate the functional resources to markets in most efficient manner, and to keep abreast of each market opportunities and threats.
3. Low product relatedness with high market relatedness	Divisionalized structure: Necessary because of different technologies and manufacturing processes inherent in the product.	SBUs to provide a strategic approach to the market and eliminate counterproductive competition within the marketplace.
4. Low product relatedness with low market relatedness	Multidivisional or holding company structure: the high degree of diversity calls for much decentralization.	SBUs, because of the large size of most of the firms in this category, the focus is primarily on goal formulation and setting on a financial basis, to place emphasis on the "stars" that are small and might otherwise be overlooked, to serve as a span or control reducer, and to overlap any interdependencies (relatedness) that might exist.

Theorists, however, have failed to show that a fit between product–market strategy and organization structure leads to high economic performance. Aside from the fact that most firms have attained this "fit," hence making it difficult to get a relevant control group, we believe that the failure to attain significant findings in this area derives mainly from the fact theorists have failed to recognize that there may be significant variation of the underlying structural variables and processes between organizations. A single example would be wide variations in centralization that might exist between firms all having the multidivision structure.

As Rumelt states,[35]

> Organizational structure consists of a great deal more than the differences that can be shown by charts. Systems of control, planning and information flow, methods of reward and punishment, the degree of delegation and techniques of coordination are among the important determinants of the way of life within the enterprise. The usefulness of the distinction between functional and multidivisional organizations depends upon the degree to which these structures are associated with consistent differences among many other organizational characteristics.

Therefore our contention is this:

First, the strategic situation consists of more than just product–market strategy. Although product–market strategy is an extremely important dimension, it is often tempered by considerations such as size, technology, and the particular contingencies in the environment.

Second, structural responses to product–market strategy are important, but performance depends upon not only the fit between product–market strategy and structure but more realistically the fit between strategy–structure and organizational processes.

Third, in today's environment the diversity in the environment has increased the role importance of these internal coordinating processes and has spurred the development of planning organizations that are designed to cope with the diversity and internal integration that the operating structure cannot handle.

Finally, the focus of the planning system will be a function of the fit, or lack thereof, between the strategic situation and organization structure.

With this brief review of the "strategy–structure" literature as a background, we will now present a simplified typology of organizations (Exhibit 6-5). This typology corresponds to the case examples that were presented in the previous section.

We begin by taking pieces of the total strategic situation. That is, we begin with the product and market strategy, specify the operating structure that should, and does in most cases, exist to fit that product–market strategy, and then show how the deficiencies in the capabilities of the particular operating structure in coping with the information processing needs of the environment would call for a different emphasis for the SBU system. We then modify the product–market strategy to include other variables to achieve a more realistic view of the "strategic situation."

NOTES

[1]Charles W. Hofer and Dan Schendel, *Strategy Formulation: Analytical Concepts* (St. Paul, Minn.: West Publishing Co., 1978), p. 25.

[2]*Ibid.* p. 4.

[3]*Ibid.* p. 26.

[4]Richard Normann, *Management for Growth* (New York: Wiley Interscience, 1977).

[5]H. Igor Ansoff, *Corporate Strategy: An Analytical Approach to Business Policy for Growth and Expansion* (New York: McGraw Hill, 1965); George A. Steiner, *Top Management Planning* (New York: Macmillan Publishing Co., 1969); Russell L. Ackoff *A Concept of Corporate Planning* (New York: Wiley-Interscience, 1970); Peter Lorange and Richard F. Vancil, *Strategic Planning Systems* (Englewood Cliffs, N.J.: Prentice-Hall, 1977).

[6]Peter Lorange, "Formal Planning Systems: Their Role in Strategy Formulation and Implementation" in Dan Schendel and Charles Hofer, eds. *Strategic Management: A New View of Business Policy and Planning* (Boston: Little, Brown and Co., 1979).

[7]Peter Lorange, *ibid.*

[8]Jay R. Gailbraith, *Organizational Design* (Reading, Mass.: Addison-Wesley, 1977) p. 5; see also Henry Mintzberg, "Organizational Power and Goals", in Dan Schendel and Charles Hofer, eds. *Strategic Management: A New View of Business Policy and Planning op. cit.*; Max D. Richards, *Organizational Goal Structures* (St. Paul, Minn.: West Publishing Co., 1978).

[9]George A. Steiner, *Pitfalls in Comprehensive Long Range Planning* (Oxford, Ohio: Planning Executive Institute, 1972); George A. Steiner and Hans Schollhammer, "Pitfalls in Multi-National Long Range Planning", *Journal of Long Range Planning*, vol. 8 No. 2 (April 1975) pp. 2-12.

[10]Richard Normann, *Management for Growth, op. cit.*

[11]Peter Lorange, "Formal Planning Systems: Their Role in Strategy Formulation and Implementation" *op. cit.* p. 224

[12]Richard Cyert and James March, *A Behavioral Theory of the Firm* (Englewood Cliffs, N.J.: Prentice-Hall, 1963).

[13]Kalman Cohen and Richard Cyert, "Strategy: Formulation, Implementation and Monitoring," *Journal of Business* vol. 46 (July 1973) pp. 349-367.

[14]Joseph Bower, *The Resource Allocation Process* (Boston: Division of Research, Graduate School of Business Administration, Harvard University, 1970); Norman Berg, "Strategic Planning in Conglomerate Companies" *Harvard Business Review* Vol. 43, No. 3 (May-June 1965), pp. 19-92; Eugene Carter, "The Behavioral Theory of the Firm and Top Level Corporate Decisions" *Administrative Science Quarterly* Vol. 16, No. 3 (December 1971) pp. 413-428.

[15]Eugene Carter, "The Behavioral Theory of the Firm and Top Level Corporate Decisions" *op. cit.*

[16]C. Roland Christensen, Kenneth Andrews and Joseph Bower, *Business Policy: Text and Cases* (Homewood, Ill.: Richard D. Irwin, 1973).

[17]Jay Gailbraith and Dan Nathanson, *Strategy Implementation: The Role of Structure and Process* (St. Paul, Minn.: West Publishing Co., 1978).

[18]Charles Hofer, "Toward a Contingency Theory of Business Strategy" *Academy of Management Journal*, Vol. 18 No. 4 (December, 1975).

[19]George A, Steiner, *Top Management Planning, op. cit.*

[20]John Child, "Organizaional Structure. Environment and Performance—The Role of Strategic Choice" *Sociology* (January 1972).

[21]Paul Lawrence and Jay Lorch, *Organization and Environment* (Homewood, Ill.: Richard D. Irwin, 1973).

[22]D. Miller, "Towards a Contingency Theory of Strategy Formulation" *Academy of Management Proceedings* (Mississippi State: Academy of Management, 1975) pp. 64-66; Dan Schendel, "Designing Strategic Planning Systems" *Institute of Economic Management and Administrative Sciences*, Working paper No. 616 (Purdue University: Lafayette, Ind. 1977).

[23]Charles Hofer, "Toward a Contingency Theory of Business Strategy" *op. cit.*; Peter Lorange, "Formal Planning Systems: Their Role in Formulation and Implementation" *op. cit.*

[24]Robert Litschert, "Some Characteristics of Long Range Planning: An Introductory Study" *Academy of Management Journal* Vol. 11 No. 3 (Sept. 1968) pp. 315-329.

[25]*Ibid.*

[26]Peter Lorange, Formal Planning Systems: Their Role in Formulation and Implementation" *op. cit.* p. 237

[27]*Ibid.* p. 238

[28]Dan Schendel, *Designing Strategic Planning Systems op. cit.*

[29]Peter Lorange "Formal Planning Systems: Their Role in Formulation and Implementation. *op. cit.*

[30]Stephen Allen III, "A Taxonomy of Organizational Choices in Divisionalized Companies" Working Paper (Lausanne, Switzerland: IMEDE 1978).

[31]Jay Gailbraith and Dan Nathanson, *Strategy Implementation: The Role of Structure and Process. op. cit.* p. 161.

[32]*Business Week* "GE's New Strategy for Faster Growth" July 8, 1972.

[33]Alfred Chandler, *Strategy and Structure: Chapters in the History of the Industrial Enterprise* (Cambridge, Mass.: MIT Press, 1962) p. 14.

[34]Leonard Wrigley and Richard Rumelt, *Divisional Autonomy and Diversification* Unpublished D.B.A. Thesis (Boston: Harvard Business School, 1970).

[35]Richard Rumelt *Strategy, Structure and Economic Performance* (Cambridge, Mass.: Harvard University Press 1974).

7
Controlling Strategic Plans

INTRODUCTION

Since the publication of Anthony's framework,[1] additional work has appeared, most of it since 1970, that attempts to explore the issues in control. Several books have been written on the general topic.[2] An attempt has been made to relate relevant quantitative techniques[3] and the systems approach [4] to the management control problem.

Virtually absent from all these efforts is any discussion of the control of strategic plans. In his three-level framework, Anthony presented few specifics on control at the strategic level, assigning most of the control functions to the two lower levels. Of the later authors cited, only Newman has singled out the strategic control area for separate treatment.

And yet the control of strategic plans is an important managerial problem. Perhaps the reason for its lack of coverage in the management literature is an incomplete understanding of the differences between strategic and lower levels of control and the implications of these differences on the tools required for strategic control. This chapter* is designed to fill this gap by discussing these differences and presenting their implications for the design of information and control systems.

To make the contrast as stark as possible, only two different levels of

*This chapter prepared by E. Gerald Hurst, Jr., The Wharton School, University of Pennsylvania.

management are discussed. Obviously, the levels of management decision are not a simple dichotomy but, rather, a continuum from the most strategic to the most operational-level decisions. Furthermore, the distinctions blur for any given decision, which in general has strategic, tactical, and operational facets. Even for what is universally accepted to be a strategic decision, some aspects of control will look operational. Nevertheless, it is fair to state that most strategic-level decisions will have the characteristics at that end of the spectrum and that they can be contrasted to the characteristics at the operational level.

DIFFERENCES

The differences between strategic and operational control are highlighted by reference to a general definition of management control. This definition is as follows: Management control is the set of *measurement, analysis,* and *action* decisions required for the *timely* management of the continuing operation of a process. The four parts of this section discuss the differences in the terms presented.

Measurement

Strategic control requires data from more sources. The typical operational control problem uses data from very few sources. In the extreme case, only the operation itself generates data; at the very most, a few environmental factors are involved. For example, in scheduling production, the bulk of the information needed to pick the next job on the machine is generated by the operation itself. Only data on deadlines and relationships to other parts of the factory do not arise from the operation itself. In contrast, strategic control typically involves data from many sources. Normally all parts of the organization contribute data of relevance, and many important data come from outside as well. For example, consideration of a merger possibility requires examination of internal factors, characteristics of the other firm, and market characteristics.

Strategic control requires more data from external sources. Related to the preceding point, strategic decisions are normally taken with regard to the external environment as opposed to internal operating factors. This gives rise to a wide variety of external sources from which relevant data must be drawn. This of course implies an increased difficulty in gathering these data and probably an increased difficulty in keeping them organized once they are gathered.

Strategic control data are oriented to the future. In one sense, all data for control are gathered in the present, as control exercised in a timely fashion and based on current data is implied by our general definition of control. Because the strategic decision upon which midcourse corrections are being made tends to be future oriented, the data gathered now are more generally used to recast the future before action is taken. This is in contrast to operational control decisions in which control data give rise to immediate decisions that have immediate impacts.

Strategic control is more concerned with measuring the accuracy of the decision premise. Operating decisions tend to be concerned with the quantitative value of certain outcomes. What is usually measured, therefore, is the value of some factor of production. The percentage of defects in a batch, the total labor content in a production run, and the number of tests performed by a hospital facility are typical examples of operating measurements. By way of contrast, strategic control normally wishes to check whether or not the assumptions made are correct. Sometimes this involves quantitative information, but it is just as likely to involve a comparison against qualitative and structural information about the market, competitors' product lines, and the like.

Strategic control standards are based on external factors. The standards against which strategic performance is measured are necessarily more external to the environment, given the nature of the strategic problem. Measurement standards for operating problems can be established fairly by past performance on similar products or by similar operations currently being performed. On the other hand, the usual standard for comparison in the strategic arena is how well a similar competitor is doing or some other external yardstick. As with the data that come from external sources, this makes the standards harder to use, both because they are less accessible and because they are not likely to be so easily comparable once they are obtained.

Strategic control relies on a variable reporting interval. The typical operating measurement is concerned with operations over some period of time: pieces per week, profit per quarter, and the like. As a result, the measurement interval is typically quite regular. Strategic events occur much more irregularly, and the measurement interval is therefore variable. This variation of the interval is related to an orientation that is discussed further in the section on timing. For now, let us simply note that the irregularity adds to the difficulty in measurement.

All these characteristics, taken together, lead to measurement that is much more difficult for strategic problems. Strategic measurements are less accessible, less regular, much more variable in their types and sources, and, in the final analysis, less measurable because they are qualitative rather than quantitative.

Analysis

The models and methods that are used to analyze strategic control problems are, not surprisingly, related to the models and methods used in strategic planning. Many of the insights developed over past years about the planning problem at this level are equally applicable in control.

Strategic control models are less precise. Strategic control models, like strategic planning models, tend to be aggregate approximations of a large world as opposed to precise representations of a small one. This is in contrast to operational control models, which are generally very precise in the narrow domain to which they apply.

Strategic control models are less formal. This is a harder generalization to make, as approximate models are used in operational control, on the one hand, and formal models are occasionally very useful in the strategic control process. However, as a rule, the models that govern the considerations in a strategic control problem are much more intuitive and, therefore, less formal.

The principal variables in a strategic control model are structural. Once the structure of an operational control problem is captured, the variations for which measurements must be made tend to be quantitative. This point was highlighted in the section on measurement. In strategic control, the whole structure of the problem, as represented by the model, is likely to vary, not just the values of the parameters. These structural variations are related typically to unforeseen events that occurred and/or predicted events that did not occur in the external environment.

The key need in analysis for strategic control is model flexibility. It follows that, because the overall assumptions are being examined and the structure of the problem is varying in strategic control, an ability to be flexible in analysis is key. That is, it is necessary to have the ability to modify the structure of the model easily. This is in contrast to operating control, for which efficient quantitative computation is usually most desirable.

The key activity in management control analysis is alternative generation. As in the analysis of planning strategy, the most important activity in strategic control is generation of alternatives, not their formal analysis. In the control problem at the strategic level, this means that the discovery of causes, while important, is hard to do in any formal analytical way. Once a cause is suggested, the key step is the generation of alternatives to deal with it. This is different from the operational control problem, in which in many cases all control alternatives have been specified in advance. The key analysis step in operations is to discover exactly what happened. Once this is done, the choice of action is normally the simple step of implementing an alternative that has been identified previously.

The key skill required for management control analysis is creativity. For the reasons given, the principal skill in management control at the strategic level is creativity. This skill is used for recognizing structural variations from the original plan, generating new models and action alternatives, analyzing them as far as possible, and having other dealings with the less structured world of strategic control. In operational control, by contrast, the formal review of outcomes to discover causes means that the key skill required is the ability to do technical, even statistical, analysis of the data received.

Action

As in the previous two sections, which deal with the measurement and analysis categories of decision in the control problem, the strategic problem is somewhat more difficult to deal with in taking action than its operational counterpart.

The relationship between action and outcome is weaker in strategic control. A frustration that is continually reported by managers at the strategic level is their inability to "turn many knobs." Those knobs that they can turn seem to have much less impact on the areas they would like to control. This is not surprising, as the most desirable area for control in strategic problems—the environment—is the least subject to direct action. However, even the internal control variables are difficult to manipulate, as outcomes are at best delayed from the time at which action is initiated. At worst, there is no perceptible impact of taking action. Operating systems are, by contrast, much easier to influence directly.

The key action variables in strategic control are organizational. Such knobs as there are to turn in the strategic problem are largely organizational, as distinct from the operational control problem, where technical factors such as labor levels, production levels, choice of materials, and the like are the predominant controllables. Corrective action in the strategic area usually means a change in organizational form or structure, a movement of personnel, or some other change in the deployment of the human and organizational resources to meet the changing or better understood environment.

Alternative actions in strategic control are less easy to choose in advance. Because each new strategic control problem presents a unique and usually different set of details, because the combinations are complex, and because the data are diffuse, it is usually not economical or even possible to choose all possible action responses to received data in advance. In an operational control problem, the few responses possible can usually all be worked out before any operating data are received. When these data are received, exercising control is a simple matter of correcting the trajectory by already established rules. In the strategic control problem, the trajectory corrections are much more difficult and the number of possibilities is much greater. It is usually not economical to anticipate action possibilities until an outcome is actually received, even if it is feasible.

The worst failing in strategic control is omitting a worthwhile action. In operating control, the most typical sins are those of commission. Complaints about too many people employed, too many defects, and too much inventory are laments commonly heard in operations. In the strategic control problem, sins of omission are much more serious. Not moving into a business opportunity when it presents itself, not undertaking a particular social program, not applying resources to meet the challenges in the best fashion are the common problems. Using a famous example as an analogy, operating control problems in a buggywhip factory would likely concern themselves with producing too large an inventory of buggywhips or producing them at too high a cost. The strategic problem is not getting out of the buggywhip business in time.

Timing

Not only do the emphases in the three major decision areas differ in strategic and operating control problems, but the issues in timing these decisions are also different.

The time frame for strategic control is longer. Not surprisingly, the period in which control has an impact is longer for strategic problems than for operating problems. The consequences of a strategic decision are larger and can be felt over a longer period, even if the decision takes place in a fairly short time. Mergers and acquisitions are a good example of this effect. They have profound effects on the basic shape of the organization for the rest of its life. The consequences of operating control decisions are shorter lived.

The timing of strategic control is events oriented. This assertion is related to the assertion about measurement interval. It simply states that discrete events influence the strategic world most markedly. By contrast, operating decisions tend to be made on a periodic basis, and they are usually measured accordingly.

Strategic control has little repetition. Strategic control problems tend to be unique. Not even the structure is the same as past problems of a like kind, much less the technical details. Operating problems, by way of contrast, tend to repeat their structure. Only the quantitative values differ from period to period. For example, the mix of jobs and the technical resources required to produce them may be different from week to week, but the basic problem of matching jobs and resources in a shop remains the same. The resources change only slowly, and the capabilities of the system do not vary much from one scheduling interval to another. The typical strategic control problem, such as responding to competition in a new product decision, is different in both structure and technical details from occurrence to occurrence.

IMPLICATIONS

The characteristics of strategic control needs just documented imply differing characteristics and emphases for the information and control systems that support these needs.

Implications for Information Systems

Strategic control requires a greater variety of data types. Because of the more complex nature of the strategic control problem and because there are more different sources of data, more data types are required. Operating control problems typically have a smaller variety of data.

The total volume of data required for strategic control is smaller. On the other hand, whereas the number of data types is larger for strategic control, the total volume associated with each data type is smaller. For example, the total market forecast by month for five years for ten different product lines comprises only six hundred data values. This is one of the larger volumes of data that would be confronted in a strategic problem. Typical volumes of actual values would be much smaller than this. On the other hand, perhaps thousands of pieces of data of each type are required for the payroll processing of even a small organization.

Strategic control data are more aggregated. Strategic problems, encompassing as they do broad segments of the organization, are not so concerned with detail. As a result, the data are typically aggregated when used. Operating data are, almost by definition, used at the most detailed transaction level, meaning that little aggregation is possible.

Strategic control data are less accurate. By the same token, data for strategic control need be less accurate. Errors of 5, 10, or even 50 percent are not atypical in such data, although for control purposes one would hope for less than 50 percent. Operating data generally need to be as accurate as possible. For example, rounding salary payments to the nearest hundred dollars is unsatisfactory, either to the organization or to the employee, depending on who is favored by the rounding. On the other hand, a value rounded to the nearest million dollars is probably sufficiently accurate when looking at overall payroll expenses by quarter to discern cost trends for a medium-sized organization.

The most important strategic control information is structural. Supporting the strategic control models discussed in the section on analysis requires information on the structure of the real world as represented by the model. Unlike the operational control area, the values of the technical variables are only of secondary importance. The sort of information to be captured by the system that supports strategic control concerns the presence, absence, or strength of relationships among components of the overall system being modeled rather than the values of the technical variables contained in the model. In short, the most critical information for strategic control models is whether or not a model segment should be present and in what form rather than the detailed values of the coefficients in that model segment. This is related to the question of data accuracy.

The receipt of data for strategic control is more sporadic. Not surprisingly, given the event-paced rather than clock-paced nature of strategic control, data for these problems are received sporadically as events take place rather than on a periodic or predictable basis. This implies that a data capture system that is designed for the regular data capture inherent in an operating control system will not in general be suitable for the strategic control problem, in which data are received less regularly.

Strategic control data are less processable by computer. Operating data that arise inside the firm are likely to be directly "machine readable." Even if they are not, they are more available by virtue of having arisen inside the organization. On the other hand, the strategic control data that arise in the environment rather than within the organization are generally not so easily available. This means that some sort of active data capture, verification, and the like must take place for them to be processable by computer. For the most part, such data need not be computerized, so this is not as serious a failing as it might first appear. It does imply that any computerization of strategic control tools must consider the important step of capturing necessary data in machine-readable form.

The key decision in information for strategic control is what data to save. The principal problem in operating control information systems design is the technological problem of efficiently capturing and retrieving data. Because of the large volumes of data, this technological design problem is very important. A miniscule saving in storage and retrieval time, when multiplied by the number of transactions in the typical operating control system, can lead to a large benefit. By way of contrast, the difficult decision in strategic control is deciding which of the myriads of data the world generates are worth saving. The typical admonition to "save everything," which is usually suggested for the operating control problem, is quite impossible in the strategic environment. The world is generating too much data in too many diverse types for that to be at all practical. One must instead be very selective in what is saved. Once the decision of what to save is made, the technological decision of how to save it is fairly straightforward, given that the volume of these data is small. Whether or not to capture the data now in machine-readable form is still an important decision, but it can be rejected now and instituted later at additional cost if and when machine-readable uses of the data develop. The key continuing decision is whether or not to save the data at all, in whatever form, at the time they are generated.

Taken together, these statements about the characteristics of the information systems required to support strategic control decisions present a rather different profile from the standard data processing information system. They present the picture of an externally oriented, much less formal process by which appropriate data are captured and saved in a variety of forms, at irregular intervals. It is little wonder that attempts to apply the methods and technology of standard data processing systems to the strategic control problem have been less than successful. The information required and the methods for capturing it are enough different in the strategic problem that very little carry-over from transaction processing systems is possible.

Implications for Controlling Formal Plans

It can be inferred from the earlier discussion that a formal plan, in the form of a documented quantitative model, is less possible in the strategic area than in lower levels of decision making. The qualitative factors that are less easy to capture in any formal sense play a much more important role in the strategic area. Having said this, it is still desirable to control carefully those segments of the strategic plan that can be documented formally. It is not possible to use the same methods for this analysis as is used for controlling operational plans, because the emphases in strategic plans are so different.

Contingency plans are less possible in strategic control. It was argued that it is more difficult to generate all possible actions ahead of time in a strategic problem, because the alternatives are too numerous and too complex. Beyond that, the whole idea of contingency plans is much more difficult in the strategic arena. As desirable as it is to anticipate all outcomes and their impact on the strategic plan, and to generate the appropriate action response, it is simply too large a problem to be feasible. This does not mean that major outcomes should not be anticipated or that plans should not be made where possible. It is only to state the sad but realistic fact that no matter how much effort is devoted to this pursuit important alternatives will be missed even if it is economical to try to find them.

Triggering contingency planning is more important in strategic control. Because of this difficulty in making contingency plans, triggering an examination of alternatives when things do not go according to plan becomes much more important. This implies both the increased need and ability to plan and the active monitoring of these situations to bring them to the attention of the appropriate managers when thing begin to go awry. It seems evident that computerized information systems for managers must move more and more in the direction of active monitoring of the environment of the managers they serve. Until this happens, humans will continue to play an important role in processing the diverse data received and determining when something has gone wrong. Even where a formal planning model has been used, a human must interpret the data and search for conclusions as well as causes.

Preprogrammed variance analysis is less possible in strategic control. It is tempting, where a formal model is available, to suggest that the computer perform all possible variance analyses (in the accounting sense). For an operational control model this might be possible. For strategic control it is both difficult technically and impossible practically. The total of all possible variance analyses is many more than can be computed economically or reviewed effectively by a human. A few key analyses can be done automatically, but, because of the nonrepetitiveness of strategic control, accounting variance analysis must remain an ad hoc and essentially humanly controlled task in the strategic arena.

A variance inquiry system is more necessary in strategic control. Based on this assertion, it seems important to have an inquiry system linked to the formal planning model with which combinations of deviations from plans can be explored by the human operator. No promising variance analyses are denied to the human, but, because of the huge number of possible analyses, the human should control those that are made and reviewed.

A variance inquiry language is more necessary in strategic control. It follows from the preceding statement that some sort of language in which the human can do variance inquiries is highly desirable in the area of strategic control. The formal strategic planning model should be a part of this analysis and should be available to generate computations using the combinations of budgeted and desired variables that lead to the desired variance results. The inquiry language should be user oriented, in the sense that the users state deviations they wish to examine in terms of their knowledge of the strategic problem and that these be translated into the computation required to display the deviations of interest.

An augmented formal planning system is more necessary in strategic control. Taken with the desirability of using a formal planning system for generating strategic plans, this leads to the further assertion that a formal planning system should be augmented with the variance inquiry language described. This would permit the same system that was used to generate the plan to be used in controlling that plan, leading to both ease of additional analysis as well as to consistency with the plan being controlled.

NOTES

[1] Robert N. Anthony, *Planning and Control Systems: A Framework for Analysis* (Cambridge, Mass.: Division of Research, Graduate School of Business Administration, Harvard University, 1965).
[2] Samuel Eilon, *Management Control* (New York: Wiley, 1972); Robert J. Mockler, *The Management Control Process* (New York: Appleton-Century-Crofts, 1972); William H. Newman, *Constructive Control: Design and Use of Control Systems* (Englewood Cliffs, N.J.: Prentice-Hall, 1975); and Allan L. Patz and A. J. Rowe, *Management Control and Decision Systems* (New York: Wiley, 1977).
[3] Alain Bensoussan, E. Gerald Hurst, Jr., and Bertil Naslund, *Management Applications of Modern Control Theory* (Amsterdam: North-Holland, 1974), and E. Gerald Hurst, Jr., "The Impact of New Techniques for Management Control on the Information System and Organization," in *Information Systems and Organizational Structure*, eds. Ernst Grochla and Norbert Szyperski (Berlin: Walter de Gruyter, 1975).
[4] Peter Lorange and Michael S. Scott-Morton, "A Framework for Management Control Systems," *Sloan Management Review*, Vol. 16, No. 1 (Fall 1974), pp. 41–56. Reprinted in Allan L. Patz and A. J. Rowe, *Management Control Decision Systems, op. cit.*

section three

Implementation in Situational Settings

chapter eight: Managing the Quality of Strategic Thinking.

chapter nine: Introducing a Formal Strategic Planning System in a Firm.

chapter ten: The Increasing Relevance of Planning: A Case Study, 1950–1980.

chapter eleven: On Acceptance of Strategic Planning Systems.

chapter twelve: Strategic Planning as a Tool for Adaptation and Integration.

chapter thirteen: Planning as a Vehicle for Strategic Redirection in a Matrix Structure.

8

Managing the Quality of Strategic Thinking

In all too many companies, strategic planning efforts produce little more than window dressing for poor thinking. Even where considerable management time and energy are devoted to the task, where a "good planning system" is in place, and where the chief executive officer is an enthusiastic supporter, insipid ideas and misleading conclusions can dominate the output. In time, the managers involved become disappointed, frustrated, and even scornful of the strategic planning process.

This chapter* examines the nature of this problem and suggests some possible remedies. Its purpose is to call attention to the general manager's task of managing his or her organization so as to generate good thinking about the right issues.

THE PROBLEM FOCUS

The formulation and implementation of business strategies is an inherently difficult task. The accomplishments of inspired leaders—such as Land of Polaroid, Lemkuhl of Timex, and Connally of Crown Cork and Seal—to conceive and to carry out major strategic moves are impressive. The task becomes much more

*This chapter is prepared by Francis Aguilar, Harvard Business School.

difficult when strategic changes depend on the involvement of many people—often separated by age, experience, and rank.

To enact a strategic change involves both insight and commitment. Someone has to discover an idea for change. Someone has to commit company resources. The less connected these two someones are in terms of trust and confidence, the more difficult will be the marriage of insight and commitment. This difficulty reflects the uncertainties and risks associated with most strategic changes. Conclusions rest on judgments and conjecture and are vulnerable to doubts and to contradiction. Under these circumstances, one person's considered opinion can easily be another's idea of nonsense.

This study, which is only partially completed, focuses on the problem of strategy making in its more complex setting—where insight and commitment involve different people. In these situations, insight is typically sought at the "middle levels" of management, where knowledge and responsibility for specific operations (both line and staff) reside; commitment is required from "senior general managers," where the power resides.

The information was gathered primarily through unstructured interviews with general managers who were responsible for corporate strategies or for business strategies and with staff managers responsible either for long-range planning activities or for formalized scanning activities (for example, corporate issues, government relations, and futures research). Where practicable, discussions were held with all or most of the relevant managers in a company. To date, about 150 managers in some twenty firms have participated in the study.

The interviews were designed to identify conditions and practices that inhibited and those that contributed to "good strategic thinking."[1] Based on the findings, this chapter discusses in turn

1. factors and conditions that suppress the creation and adoption of new strategic moves, and
2. ways to reduce the barriers to initiative and to encourage risk taking and change where appropriate.

A Conceptual Map

While the problem of generating strategic changes must be viewed in its entirety, I find it helpful for purposes of analysis to break it apart along several dimensions.

1. As already mentioned, strategic change requires both the act of creation, or insight, and the act of commitment. The difficulties associated with each task, while closely interrelated, are sufficiently different to justify a separate consideration of the two tasks.
2. Basically, when all is said and done, managers fail to generate good strategic moves because they are unable or are unwilling to do so. This distinction between ability and volition has practical significance because the reasons for inaction and ineffectiveness differ, as do the ways to overcome the problem.
3. The source of the constraints on a manager's ability and volition, either to conceive or to commit to new strategic moves, can provide another useful distinc-

tion. Broadly speaking, there are conditions in the organizational context that hinder or suppress strategic thinking. Strategic thinking is also limited by the particular capabilities and attitudes of the individual managers involved.

A map of the territory to be covered, then, might be represented by the three-dimensional matrix shown in Exhibit 8-1. The arrows are to remind us that each cell is strongly interrelated with every other cell in this conceptual breakout of the problem.

BARRIERS TO GOOD STRATEGIC THINKING

The search for conditions and practices that inhibit good strategic thinking can be intensified by giving separate attention to each cell in Exhibit 8-1. Viewing a particular type of difficulty from the different perspectives can help to uncover subtle but important considerations. To simplify the reporting in this paper, the barriers to good strategic thinking are subdivided only between those having to do with ability and those with volition.

The Problem of Inability

Not surprising, a common reason for poor strategic planning was a lack of ability. The managers called upon to generate new strategies did not possess the

EXHIBIT 8-1

Principal Dimensions for Analyzing the Strategy-Making Process

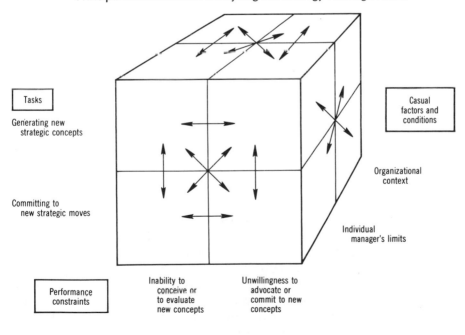

Tasks

Generating new
strategic concepts

Committing to
new strategic moves

Casual
factors and
conditions

Organizational
context

Individual
manager's limits

Performance
constraints

Inability to
conceive or
to evaluate
new concepts

Unwillingness to
advocate or
commit to new
concepts

skills to do this work.[2] After all, just because a person is good at running an ongoing operation does not ensure that he or she can conceptualize new approaches.

A manager's ability to conceive new strategic concepts would seem so obviously a needed element that it need scarcely be mentioned. That might be true if conceptual abilities were not so often overlooked in practice when planning assignments are meted out. Actually, the reasons for limited abilities and the possible corrective actions are neither straightforward nor simple.

The individual manager's intellectual capacity and his or her developed skills for dealing with strategic concepts are obviously relevant. But a manager's abilities to think about new strategic moves are also influenced by contextual considerations.

For example, the individual manager's ability to think along fresh lines is strongly influenced by the established views held by others in the organization. These views can pertain to the nature of the business, how to compete, what the product should be, and how to run the organization. The more strongly these views are held, the more inhibiting they are likely to be with respect to new ideas. "The repressive powers of the corporate mythology" was the way one senior executive put it.

In companies located away from industrial and commercial centers, managers frequently complained about the problem of parochial thinking resulting from their isolation. A successful history of performance also tends to reinforce myopic thinking about the business. Hugh Schwarz complained of this problem when he served as director of Corporate Planning for the Coca-Cola Company:

> If a person is happy with the present situation, he will not want to change. The very success of The Coca-Cola Company works against its planning for change.

Vermont Royster, columnist for *The Wall Street Journal*, recently touched on this same point:[3]

> The American auto industry was enormously successful for years making the kind of cars it made. . . . That very success built up inertia against change until forced to change by foreign competitors who had to offer something different to penetrate the market.

The kind of information made available to a manager also affects his or her ability to generate or become committed to new strategic ideas. Thus, environmental scanning practices, the openness of internal communications, and the explicit delineation of issues and priorities are importantly relevant to the problem.

Ironically, formal planning often has the effect of inhibiting conceptual thinking rather than enhancing it. The result can occur for several reasons. Many managers are confused and distracted by the mechanics and terminology (jargon) of the elaborate planning systems increasingly in vogue today. This problem is especially true in companies in which the planning system is in a continual state of revision. More time goes into trying to figure out what is wanted than into thinking about the business.

Planning concepts can also create new corporate myths as repressive as the old. In several large industrial firms in which portfolio planning approaches had been firmly implanted, senior managers complained that operating managers had become so conditioned by their assigned "cash cow" business role that they were not sensitive to possible growth opportunities in segments within the overall charter of their unit. A related pitfall is that the planning effort and the resulting plan can give a manager the illusion of having done planning when no constructive or imaginative thinking has taken place.

Insight versus commitment. These comments were directed largely to the task of generating new strategic concepts where creative insight was called for. Key ingredients are the manager's abilities to detect new opportunities and threats (discover the problem), to conceive new combinations and new approaches, to sense implications, and to assess the business risks. The senior manager's task of commitment requires similar abilities, but with a different emphasis.

The problem for senior managers is to evaluate someone else's ideas and judgments with limited firsthand knowledge of the facts. This problem is intensified in multibusiness companies for those activities where the senior managers have not had direct experience. Fred Borch, a former president of General Electric, expressed the problem as follows:

> With hundreds of products ranging from electric pencil sharpeners to diesel engines and nuclear plants, it is difficult to do an effective job of planning. It is, in fact, impossible for management to have a direct, personal feeling and knowledge about so many business environments.

In effect, the senior manager has to assess both the quality and the appropriateness of new ideas, in many or most cases with very limited understanding. Weakness in a manager's ability to evaluate the merits and to assess the risks associated with a new strategic approach involving major commitments of time and resources leads to temporizing or to its rejection.

The problem for senior managers is exacerbated by the unknowns surrounding the proposal under consideration. This difficulty in its most direct form concerns the relative merits of possible alternative approaches for the strategic move in question. William Wommack, deputy chairman of the board of directors for the Mead Corporation, saw this as a major problem for senior management:

> The idea that the organization will present strategic alternatives to top management is a fiction. If alternatives are ever generated, they get eliminated as they move up the organization. Top management is then faced with accepting or rejecting the one proposed plan that survives the organizational screening.

A broader problem of context concerns the need for senior management to assess how the business strategy in question fits into the total range of concerns for the corporation. How does the proposed move relate to the other known corporate business activities and concerns in terms of importance and possible interactions? Are other issues of importance to the corporation being overlooked? These questions are not easily answered.

The Problem of Willingness

For managers, to be able to conceive and to commit to new strategic concepts is not enough. They must also want to advocate new ideas. A wide variety of factors influence the manager's decision on how far to go and on how hard to push. These factors can be grouped as having to do with motivation and with personal risk as defined by the individual manager and by the organizational context.

Individual considerations. Some people are natural riverboat gamblers, and others find comfort wth the celluloid cuff of the bookkeeper. Some people want to lead the pack, and others prefer to follow. In like manner, managers' positions differ greatly with respect to their motivation for recognition and reward and their willingness to bear personal risks.

Although probably relatively little can be done to change the individual manager's proclivities in this regard, an explicit awareness of them can be important for the design of corrective actions. In this connection, just how an individual manager will act in a given situation depends on the organizational context.

Contextual considerations. In companies in which strategy making was actively and constructively underway, managers would typically single out the CEO (or some other senior manager close to the CEO) as the prime mover. The converse also held. Blame for the failure of strategic planning was usually attributed to the top executive. The senior executive's marked influence manifests itself organizationally in several ways.

The clarity of the goals for change had a major effect on strategy making. The healthiest situations were those in which the CEO and other senior managers held in common a clear idea of the desired direction, degree, and urgency of strategic change and in which this definition was clearly promulgated to the line and staff managers responsible for business strategies. In these situations, middle managers were able to calibrate the personal risks attached to strategic ideas and could feel some security in advocating changes that were in line with senior management's goals. When top management was unclear and vacillating in its position with respect to strategic change, the risks of advocating new ideas escalated.

New strategic ideas are often in need of modification and almost always vulnerable to second-guessing. The way in which senior managers reacted to strategic ideas greatly affected the perceived risks of advocacy. No one cares to be embarrassed or punished. A great many managers are very senisitive to criticism. The hard-nosed executive who likes to "lay it on the line with no punches pulled" can turn off a lot of potential ideas.

The fate of the "fathers" of unsuccessful strategies is obviously another telltale sign of the personal risks involved. In one company in which the CEO had a habit of firing division managers when new strategies did not work out, it came as no surprise to find managers throughout the company petrified to advocate any changes. Admittedly, how to deal with a manager who has advocated a strategic move that proves to be a flop is not a simple matter.

The formal measurement and reward systems also influenced the climate for change. In most companies, great attention and effort go into budgeting. Managers are evaluated and often compensated by how well they do with respect to yearly profits. This stress on short-term results was often cited in practice as a deterrent to good strategic thinking. One reason was that concern with "making budget" often left little time for thinking ahead. Another reason was that the pressure for profits tended to give disproportionate importance to moves that gave near-term profits.

The mismatch between planning intentions and the administrative systems used to evaluate and reward managers is understandable. These systems in large companies are ponderous and deeply rooted. To change them requires great effort and time and can be upsetting to an organization. Moreover, management still has to run the company's operations, and the requirements for this task do not necessarily coincide with the requirements for encouraging new strategic moves.

FACILITATING GOOD STRATEGIC THINKING

While each barrier to good strategic thinking has corresponding solutions, managers must deal with an entire approach of interrelated practices for their company. The practices aimed at overcoming specific barriers must also fit with each other. For this reason, the discussion on facilitating good strategic thinking will start with a look at the overall approaches in two companies. These accounts will be followed by a description of other selected practices that appeared to contribute to improved strategic decision making or to have the potential to do so in the other firms studied.[4] This paper will not comment on many important practices that are rather obvious responses to specific problem barriers (for example, the use of business education programs to improve managers' analytical skills).

Two Approaches

Improving strategic thinking is a matter of getting managers more able and more willing to generate good strategic ideas and to become committed to them. There are really only two basic ways to accomplish this: (1) placing people who already have these capabilities in position of responsibility and (2) developing these capabilities in the people who already hold positions with strategic responsibilities. Although neither approach is ever used exclusively, deciding on a balance between these two approaches is of fundamental importance to a company embarked on improving strategic thinking.

Among the companies studied, two large successful firms competing in the same industry provide good illustrations of the two approaches. In both cases, major efforts to improve strategic planning were launched under the leadership of newly appointed CEOs. The different approaches in the "Alpha" and "Zeta" companies are described in turn.

The People-Changing Approach

The chief executive officer of Alpha summarized his program for improving strategic planning in the following words:

> I believe that it is necessary for me to accomplish two things to improve strategic planning in Alpha. One is to establish an environment to encourage and support planning. The other is to put "spark plugs" in key positions to get good planning done.

The effort to create a proper environment encompassed a variety of moves. For example, the CEO made crystal clear his intention to require strategic planning. Pressure was put on the senior managers to work on it. Financial models for planning purposes were developed. Staff support for strategic planning was beefed up.

The principal means of exploiting the new planning set-up was to put "fresh blood" in key positions. These people were to be the spark plugs for change.

In most cases, company people were moved up and around for this purpose. The following comment by the CEO gives some idea of the thinking behind these moves:

> We promoted [Bob] to head up the _____ division, even though he hadn't been in his previous job very long, because he has shown himself to be smart and aggressive over the years. The former divisional manager had been in that post for many years and was rather too settled in his ways. He was moved up to an EVP position where his experience could be tapped, but where his conservatism could be circumvented. People were also brought in from the outside to take over key positions at all levels, including that of President and Chief Operating Officer.

The People-Improving Approach

The Zeta Company's approach was primarily one of getting the people already in positions of responsibility to do a better job of strategic planning. The following excerpts from a case in preparation describe the salient features of this approach.

In early 1973, soon after his appointment to the position of chief executive officer for Zeta Company, John Ripley initiated a series of meeting with his senior managers to deal with his company's lackluster performance in recent years and with the lack of direction he had perceived. He opened the first meeting with the following statement:

Our current efforts to plan beyond one year are ineffective. The five-year plans are, to a large extent, mechanistic projections of our current numbers. We don't seem able to stimulate new ideas for our businesses, nor do we seem able to generate any sense of commitment to change. We lack a clear overview of the pieces. To my mind, one of the key tasks we have before us is to make our planning meaningful.

One of management's early decisions was to develop planning in stages, starting with divisional operational planning, then moving to divisional strategic planning, and finally to corporate strategic planning. After five years, the company was about to start on the third step. Ripley had this to say about the deliberate sequencing:

The evolution of planning at Zeta might be seen as rather conservative. In my view, you cannot change a large corporation quickly, especially if it is successful. While there was plenty of room for improvement in the early 1970s, there was no real crisis to help us unblock the norms and procedures followed in managing the operating divisions.

The role of corporate staff.   One of the distinguishing characteristics of the planning process at Zeta was the highly active role of corporate staff in the divisional planning activity. Members of the planning staff were assigned to work closely with operating units in the preparation of operational and strategic plans.

An operating general manager gave the following view of this practice:

The concept of having a corporate planner working with us in depth makes a lot of sense. His liaison role is of particular value to us. I appreciate the opportunity to try out new ideas on one of these people rather than trying to spring a full-blown new idea on top management without this earlier testing. Not only can the staff coordinator help me to shape my ideas in a way that will be most convincing to senior managers, he also can be very helpful in explaining to senior managers what we are doing.

The manager in charge of the staff planners had this to say about the operation:

One of the important features of our approach is that we do not have professional staff. The staff positions for planning are seen as development jobs for our brightest and most capable line people. These people serve as staff planners for three or so years and then return to the line.

We have a general policy among our staff to tell operating divisional managers beforehand anything that is going to be said to senior corporate officers which might be construed as critical. We feel that it is very important not to spring surprises on the operating managers.

There is no doubt that we are plan driven in our management process. Nonetheless, we do not get carried away with the formal numbers as seems to be the case for a company like ITT. One reason for this difference is that we have access to each other reasonably easily. So far, we have been able to avoid doing dumb things to make the numbers come out.

Issues identification. Getting operating managers to take planning seriously was one of Ripley's central concerns in his efforts to develop useful planning for Zeta. A second major concern for Ripley was to have management planning with respect to the right issues. Over the years, a number of activities were instituted to achieve this second aim.

Each January, Ripley would launch the planning cycle with a memorandum to operating divisional managers in which he laid out the major issues to be addressed. Some seven or eight pages in length, this memorandum served as the basic reference for evaluating the quality of divisional plans.

Events leading to this memorandum stretched over a period of several months. Some time in November, a senior staff executive with responsibility for strategic planning activities began meeting with senior-level executives on an individual basis to get their ideas about issues that should be addressed in the coming round of planning. He referred to this process as "polling the congregation." Based on these interviews, he would prepare a working paper and collect other relevant documentation to be used at a management meeting held to discuss these issues. The senior management group of Zeta, comprising some eight to ten individuals, would meet for three days to discuss these issues of future importance to the company. In these discussions, they would try to arrive at some agreement as to what goals should be set with respect to key problems and opportunities.

One of the most noticeable of management's efforts to identify issues of importance to the company was the creation of a Government Affairs Department. Ripley had long been of the opinion that management was failing to keep closely enough in touch with developments in the federal and state governments which could affect Zeta's businesses.

In mid-1976 a new Government Relations Department was created. Its charge was to help management to become aware of major governmental issues and to help it respond effectively to such developments. One of the early outputs from the Government Relations Department was a lengthy memorandum identifying and describing ten major government relations issues for management's consideration. To assist managers in their efforts to deal with these issues in their operating and strategic plans, special staff assistants worked with them in a manner similar to that employed for planning.

A weekly Monday-morning senior executive meeting also contributed to management's efforts to identify issues for attention. The meeting was held in a special room equipped with audiovisual devices for presentations.

The practices at Zeta can be related to the various barriers described earlier. For example, the explicit definition of planning issues that have to be addressed and the extensive involvement of a strong corporate staff planner both serve to motivate middle-level general managers to spend time and energy on strategic considerations. These inputs can also strengthen the middle managers' abilities to do good planning.

The corporate staff planner also can reduce the risks that inhibit innovation, not only by serving as a sounding board for the middle manager but also by being able to act as a "friend in court" in arguing the merits of the strategic plan with senior managers. In his or her liaison role, the corporate staff planner can also contribute to senior managers' confidence in the new ideas by having served as a corporate agent in the process.

The extensive efforts in Zeta to seek out new issues of importance to the company also provides senior management with some reassurance that the planning being done is what is most relevant to the company's needs.

Dealing with Personal Risks

Many of the practices that facilitated insight and commitment to new strategic ideas had to do with lowering the personal risks for the people involved. The following discussion makes special reference to two risks: the risk for the middle manager of an embarrassing rejection of a proposed strategic move and the risk for the senior manager in evaluating proposed strategic moves.

One way for the middle manager to reduce the risk of having his or her proposal cut to pieces by or before his or her superiors was being able to test those ideas early in their formation with senior managers. When this was possible, a manager could "try out a new idea for size." A manager could then drop it, modify it, or push it, depending on the nature of the response received.

Open and informal communication between middle and senior levels of management provided the best way to accomplish this. In one company, where such open communication was limited, the use of task teams involving senior-and middle-level managers to deal with specific strategies issues provided the mechanism for the needed informal exhanges.

These early and repeated exchanges also served to give senior managers confidence in a new idea. By being exposed to a new idea as it grows over time, the senior executive has an opportunity to shape it and to become comfortable with it. As was true for Professor Henry Higgins of *My Fair Lady* fame, the senior manager has to become "accustomed to her face."

Many of the planning concepts that have been gaining popularity in recent years have been particularly helpful to corporate management for testing strategic ideas. For example, the portfolio planning approach, in its several variations, provides senior management with a powerful tool with which to evaluate a business strategy in the context of total corporate cash flows.

The PIMS program is designed to provide management with an indication of the likely effects of various strategic changes. In its 1978 annual report, the Norton Company devoted a full page to describing this system. In the following excerpt, the CEO explained how it helped him to gain confidence in assessing business strategies:

> Imagine for a moment this situation: As a manager, you are faced with the question whether or not to invest in a new product just developed by your research people. You know about the costs involved, the market, the competition, etc. You can guess at how your investment might pay out, but it would be only a

guess. Now imagine that you are given an opportunity to learn what actually happened to hundreds of other companies that made similar decisions under similar conditions during the past ten years. There is no guarantee that your experience will parallel that of others—but you now have a much clearer picture of the odds. Your risks are reduced, and your decision can be made with far more confidence.

Even simple concepts can provide a helpful structure for analysis. The management of a large company manufacturing industrial products employs a "test for winning strategies." The idea is that a strategic proposal must show a clear competitive advantage with respect to at least one of the following considerations: input factors (raw material and labor), process, product, selling and distribution, service, or special. "Trying harder" was ruled out explicitly as a basis for a winning strategy. With this simple checklist, management was able to shift some attention from what was going to be done to why it would succeed. In practice, this outward orientation helped to spawn new strategic ideas.

Aids to Thinking About Strategy

"Daily routine drives out planning."[5] Strategic thinking is certainly one of the most vulnerable aspects of planning in this regard. It needs constant nurturing and protection. Otherwise, it will die or be stillborn.

Emphasize the strategic concept. One way in which to focus attention on the strategic concept is to single it out from the rest of long-range planning for special consideration. The notion of "winning strategies" described earlier did this to some extent.

In the Monsanto Company, this singling out of the strategic ideas is carried further. The basic strategic concept for each business is stated and evaluated separately from the long-range plans for that business. In contrast to the yearly updating of the long-range plans, the "business direction paper" that contains the basic business strategy is "evergreen." It is reviewed whenever a significant change is to be made to the strategy. The separate existence of the strategy statement helps to keep it from being submerged in the welter of planning considerations.

Separate reviews. Another way to increase attention to the strategic concepts is to schedule enough time for a thoughtful interchange between middle and senior managers in the review process. The all-too-common practice of scheduling an annual marathon of planning reviews tends to be self-defeating. Almost always, there is too much ground to cover in the time available. There is little opportunity to explore the strategic concepts in depth.

To get thoughtful and thorough reviews in the Norton Company, business strategy review sessions were spread throughout the year so that only one business would be reviewed at a time. In this way, senior managers had time to become deeply engrossed with a particular strategic proposal. If more time was needed for discussion, there was no "next planning session" to rush the closure.

A newcomer to Norton's top management ranks gave his impression of this practice:

> I really like the idea of holding strategic review meetings for different businesses at different times during the year. By looking at one business at a time, we get a chance to focus our thoughts and to concentrate on the distinctive aspects of that business. Oddly, the opportunity to go into depth in a given business has also helped us to gain new insights for some of our other businesses.

Coaching. The introduction of good planning concepts, the identification of planning issues, and better information about relevant developments in the competitive world were important underpinnings for efforts to improve the quality of strategy making in the companies studied. But for most managers the improved tools were not enough. They needed help in using them.

The planning instructions and planning manuals on which many companies rely for instruction were typically grossly inadequate to the need. In at least one respect, strategic thinking might be likened to tennis. While some people might be able to learn good tennis from a book, most need coaching, and lots of it. This need for coaching seemed to hold true for strategic thinking as well for all levels of management.

CONCLUSION

Managing an organization so as to improve the quality of strategic decision making is a very different task from managing an organization to implement a strategy. The central issue changes from one of "how to organize resources so as to achieve a strategic concept" to one of "how to get people to discover new ideas and to act on them." Because the requirements for these two tasks differ, and possibly conflict, the overall job of the senior general manager is to find a way to accomplish both.

Management has to be realistic as to how far it can and should go in activating strategic thinking. Exhibit 8-2 gives some idea of what the managements in the Alpha and Zeta companies were attempting to accomplish, each in its own way.

How far to push the curve to the right in Exhibit 8-2 has to be considered. The CEO of one of the largest insurance companies put the dilemma in this way:

> There is a need for a delicate balancing act between getting people to look ahead and at the same time making sure that someone is minding the store.

Deciding on the right balance is complicated by the fact that some innovative moves can be more disruptive and distracting than they are constructive. Management would naturally like to suppress the former and support the latter. The problem of course is that managers often have difficulty in knowing which is which. Under those circumstances, the easiest way to reduce troublesome new ideas is to reduce all new ideas.

EXHIBIT 8-2
Distribution of Innovative Managers

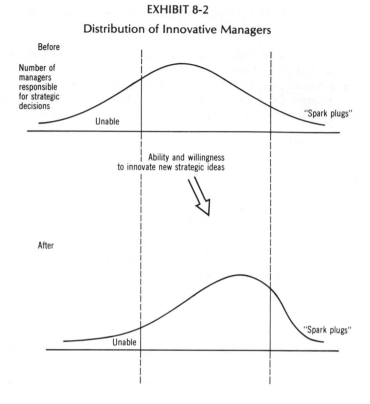

That management should act to improve the quality of strategic thinking is clearly desirable, and for most companies sorely needed. This paper has tried to show the complexities of the problem managers face in this regard. There are no hard-and-fast rules on how to achieve such improvements. As Ogden Nash so eloquently noted in one of his poems:

> In the land of mules;
> There are no rules.

The realm of strategic thinking lies in the land of mules.

NOTES

[1]In the interviews, I often used the terms strategic thinking and strategy making rather than strategic planning so as to broaden consideration beyond formal planning efforts. My interest is to examine the whole process leading to changes in strategic commitments. Such commitments usually involve the long-term deployment of company resources (people, money, assets, and relationships). For me, strategic thinking is concerned with the question of what businesses to be in, involving decisions with respect to entry, exit, and the relative emphasis among several businesses. Strategic thinking is also concerned with how best to run an ongoing business where decisions involve consideration of major new approaches to competing or moves to defend against new threats such as might be imposed by government regulations.

[2]To give an example, a group of experienced business managers had spent months trying hard to come up with a strategy to reverse the serious decline of a key product. The resulting plan, couched in the technical language and format of a perfectly good planning system, was little more than old wine with new labels. It contained little in the way of new or imaginative ideas, despite the considerable effort made. A consultant subsequently suggested an entirely different way of viewing the business using the same information. The managers involved readily saw the advantages of the new concept over the old and adopted it. One of them lamented, "There the solution was, right before our very eyes, and we never could see it."

[3]Vermont Royster, "Thinking Things Over: Inertia and Innovation," *The Wall Street Journal,* September 12, 1979, p. 20.

[4]Many of the practices described were newly introduced and consequently still had to prove their merit.

[5]James March and Herbert Simon, *Organizations* (New York: Wiley, 1958), p. 185. The authors go on to explain this point: "When an individual is faced both with highly programmed and highly unprogrammed tasks, the former tend to take precedence over the latter."

9

Introducing a Formal Strategic Planning System in a Business Firm

INTRODUCTION

This chapter* is designed to describe the development and implementation of a formal strategic planning system in a European company, to be designated as the W Company, which is wholly owned by a Japanese corporation.

First, a brief conceptual framework for strategic planning is presented. That framework summarizes the overall approach that we use to guide the strategic planning process at W. Then a short, historical background of the W Company is presented to help in understanding its evolution and stage of development at the time we introduced the planning system. Next the competitive environment in which W operates is described and broad statements of the objectives and strategies for its major businesses are provided. This is followed by a discussion of the segmentation of W's businesses, leading to the definition of its strategic business units. Then the organizational changes that have to be made to provide a meaningful strategic focus to W's actions are identified and the resulting strategic business cycle is analyzed. Finally, a brief conclusion is given.

---

*This chapter is prepared by Arnoldo C. Hax, Alfred P. Sloan School of Management, Massachusetts Institute of Technology, and Gerhard Schulmeyer, Vice President and General Manager, Europe, Motorola, Inc. Automotive Products Division.

CONCEPTUAL FRAMEWORK

Basic Cycle of Strategic Planning

Many firms have recognized the need to carry out a formal strategic planning process. Normally, a number of activities are scheduled over a full calendar year, starting with the release of general guidelines from corporate headquarters and culminating in a well-defined budget for the following period. The completion of one cycle of strategic planning is followed by the starting of a new one. In this way, strategic decisions may be viewed as a final product of a process that may span many years rather than as an unexpected and isolated change in direction.

A formal strategic planning system is focused on the one-year cycle. In its initial stages, it is important to recognize the structural components that define the setting in which the planning process should be conducted, as they condition the overall strategic actions of the corporation. For this reason, we will refer to these components as the *structural conditioners* of a strategic planning cycle. There are three such conditioners: the *internal structure* of the firm, the *environmental structure* that affects the totality of the firm, and the composition of the *strategic business units*, which identify the businesses in which the firm is engaged.

A formal planning system addresses, first, the characteristics of each one of the three structural conditioners and, then, the basic stages of the strategic planning cycle: *objective setting, strategic programming,* and *budgeting.* These elements are portrayed in Exhibit 9-1.

EXHIBIT 9-1

The Fundamental Elements in Formal Strategic Planning

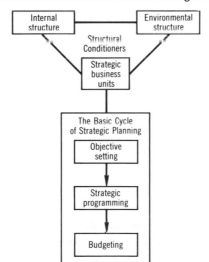

Identification of Strategic Business Units

The primary focus of the strategic planning process is directed to a well-defined unit of the organization, which is given the name of strategic business unit (SBU), strategic center, or business segment. A strategic business unit, is "composed of a product or products lines with identifiable independence from other products or products lines in terms of competition, prices, substitutability of products, style and quality, and impact of product withdrawal."[1]

The role of the SBU as the subject of attention in the strategic planning cycle may be appreciated when contrasted to attempts to provide strategic objectives for the overall firm. Normally, objectives that are stated at the corporate level do not carry any operational meaning; for example, "we want to grow at 7 percent per year" or "we have to achieve a 12 percent ROI after taxes." Expressions such as these, which are commonly offered as corporate objectives, are simple motherhood statements with very little, if any, practical value. However, by lowering the attention to the SBU level, one can begin to perform a rich analysis of the existing strengths and weaknesses of each unit as well as opportunities and threats in the environment. The condensation of all this analysis in the formulation of a strategic program will carry a wealth of managerial information.

The identification of an SBU demands an exhaustive analysis of the segmentation of the overall businesses of a firm. Several criteria can be used to characterize a business unit.[2] Some firms define an SBU as a reasonable autonomous profit center with its own general manager. This normally calls for a self-standing unit in terms of manufacturing, sales, research and development, and other functional departments. Some other firms conceive of an SBU as having a clear market focus and identifiable strategy and an identifiable set of competitors. In either case, the important concept to bear in mind is that the business strategy is delegated to the SBU level.

The crucial issue to be addressed in defining an SBU is finding the largest monolithic segment that allows for a proper assessment of internal strengths and environmental opportunities and that can be treated as a separate entity in terms of the resource allocation process. Of foremost importance is the ability for strategic business managers to operate an SBU with a high level of independence with respect to other business units in the firm, to respond in an effective way to competitive pressures.

A later section of this chapter contains a detailed discussion on the segmentation of the W Company's business leading toward the identification of its SBUs.

Basic Strategic Planning Cycle

The internal structure, the environmental structure, and the definition of SBUs constitute the fundamental premises that have to be recognized when initiating the strategic planning process. Our attention now will be focused on the generic tasks to be undertaken for the development of formal strategic planning.

Process description of the strategic planning cycle. A first conceptualization of this process may be established by distinguishing two hierarchical levels in business firms: the corporate, or central, level and the business, or SBU, level.

The primary roles assumed by the corporate level are, first, to provide initial expectations, guidelines, and directives and, second, to consolidate and sanction the proposals being presented from the business level. At the SBU level, the initial guidelines provided by the corporation are translated first into broadly defined strategic options (action programs). In turn, these are reviewed by corporate officers to ensure their consistency with corporate resources and goals. After this initial stage, more specific and detailed strategic programs emerge at the SBU level that must go to a second round of corporate consolidation. The process finally terminates with the preparation of detailed budgets.

Exhibit 9-2 illustrates the interaction existing between corporate and SBU levels in the realization of the strategic planning process along the three major stages of objectives setting, strategic programming, and budgeting.

Although the previous discussion merely recognizes two hierarchical levels in the planning process, some corporations tend to insert one or more intermediate levels to coordinate the activities of related business units. Later we address the definition of the strategic planning cycle for the W Company, which involves four hierarchical levels.

Moreover, the process captured in Exhibit 9-2 does not detail the role played by hierarchical levels below the SBU. These levels typically functional units, contribute the detailed disciplinary knowledge required to flesh out the strategic programs and budgeting stages. By collapsing the role played by the SBU manager and the functional departments into one single hierarchical stage in our discussion, we are stressing the need to reconcile two main issues in the strategic planning process: the corporate portfolio and the development of each individual business of the portfolio.

Another notion emerging from Exhibit 9-2 is the recognition that strategic planning is neither a top–down nor a bottom–up process. Rather, it involves a complex iterative interaction among the hierarchical levels in the firm. The full extent of this interaction is not captured in that figure, which presents only the major tasks that the formal planning process is supposed to complete along one realization of a planning cycle.[3]

Major tasks in the strategic planning cycle. The major tasks to be undertaken when implementing a full cycle of the planning process are presented in Exhibit 9-3. The sequence of these tasks closely follows the outline in Exhibit 9-2 showing the participation of different hierarchical levels along the stages of the planning process. (The numbers in both figures are consistent.)[4]

A BRIEF BACKGROUND OF THE W COMPANY

The W Company was founded in 1923 in Stuttgart, West Germany, as a family-owned company. At the beginning, the company concentrated on developing and manufacturing radios. The expansion of the company's product line was linked

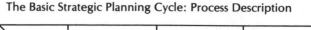

EXHIBIT 9-2

The Basic Strategic Planning Cycle: Process Description

Stages / Hierarchical Level	Objective Setting	Strategic Programming	Budgeting
Corporate Level (portfolio)	① ③	⑤	⑦
SBU Level (business)	②	④	⑥

Major Tasks:
① Formulation of general guidelines
② Formulation of board strategic action programs
③ Consolidation of action programs
④ Generation, evaluation, and selection of strategic programs
⑤ Consolidation of strategic programs
⑥ Development of tactical programs and budgets
⑦ Consolidation of budgets

closely with the technological developments of the electronic industry in Germany. W never had its own basic research unit.

From the start of World War II until the 1950s, company sales were well below 10 million DM, an extremely small business even at that time in the industry. With the introduction of TV broadcasting in Germany in 1955, W entered that market and total sales escalated to 20 million DM by the early 1960s.

A major change in the company's strategy took place with the entry of the grandson of the founder into a top management position. W changed its policy from that of a trend follower with low profitability and low profile to that of a high-quality brand position with a very contemporary design. The distribution policy changed from a very broad coverage to a highly selective dealer network, while at the same time building an export market. Technologically, it remained dependent on the large component manufacturers, as the company did not have resources to fund its own basic research.

This strategy of high quality, excellent design, and selective distribution resulted in a rapid increase in sales to 100 million DM by 1971. To absorb the sales growth, considerable investment was made in 1973 to expand production capacity.

EXHIBIT 9-3

The Basic Strategic Planning Cycle: Major Tasks

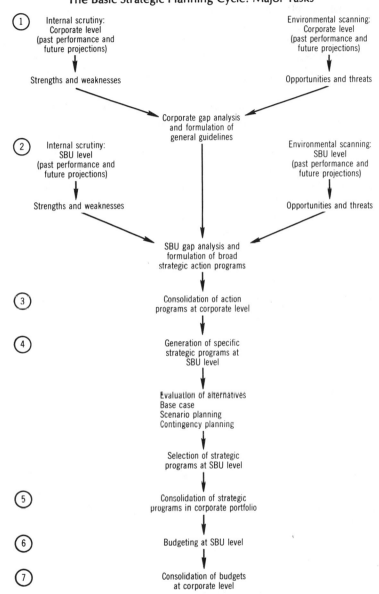

① Internal scrutiny: Corporate level (past performance and future projections)

Environmental scanning: Corporate level (past performance and future projections)

Strengths and weaknesses

Opportunities and threats

Corporate gap analysis and formulation of general guidelines

② Internal scrutiny: SBU level (past performance and future projections)

Environmental scanning: SBU level (past performance and future projections)

Strengths and weaknesses

Opportunities and threats

SBU gap analysis and formulation of broad strategic action programs

③ Consolidation of action programs at corporate level

④ Generation of specific strategic programs at SBU level

Evaluation of alternatives
Base case
Scenario planning
Contingency planning

Selection of strategic programs at SBU level

⑤ Consolidation of strategic programs in corporate portfolio

⑥ Budgeting at SBU level

⑦ Consolidation of budgets at corporate level

Unfortunately, the economic recession in 1974 strongly affected the electronic market and sales did not grow beyond the 140 million DM level, which was insufficient to provide adequate returns to the new capacity investments. This situation, compounded by an erosion of quality standards resulting from the expansion of color TV businesses and the product variety in the audio businesses, forced the family to sell the company.

W was acquired by a Japanese corporation, which sought an opportunity to establish a manufacturing base in Europe. The strategy behind this acquisition was to provide research and development and production support to the W product brand, which was positioned at a market different from that of the existing Japanese brand.

The former owner of W was kept in place as general manager and was given added resources to strengthen the development of the W brand. However, he did not adjust himself to the new conditions imposed by the large multinational Japanese corporation and resigned in 1976. By then the company had lost its direction and had a significantly weakened brand position.

A professional manager was hired to assume the responsibilities of restructuring the W Company. His charter included the building of all the managerial talent required to regain the W brand's identity, which was very much in danger. The task of hiring the appropriate managers and structuring their responsibilities took about a year to be consolidated. After this was accomplished, a commitment to introduce a formal strategic planning process in the company was made.

To facilitate that effort, three professors from M.I.T.'s Sloan School of Management were invited to conduct a one week workshop with all the top managers of W. The primary objective of the workshop was to provide an educational experience leading to action in the company. To satisfy this objective, two basic goals had to be accomplished. First, the fundamental concepts, techniques, and processes related to planning and control were instructed. Second, a complete cycle for the planning and control process was conducted with the active participation of the executives represented in the workshop. This led to a recognition of the major activities that had to be undertaken in the development of a formal planning and control system at W.

A point worth stressing is the role played by six young professionals who were hired directly from universities to provide staff support to the W managers in this effort. These trainees were assigned to gather all the necessary data prior to the seminar, which they attended. After the seminar, they were in charge of providing day-to-day support to the management team in all the aspects pertaining to the design and implementation of the formal planning system.

W. COMPANY'S OBJECTIVES

Audio and Video Businesses

Prior to providing a statement of the W Company's objectives, it is important to understand the overall nature of the audio and video businesses. The market of consumer electronics can be divided into five major product categories:

1. color TV
2. home video

3. hi-fi
4. mono radio, including portable radios and clock radios
5. accessories

In the world market there are three regions of supply and three main regions of consumption:

1. Japan and Southeast Asia
2. North America
3. Europe

Exhibit 9-4 summarizes the position of the three major suppliers in the world market by product category.

EXHIBIT 9-4

Significance of Industry Groups in the Main Markets

Industry Markets Product Category/ Stage in Life Cycle	American Industry			Japanese Industry			European Industry		
	USA	Jap	Eur	USA	Jap	Eur	USA	Jap	Eur
Color TV/mature	+	—	—	°	++	°°	—	—	++
Home video/Embryonic	—	—	—	++	++	++	—	—	°°
Hi-fi/mature	°	°°	°	++	++	++	°°	—	°
Mono-radio/mature	°°	°°	°°	++	++	+	—	—	°°
Accessories/growing	+	°°	°	+	++	°	°°	—	+

++ Leading position
 + Strong position
 ° Average position
°° Weak position
— No position

It is important to recognize the position of each of the product categories in each of their respective life cycles. Color TV, hi-fi, and mono radio are in a mature stage; accessories, especially tapes, are in a rapidly growing stage; home video is in an embryonic phase.

Regarding the position of the W Company in those markets, W only produces color TVs and hi-fis, each product category accounting for roughly the same sales volume. However, the Japanese mother company has complete product coverage.

The W Company's total color TV line is based on one screen size (26″) and one chassis. Model differentiation is mainly done through design and feature changes. The 26″ screen size represents 78 percent of the total European continental color TV market, which explains W's concentration on that size screen. In research and development and manufacturing, there are close ties to the mother company, but, in marketing and sales, both brands compete with each other in the

European market. All color TV models are final assembled in the W Company's own facilities, because of technological differences and certain patent and import restrictions. W has considered an extension of the product range, including entry into the home video business (adopting different screen sizes) and adding a monitor business.

The product range of the W Company in hi-fi is much wider and spans from single-end components to low-end compacts. Audio products range from those that are completely designed and manufactured by W to those that are totally procured from the mother company. The support being given from Japan is essential to W, as the audio business is characterized by large product variety and short product life cycles. Also, W's and the mother company's brands compete in the audio market.

Primary Objectives of the W Company

The W Company has three primary objectives:

1. To have an active presence in both the audio and video businesses. This is desirable because of great synergism between those two businesses. From a production standpoint, efficiencies are obtained from joint parts procurement, incoming inspection, automatic parts insertion, and so on. From a market and sales standpoint, synergism is obtained through the sharing of distribution channels, sales forces, and consumer groups.
2. To keep a sound business base in Germany. This results from long-term strategic interests of the mother company and from existing patent and import constraints that prevent certain Japanese products from penetrating in some European markets. For example, Japanese manufacturers cannot export color TV sets of 26" or 22" to Europe, and they face import restrictions for tuners in France and Italy.
3. To improve its current profitability. In color TVs, this implies achieving at least a minimum sales volume to sustain a reasonable profitability with its one-chassis product. In audio, it is required to offer a broad product line that keeps up with fast-changing trends, necessary for recognition as a hi-fi manufacturer.

W's Distinct Positioning

W operates in a competitive environment, which in the color TV business is dominated by large European manufacturers and in the hi-fi business is dominated by large Japanese manufacturers. What can a middle-sized company such as W do? Because it is impossible for such a company to compete across the board with the leading corporations, it is mandatory to assume a distinct positioning in those businesses. This is what is referred to commonly as "finding a niche."

There are three primary elements of W's business position: attractive design, high quality, and a total user's concept. A brand-image study conducted by W showed that the company had a very strong image for its unique and attractive design, which was one of the strongest historical features of W's line. However, the study also indicated a fairly poor ranking on technical quality. In color TVs, quality is mainly attributed to good picture image and high reliability. In the hi-fi business, quality encompasses a much wider range of issues linked to advanced technology, features, outside finishing, and performance.

Maintaining its tradition for good design is an obvious strategy on which W can build, because there is a broad discriminating market willing to pay a premium price for a product with superior aesthetic design. Moreover, by channeling its efforts in this direction, W will be confronted by only three potential competitors, only one of which operates in both the color TV and hi-fi businesses.

With the additional available resources generated by the Japanese mother company, it makes sense to adopt a second dimension of strategic positioning concerning a high-quality image.

The third dimension for the distinct company position, as an umbrella for all products, is the so-called user's concept. In an industry that is plagued by an extraordinary segmentation of individual products, W has the philosophy of the concept of the total package, targeted to individual customer groups. Rather than selling speakers, tuners, amplifiers, cassette recorders, and so on as independent products, W has developed total systems for well-defined market groups. For example, there are W system components oriented primarily toward the youth market—low in price, fashionable, and aggressive in design. There are low-priced concepts for more conservative target groups at a lower end of the income level who are seeking a complete one-piece solution. There are middle-price components with clean and functional designs for those with high aesthetic standards looking for long-lasting goods. The total systems produced and marketed by W cover a wide range of values from U.S. $600 to U.S. $8,000.

Design and Quality of all different product families are made under the same standards; however, they reflect the specific needs for the different target groups. The advertising and merchandising is done along the different system positionings, maintaining some common guidelines to keep a distinctive company identity.

Description of W's broad strategies

Having explained the principal objectives of the W Company, we now turn our attention to the broad strategies that would allow W to attain its major objectives. The primary issues to be addressed are what markets to serve, what products to use in those markets, what new products to develop, and what production technologies to use.

Markets. With regard to the geographical locations to be covered, W will concentrate on Europe as the main target area. In Germany, France, and Italy, W is committed to having its own sales force and logistics capabilities. In other European countries, W will be represented by qualified agencies. Some flexibility has to be maintained to seize opportunities available within Europe as they emerge. From a pricing standpoint, W will concentrate on the middle and high ends in color TV and hi-fi. In the remaining product categories, there is an intent to penetrate in the home video market as soon as possible. In the accessories business, it should be studied whether the available resources from the mother company can be utilized by the W brand.

Color TV product line. W should concentrate on the one-chassis color TV line to achieve high productivity resulting in low costs. During the first stage, production should be concentrated in one of W's plants, to permit high manufacturing volumes. All color TV products should meet the highest standards in picture quality, design, and reliability. The high-end products should also present the state of the art in tone quality and features for convenience, including tuning and remote control. W should provide both wood and plastic cabinets to satisfy specific consumer needs. The total user concept applied in the audio business should be included in the development of the home video business. It is expected that W will enter the small-screen-size color TV market on an original equipment manufacturing basis by 1980, maintaining the same criteria for design, quality, and user concept.

Audio product line. The total user concept should be the anchor of W's strategies in this business. All income levels should be covered, but special emphasis should be given to the youth segment. The high-priced products should integrate all state-of-the-art features and technologies; the low-priced products should concentrate on trend features and trend specifications. All products should have a high standard in design, quality, finishing, and reliability. By 1980, middle- and high-priced products should be developed and manufactured by W. Middle- to low-priced products, which can only be manufactured competitively in large quantity, should be based on the mother company's concepts and manufactured in low-cost countries. All W products should be distinctly different from the mother company's products and should satisfy the German standard for hi-fi products.

New products. Home video and accessories are the new product categories to be introduced in 1979 and 1980. They should be distributed through the existing channels and be consistent with W's strategic position. Accessories, especially video and audio tapes, microphones, headphones, and pickup systems, should constitute a new business entity ready to develop other businesses.

Production. The two existing W plants should be integrated into the overall international production capabilities of the mother company. One plant, concentrating on the production of color TV, is expected to double its output over the next two years. This will require a change in the plant layout and a significant capital investment, whose payback period should not exceed three years. The second plant should concentrate on manufacturing high-priced audio products and speakers for the W brand as well as speakers and tuners for the mother company.

SEGMENTATION OF THE W COMPANY'S BUSINESSES

A fundamental step in the development of the planning system is the recognition of the various business segments in which the company is engaged. We found it useful to consider two different dimensions in which to perform this segmentation for W. The first is the traditional product–market structure. The second looks at the customer needs that are satisfied by the various W products.

Segmentation Based on Product and Market Structure

To characterize W's business segmentation based on this dimension, we identified three hierarchical levels of increasing detail for each one of the three major industries in which W operates: audio, video, and accessories.

Level 1	Level 2	Level 3
Audio	Product group	Individual product line
Video	Product group	Individual product line
Accessories (in planning stage)	Product group	Individual product line

First level of segmentation: Industry characteristics. The broadest classification of W's businesses is in accordance with their respective industrial characteristics: audio, video, and accessories (in the planning stage). These three different industries have distinct characteristics, not only from a technological point of view but also from their saturation levels, consumption needs, life-cycle considerations, competitive structure, and so on.

The video industry, composed primarily of color TV and home video, has the following general characteristics:

1. long model life cycle (three years)
2. few competitors (ten to fifteen)
3. relatively stable market shares
4. different regional standards
5. dominance of local industry
6. high saturation and mature markets
7. uniform price structure
8. small product differentiation

The primary characteristics of the audio industry are

1. short model life cycle (below one year)
2. many competitors (more than a hundred for most categories)
3. fluctuating market shares
4. international standards
5. dominance of Japanese industry
6. still-growing markets but starting to mature
7. high product variety with fashion trends
8. high differentiation performance and price

Second and third levels of segmentation for audio industry. A second level of segmentation recognizes the different product groups in a given industry. For the W Company, the audio product groups are divided into three major categories:

1. middle- and high-priced product lines developed and manufactured by the W Company
2. middle- and low-priced product lines based on product concepts of the mother company and manufactured in low-cost areas
3. speaker product lines

Each of these product groups can be segmented further into individual product systems based on distinct user concepts. This differentiation is captured at the third level of segmentation, which defines the individual strategic business units for the audio industry.

Second and third level of segmentation for the video industry. A similar criteria for the second and third level of segmentation can be applied to the video industry.

The second level represents four major product groups:

1. the color TV, one-chassis product line, developed in partnership with the mother company and manufactured with W Company's own resources
2. original equipment manufacturing product lines, which constitutes a new business area for W
3. home video product line, a category just being developed, with market characteristics similar to those for color TV
4. video monitor product lines for semiprofessional and professional use

Each of these product groups are differentiated further at the third level of segmentation, based not only on different user concepts but also on the specific markets they serve. This last differentiation emerges from the different specifications of the broadcasting specifications of the various European countries. As was the case in the audio industry, the third level defines the different SBUs for the video industry.

Accessories. This business entity is still in the planning stage and a detailed business segmentation has as yet to be developed.

The segmentation just proposed is extremely helpful in identifying specific objectives for the development of each individual business of the W Company in accordance with the opportunities that each business provides. The SBUs identified as a result of this segmentation process constitute the primary focus for strategic planning and for the allocation of the overall resources of the company to each SBU.

Segmentation Based on a Discretionary Spending Analysis

An entirely different view of W's businesses starts with the recognition that W is competing for funds that fall into the broad category of discretionary spending. We therefore looked at how the various product lines of W contribute to satisfying consumer needs associated with discretionary spending. The areas of such spending were classified as follows:

1. traveling
2. entertaining
3. hobby
4. physical exercise
5. fashion
6. education
7. convenience
8. art
9. status symbol
10. home improvement

Because W products belong directly to the entertainment category, we dropped this dimension as a discriminator among the different product lines. Moreover, the art and physical exercise categories were also dropped as W products did not seem to contribute there.

For the purposes of this analysis, W products were classified in the following ten categories:

1. color TV line "object"
2. color TV line "integral"
3. color TV portables
4. home video recorders
5. system component line "JPS"
6. compact line "40/41"
7. component line "module"
8. component line "lab zero"
9. speaker line "direct"
10. compact line "concept"

A product line not considered in this approach is the color TV monitor line, as it has a very specific market outside the general consumer business.

Exhibit 9-5 depicts what specific consumer need, in addition to entertainment, is partially fulfilled by each product line. The classification of a color TV table set as a status symbol, a color TV portable as a convenience item, or a system component family as a fashion item leads to quite different segmentation from the one suggested before. Because this positioning concept is central to the W Company, we found it important to consider this dimension in the structuring of the formal planning process.

Strategic Resource Units

To ensure that the consumer needs dimension is brought into strategic planning thinking at W, seven "strategic resource units" (SRUs) were formed along the seven areas of discretionary spending identified in Exhibit 9-5. Each of

EXHIBIT 9-5

Contribution of W Product Lines to Consumer Needs for Discretionary Spending*

Product Lines \\ Consumer Needs	Color TV table "object"	Color TV table "integral"	Color TV portable	Home video recorder	"JPS" system components	Compact line "40/41"	"Module"	"Lab zero"	Speaker line "direct"	Compact line "concept"
Traveling			x							
Hobby				x	x	x	x		(X)	
Fashion			x		(X)		x			
Education	x	x		x						
Convenience	x	x	(X)	(X)		x				x
Status symbol	(X)			x	x		(X)	(X)		(X)
Home improvement	x	(X)		x		x				x

*The crosses indicate a certain contribution of the individual product line to consumer needs to each category. The circles indicate a significant and direct contribution. If there is no circle for a product line, the entertainment need is dominant.

these groups is composed of eight people, from different hierarchical levels and functional areas, interested in the given segments.

The SRUs work under the given guidelines of the general company's strategies. Their objective is to find out to what degree existing product lines can be improved in their positioning to fit better into certain consumer need categories and to identify potential consumer needs that are not yet covered properly.

Frequent discussions in these groups and biannual presentations to the W Company's operating committee should ensure that the structuring of the business in consumer concepts is maintained as a specific strength of the W Company.

THE ORGANIZATIONAL STRUCTURE

A Business Orientation in the Organizational Design

Prior to the introduction of strategic planning in the W Company, its organization was structured in a very conventional functional form, as presented in Exhibit 9-6. A change in this organizational structure was needed to facilitate the implementation of a strategic planning process, with a strong commitment toward the development of the various business segments of W. This change called

EXHIBIT 9-6

Original Organization of the W Company

for a formal recognition of audio, video, and, subsequently, accessories, as distinct entities of the total company's business.

A straightforward solution to facilitate the emphasis on the development of this business would have been to adopt a fully divisionalized structure having audio, video, and, subsequently, accessories as autonomous units with full and independent functional support. This solution, however, was unacceptable due to the small size of the W Company. A compromise between a fully functional and fully divisionalized structure had to be found.

The solution accepted is shown in Exhibit 9-7, which recognizes three different types of managerial functions:

1. service functions, which are finance, and personnel, and organizational
2. operational functions, which are production and sales, and
3. business functions, which are audio, video, and, subsequently, accessories.

There is a strong need to integrate these functional activities, which is accomplished by the strategic planning process, by committee work, and by various coordinating mechanisms.

The business function managers are the key individuals responsible for the coordination of their corresponding business strategies. The audio and video functions are differentiated further to reflect the second and third segmentation levels of each of these businesses, as described in the foregoing section.

The primary organizational responsibilities are as follows:

General manager. His major role is to contribute to the definition of broad objectives for the W Company; to set up the initial guidelines for the planning process; to provide consolidation, validation, and final sanctioning of resource allocation among business and functional areas; to approve the operational budget; and to monitor overall performance of the W Company.

W's operating committee. This is the key coordinating body of W. The committee is composed of the general manager and the managers of each function

EXHIBIT 9-7

Present Organization of the W Company

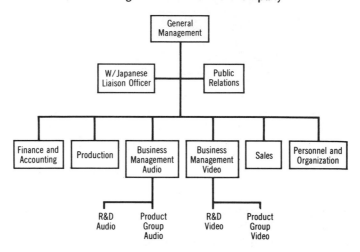

of W (service, operational, and business). The committee formulates specific company objectives, balances the portfolio of the total company businesses, oversees the preparation of the company budget, and develops and implements appropriate control instruments. This committee has the strongest influence in shaping W's strategic directions. Each of the six functional managers has one trainee in his or her personal staff. These trainees are essential to providing technical inputs to the planning process. Clearly, the managerial responsibilities rest on the functional managers, but the trainees are a great source of technical support in the detailed matters pertaining to the preparation and evaluation of the strategic programs and budgets. Moreover, because the trainees meet regularly among themselves, they provide an important second level of coordination in the planning process, which assures consistency and uniformity in the individual programs and budgets.

The business managers. The primary responsibility of the business managers is to coordinate all managerial activities pertaining to their individual businesses. They are responsible for setting strategic objectives and allocating resources among the various product groups within their businesses. In the budgeting process, they are ultimately responsible for obtaining well-balanced marketing and research and development funding to support their respective businesses.

Product Group managers and R&D managers. Each business manager has Product Group and R&D managers reporting to him or her. It is at this level in the organizational hierarchy at which the SBU responsibility is located. Product Group managers and R&D managers are trained to influence the direction of the individual product lines, within their product groups, in accordance with market needs and technological developments. This close linkage between R&D and Product management is necessary in an industry characterized by a very high speed of technological innovation. The focus of responsibility for a given SBU normally resides in the Product Group manager. However, in those product lines strongly affected by rapid technological changes, the responsibility might shift to the R&D manager. This requires both the Product Group manager and the R&D manager to work very closely and to assume joint responsibility for the development of the SBUs. Often the technical developments, more than real consumer needs, influence the cost structure of a product line, which is paramount to the success of an SBU.

The strategic resource units. As has been discussed, the SRUs are not integrated formally in the hierarchical structure. They are, rather, ad hoc groups of people who generate creative ideas involving and identifying the total potential of the company's employees in the strategic planning process.

The Formal Planning Cycle

As we have indicated, the implementation of strategic planning rests heavily on the definition of a formal planning cycle. The cycle identifies the inputs to be made by the key organizational levels in accordance with a well-prescribed sequence.

Exhibit 9-8 illustrates the planning cycle adopted by W. Due to the need for

EXHIBIT 9-8

W's Formal Planning Cycle

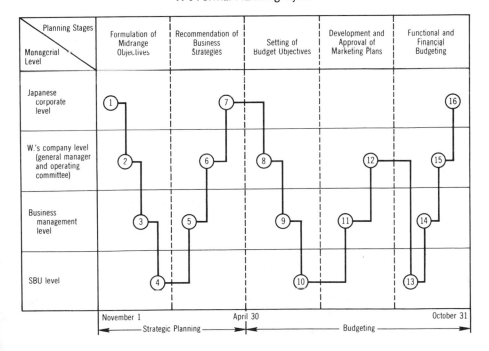

final approval by the Japanese corporation, and the strong coordinational requirements because of the rapid rate of change in the technological environment of W, it is not surprising to detect a high degree of complexity in the planning cycle. The numbers in Exhibit 9-8 characterize key decision points that can be summarized briefly as follows:

1. Formulation of planning guidelines for the W Company by the Japanese corporation.
2. General midrange objectives for the business and line functions at W's company level.
3. Specific midrange objectives for the product groups by the business managers.
4. Strategic programs recommended for specific product lines and consolidated into product group strategies by SBU managers.
5. Evaluation and approval of resource allocation for each SBU; consolidation of SBU plans into a general business strategy.
6. Review of business plans; consolidation of company strategies; allocation of company resources.
7. Corporate review; approval of company strategy; allocation of corporate resources.
8. Definition of company's budget objectives.
9. Development of marketing strategies for the audio and video businesses.
10. Development of marketing plans for product groups.
11. Consolidated marketing plans for the audio and video businesses.
12. Company review and approval.
13./14. Functional and financial budgeting, involving business, service, and operational functions.
15. W Company's review for all functions approval.
16. Company budget approval by Japanese corporation.

CONCLUSIONS

The major emphasis in this chapter has been the description, in fairly conceptual terms, of the efforts undertaken to develop and implement a strategic planning process at W. It is important to underscore that, from the outset, we had a framework to provide us with concrete guidelines in this difficult task. At several stages in our work, we found a great need to refer back to that framework to redirect our efforts. We wanted to share broad concepts and ideas with our readers, skipping the host of technical details that would have, perhaps, obscured our message and divulged confidential information. We had also decided not to elaborate on the variety of tools pertaining to portfolio analysis, business profiles, competitor analyses, financial analyses, and budget preparation. To do so would have expanded this chapter prohibitively. Moreover, such tools have received extensive coverage in other published sources.

The most important outcome of this task, which was initiated by an intense one-week seminar with the total involvement of the key managers of the W Company, was a strong attitudinal change on the part of those managers. When we started our project, we met a group of very competent managers with strong functional orientations. They were extremely knowledgeable in their respective fields of specialization (research and development, production, sales, marketing, finance), but they had little awareness of the broad and complex managerial tasks necessary to provide a strategic direction to the W business. After a full year of intense work, which included an important educational experience, a significant reorganization, and an active participation in an orderly planning process oriented mostly to motivate creative thinking, those managers had developed a mature understanding of the general management problems. This seemed to us to be the most significant payoff resulting from the implementation of a formal strategic planning system.

NOTES

[1] Arthur D. Little, *A System for Managing Diversity* (Cambridge: Mass.: Arthur D. Little, December 1974).

[2] D. F. Abell and J. Hammond, *Strategic Market Planning: Problems and Analytical Approaches* (Englewood Cliffs, N.J.: Prentice Hall, 1979).

[3] This interactive view of the planning process was first formalized by Richard F. Vancil and Peter Lorange, "Strategic Planning in Diversified Companies," *Harvard Business Review*, Vol. 53, No. 1 (January–February 1975), pp. 81–90. For a discussion of pitfalls commonly observed in the practice of planning, see Peter Lorange, "Implementation of Strategic Planning," Chap. 3 in Arnoldo C. Hax, ed. *Studies in Operations Management*, (Amsterdam: North-Holland, 1978).

[4] For a detailed description of each individual task, refer to Arnoldo C. Hax and Nicholas. S. Majluf, "Towards the Formalization of Strategic Planning—A Conceptual Framework," Randall Schultz, ed. in *Applications of Management Sciences*, Vol. 1 (Greenwich: JAI Press, 1981).

10

The Increased Relevance of Planning: A Case Study, 1950-1980

INTRODUCTION

Of all the cries heard from strategic planners, perhaps the best known is that for consideration of "the long-term" and a protest of "the short-term" focus they continually observe to be the emphasis of management systems, management concerns, and management decisions. On the other hand, most of the examples, case studies, and illustrations used by planners deal with the design of a strategic planning system to meet the firm's planning needs *at the moment*. Little attention is paid to the relationship among the changes in the firm (which can be wrought by changes from without *or* from within, including the successful implementation of strategy), the resulting changes in the need for strategic planning, and the changes in the strategic planning system that would be appropriate in maintaining its usefulness to the firm and its management.

The result of this kind of analysis is a tendency for "long-range planners" to view the long-range needs of the firm and ignore the long-range dynamics of their own function. This chapter*is an experiment in viewing the generation and evolution of strategic planning in a firm from the long-range perspective. The importance to the reader is intended to be the nature of the experiment rather than

---

*This chapter is prepared by Ben C. Ball, Jr., Alfred P. Sloan School of Management, Massachusetts Institute of Technology.

any intrinsic value of the case itself, although, of course, it is hoped that the particulars of the case are not without significance, applicability, and interest.

The experiment here is to begin developing a method for taking the broad historical perspective on the evolution and relevance of planning systems. This should enable strategic planners to move in the direction of taking a broad, future perspective on their own function rather than to "make it" through each day, one day at a time, immersed in pushing management toward looking more to the future and urging them not to get bogged down in day-to-day matters.

LONG-TERM TRENDS: AN EXAMPLE

This case study is something of a diary, the author having been associated with the planning activities and their changes in Gulf Oil Corporation from 1954–1978. The dates in the title are therefore intended to be imaginal rather than precise. This thrust toward imaginal authenticity rather than precision of data is endemic to the chapter, for what we seek here is a picture of the various concurrent trends and how they interact with the strategic planning process. We will examine not events but, rather, long-term trends in the natures of the environment, of the business of the management, and of planning as a part of the planning system. In this, our approach is truly an experiment, and its context must therefore be appreciated for its objectives to be appropriated.

Gulf, of course, is a large, mature, technically oriented, publicly held firm in a mature business that is coming into increased public view and is becoming increasingly regulated. This same description fits a significant number of the firms in the "Fortune 500," including automobiles, steel, chemicals, food, computers, and air transportation. The implication is that an examination of Gulf, as a case study, could have significant importance to a high proportion of business, especially if the percentage is taken on the basis of gross revenues. That is, most of the revenue of the Fortune 500 is accounted for by businesses fitting the description just given. Therefore, it is not unreasonable to expect that the case study undertaken here has very broad applicability.

POPULAR PLANNING

My colleague, Don Collier, in Chapter 12 of this book, quite effectively throws down the gauntlet to these kinds of firms and demonstrates in an exciting way in which they in fact can, consciously and deliberately, reap the benefits to be derived from exercising the discipline of strategic planning. However, Borg-Warner's experience is the challenge for the very reason that it is the *exception*. We will present here what amounts to the other side of the coin; that is, "useful" planning happens, and must in fact happen, to some significant degree in all such firms, even with little or no conscious effort and with even less acknowledgment or recognition. The argument that this leads to is the following: Because "planning" is *inevitable,* a conscious effort to (1) systemize the effort and (2) manage its evolution is preferable to an amorphous and unmanaged natural evolution.

Planning Defined

Key to this argument is an arbitrary but highly pragmatic (although not satisfying academically or theoretically) definition of "planning." We mean here by "planning" the de facto procedure, formal or informal, by which the *direction* of the firm is managed, consciously or unconsciously. It is real rather than "good," used rather than "imaginative." The definition applied here attempts to eliminate the value judgment pertaining to the quality of the planning and focuses only on its utility. It deals not with the "ought" but, rather, with the "is." This definition asks only with old-fashioned simplicity, "What decision-making process is used by the principle decision maker" and does not require that the process be housed in some organizational unit? How does the CEO spend his or her time? The answer may well be more cultural than formal. It may be that this kind of definition can only be applied from the historical perspective. A corollary may well be that it can be applied better by someone outside the firm. At least, that is the perspective applied here as the foundation that "planning" is natural and even unavoidable. The only real choice is between conscious (managed) planning and unconscious (evolution by trial and error, i.e., natural selection) planning. It is from this view that we shall set out to track "planning."

Relevant Planning

In this tracking of "planning," it is the "relevance" we wish to consider—whether it increases or decreases. As used here, the dynamic of relevance has two dimensions: the criteria and the elements. The criteria fall into three categories.

Relevance Criteria

The first criterion of relevance is the replicability of decisions. That is, they are thought through and are not the result of inspiration, genius, or "seat of the pants" judgments. For us to consider planning relevant here, the decision-making process should be transferable and, therefore, not essentially dependent on the particular individuals involved. It must be able to be described and therefore changed.

The second criterion of relevance is the conscious consideration of the future implication of a decision. The decision, therefore, must be from other than habit and directed beyond the operational mode.

The third, and most important, criterion is a comfortable usage by the executives. This usage might even be internalized. But it is neither imposed upon them nor is it given only lip service. It is the one that is really used.

It can be seen from these criteria that planning need not always be relevant or that it can vary in relevance from time to time. For example, a classic bureaucracy would be judged to have planning of low relevance in that decisions emerge amorphously from middle management and flow downward for execution while they flow upward for de jure approval. Top management has no de facto ability to initiate or control, although it may occasionally (but not too often) exercise veto. In essence, no one is in charge. Decisions occur, but without meeting any of our three criteria. In the top–down, bottom–up taxonomy, this type of management might be called middle–up. At best, upper management acts as a sort of filter.

Another sort of management that would exemplify low relevance would be the one-man, near-mystical style of the kind attributed by the press to Howard Hughes. Although this may seem a caricature, it serves to illustrate the kind of management exercised by many an executive who depends for input for his or her decisions only upon his or her own experience and the advice of his or her personal guru, meditative council, or brain trust.

Of course, at the other end of the spectrum are the firms with highly articulated planning systems imbedded in future orientation and forming a right arm of the top executive. In these General Electric- and Texas Instruments-type firms, planning is certainly relevant by our criteria. However, to use them as examples of relevance for I might give the reader the idea that "professional planner's" agreement with the de facto strategy or his or her acceptance of the process by which it is selected has anything to do with what we mean here by "relevance." Here, "planning" could be a professional planner's nightmare, and no one in the firm need admit to or know anything of strategy—and it still has relevant planning by our criteria—if the firm's decisions are replicable, future oriented, and internalized by the executives.

Elements of Relevance

The other dimension of planning relevance is contained in its seven elements. The first is the organizational basis for the firm. That is, upon what criteria is the firm organized—what characterizes the overriding framework for the organization? Examples here might include geographical, functional, historical, business, customer, market, and so on.

The second is the kind of planning issues (i.e., planning tools) that are considered by the firm, whether or not they are considered to be planning issues or tools, and regardless of the name by which they are called. These range from operational coordination to strategic redirection.

The third is the type of management issues of concern to the executive. This is the element that refers to the substance of the business that is in the center of management consciousness and could include growth, profitability, narrowing of options, explosion of options, and so on.

These first three elements relate to the content of planning. The remaining four relate more to the process.

The fourth has to do with planning styles, that is, decision-making style. Is it Theory X or Theory Y, top–down or bottom–up? The fifth is the planning form, the dynamics and tools within the planning system. The sixth is the planning organization itself and its relationship to the corporate organization. Where is the staff support located organizationally? Is the planning organization centralized or decentralized, discrete or integrated vis-à-vis other management, staff or line.

The seventh element of planning relevance, often called "internal consistency," is very close to planning relevance itself. It has to do with the breadth and depth of use of what we are calling planning. It also has to do with the degree of integration and compatability of this planning with the total management system of the firm: organization, rewards, personnel, accounting, control, and so on. This element is intended to deal with the "ad hocery" of decisions, on the one hand, and their assimilation into the culture and nature of the firm, on the other.

GULF OIL CORPORATION, 1950–1980

The content of each of these seven planning relevance elements for Gulf Oil Corporation for the period 1950–1980 appears in Exhibit 10-1. This is intended to be something of an imaginal view rather than an historical revelation, the objec-

EXHIBIT 10-1

The Relevance of Planning

THE RELEVANCE OF PLANNING

Element / Period	Organizational Basis	Planning Issues	Management Issues	Planning Style	Planning Form	Planning Organization	Internal Consistency
1950-55		Volumes and facilities		Bottom-up Top-down			Low High
1955-60	Functional	Capital budgeting					
1960-65		Profit budgeting	Long on cash, short on opportunities		Forecasting	More decentralized	
1965-70		Functional					
1970-73	Geographical	Interfunctional					
1974		Resource allocation	Change, short on cash, long on opportunities; binding constrictions				
1975	Business	Strategic options	Opportunities vs threats; diversification		Portfolio	Centralized	
1976		Strategy development	Direction of the firm				
1977	Business-functional	Strategy execution	Concentration on traditional business			Less decentralized	
1978-80		Cash management	Recommitment to traditional business		Projecting		

tive being to track what we are calling "planning" in the context of its elements, so that we can discern the direction of its relevance from the trends we observe.

Do not be misled by the nonlinearity of the ordinate. The uneven spacing of the time coordinate was selected to accommodate the data and discussion that are presented here. No apology is offered regarding the perspective that is obviously reflected therein, that is, that more clarity is perceived, more importance is attached, and finer delineations are therefore possible the more recent the period under study.

Before 1974

Gulf was organized functionally until 1965. Correspondingly, all the planning issues were functional, although the degree of sophistication increased from volumetric integration to capital budgeting to profit budgeting. This progress was much slower than in the other "defense" industries coming out of World War II, probably because of the cash-rich position of all oil companies from World War II through 1974. Although they were subject to business cycles, investment opportunities simply did not keep pace with internally generated cash. Among other things, this resulted in huge investments in refineries and in marketing facilities operated at little or no profit. In retrospect, we can now see that the underlying issue was the leveling of U.S. reserve position, leading to the peaking of production and almost inevitably resulting in a shortage of good investment opportunities, an excess of cash, and little perceived need for sophisticated management or control systems.

About 1965, Gulf was reorganized along geographical lines, but with each geographical entity organized functionally. Whereas prior functional planning had led intrinsically to suboptimization, the functional planning now led to suboptimization by geographical areas. This highlighted the problems and led by 1970 to interfunctional planning on a geographical basis, that is, business planning by geographical area, with volumetric coordination among areas.

All during the period since World War II, the environment of the petroleum industry had been evolutionary, and forecasting (i.e., projecting the future on the basis of the past) was an adequate planning form. However, as is generally true in this type of environment, the "hockey stick" syndrome was unavoidable: We will solve all our problems in the next few years, which will depress profits; then, profits will climb without limit, forever.[1]

The planning organization was highly decentralized, determined largely by the bottom–up (or middle–up) planning style.

In addition to the obvious disruptions of the 1973–1974 embargo, the pivotal change of 1974 was a significant shortage of cash relative to investment opportunities or even relative to investment obligations. Thus, a firm and an industry, that had never been required to deal seriously with debt and finance issues now found itself forced to deal with huge resource allocation issues. This was accommodated within the element of planning issues by shifting from project evaluation to the assignment of priorities to programs and within the elements of planning organization and style by moving toward more centralized planning and more top–down direction setting.

This shifting in the nature of planning brought to the attention of management the implications of a shift in its role. Establishing program priorities on a portfolio basis was seen as a more powerful and appropriate management style than was project approval. It was seized as the instrument for reorganizing the firm along business or "strategic" lines in preparation for more effectively dealing with the world of the 1970s and 1980s.

In 1975, this reorganization was accomplished, the central planning issue being as follows: What is the direction of the firm to become, and what role will each organizational unit play in moving in that direction? The management issues were of evaluating opportunities and threats and alternative responses thereto and of considering various diversification moves. Both planning style and organization became quite top–down and centrally oriented, as fundamental issues were being dealt with in every functional, geographic, and business area.

In a very real sense, 1975–1976 was the period of intense and fundamental analysis and soul searching. During 1976, some of the intense questions that were being raised seemed to begin receiving answers, and some of the fundamental issues being grappled with seemed to begin being put to rest. As reflected in Exhibit 10-1, planning issues moved from the consideration of strategic options to the strategy development of the selected options into concrete alternatives. The management issues, correspondingly, dealt with directing the firm along the chosen course.

By 1977, the "business–strategy" organization had moved to "business–functional." Admittedly, this dynamic is especially difficult to track, because the business–strategy reorganization of 1975 followed lines of demarcation not different from those one might have drawn using functional criteria. Only the intent was new, not the lines themselves. The planning issue was execution of the selected strategy and the development of appropriate performance controls. The direction of the firm was primarily a concentration on the traditional business. The planning organization became less centralized, and planning style began to become more homogeneous throughout the hierarchy as strategy and direction stabilized.

In the present (1978–1980) period, the central management issue is recommitment to traditional business, and the regrouping and consolidation of all forces and resources is around this direction and thrust. The central planning issue is cash management and the fine tuning of marginal resource allocations. Projecting is the principal planning form, suitable for the same kinds of reasons that forecasting was suitable prior to 1974. The planning organization becomes increasingly decentralized, appropriate to the planning style typical of a stabilized, homogeneous strategy, a planning style that could be characterized as monolithic.

Internal Consistency

The argument here is that, in its long-range aspects, planning is, in fact, consistent internally with the business environment as discerned by management and with the style that management adopts to cope with that environment. More important, we argue that, in general, consistency increases with time. That is, any friction or divergent trends that might cause inconsistency or decrease consistency are swayed, in fact, toward conformity. Perhaps it is only in retrospect that this can be seen, for in the short term the debates can be heated, new approaches strongly defended and strongly attacked, and changes in process adopted without real effect.

It seems upon reflection that what we have just said here must necessarily be so. The alternative to increased internal consistency would be a move toward anarchy, which in itself would be quickly self-correcting in any firm that is required to operate in the public view and within the rigors of the marketplace.

CONCLUSIONS

We have tried to illustrate here, if not to prove, that planning in a firm will change as a function of management issues, management style, and management itself. In a firm that is to be ongoing, we have also tried to illustrate that planning will also increase in relevance. Planning, as we have defined it, is in fact relevant; it is that portion of the decision-making process that is in fact relevant.

The interesting issue, then, is whether or not planning will lead or lag changes in management issues, management style, and management itself. Planning is an unavoidable reality within a firm, as is, say, communications. The question is, Will it be allowed to evolve, by trial and error, with the survival of the fittest (i.e., most consistent, most relevant) or will its changes be managed?

It seems that there are great possibilities for leverage in managing the change in planning as a method of managing the firm. There are significant costs associated with planning either leading or lagging changes in management perceptions at all levels throughout the firm and significant advantages to be gained in terms of maintaining maximum consistency and relevance for planning. One would expect the effort expended in maintaining this consistency and relevance should be small in relation to its benefits; however, it is only top management that can effectively perform this function. Staff and support work is possible and even necessary, but management of the decision-making process, and of changes to it, requires the attention, involvement, interest, and commitment of the CEO as a part of his or her management responsibility, or else this function becomes simply another facet of the trial-and-error evolution of planning.

Perhaps planning, as a function and as a discipline, is unique in this way. We say this, it is hoped, without being egotistical or parochial. Perhaps it is because of the early stage of planning as a discipline. Perhaps other functions, such as accounting or operations, contain within themselves self-correcting adjustment procedures so that they automatically change in these management elements. As yet, planning does not. Our perception is that, on the whole, "planning" happens, naturally, with or without a formal recognition or system. Usually the system does not conform to reality and therefore is at best a burden and at worst a hindrance to management. As the management elements change, planning changes, with lead or lag, but the system does not change.

An acknowledged and conscious management of planning and the appropriate system or systems would assure greatest possible use of the firm's resources in making the decisions that are important to the firm's future, as perceived by the management. This would involve not only anticipating possible changes in the business environment and in the issues that will be facing the firm, but also anticipating the changes in management style and in the process of decision making that will permit dealing with them in the most effective ways.

The development of this ability could very well provide the firm with a significant advantage over its competition, which would be very difficult to emulate. Perhaps we are all now aware that change is the important reality of our time and that the key to success is effectively managing this change. The conscious management of planning offers the opportunity of managing the management process so that change itself can be managed most effectively by the firm.

NOTES

[1]The term "hockey stick" or "checkmark" comes from the shape of the profits or cash curve when plotted against time. It decreases steadily for a couple of years, then climbs steadily thereafter. Then, the same projection is repeated, year after year.

11

On Acceptance of Strategic Planning Systems

INTRODUCTION

The question addressed in this chapter* is how to get an organization to accept a formal system of strategic planning. The observations presented in response to this question are based on direct experience with a strategic planning system at EG&G, Inc.

By way of background, EG&G is a highly diversified, high-technology company serving specialized industrial and government markets. In 1978, EG&G became one of the "Fortune 500" companies, and sales reached $400 million. From a 1972 base, this represents a sales growth of 23 percent per year. During this same period, reported earnings per share increased from $0.65 to $2.45 per share for an arrival growth rate of 24 percent. Return on equity has increased steadily and reached 26 percent after taxes in 1978. In the most recent listing of the "Fortune 500," EG&G ranked eleventh among the five hundred companies in return on equity and twenty-second in total return to investors.

A strategic planning system was introduced on a companywide basis in 1971. Although evolutionary improvements have been made since that time, the essentials of the 1971 system have remained unchanged. By the end of this year, we will have completed nine annual planning cycles. The planning system has become a basic ingredient of the management style used.

*This chapter is prepared by George H. Gage, Vice President, EG&G, Inc.

Strategic planning, at its present state of the art, means different things to different people. As a consequence, very different kinds of strategic planning systems based on different concepts are in use today. Before presenting any observations on the original question of acceptance, therefore, we will describe the underlying concepts and characteristics of the EG&G system on which our observations are based.

To do this, the initial negative predisposition of an organization to the establishment of a formal planning system is discussed first. Then the rationale of an approach to overcome this resistance and to contribute value to the management of the organization is presented. These considerations lead to the two principles that underlie the EG&G system. The way in which these principles are applied is expanded upon and the conditions that appear to be necessary for this type of planning system to be effective are presented.

For the planning system thus described, the potential benefits are then delineated, and the issues related to initial and ongoing acceptance are discussed. This discussion is then extended to the related issue of need for flexibility in the system.

THE BASIC PROBLEM

To expect an organization to accept a formal planning system is to expect a great deal. The predisposition of a typical organization to such a proposed system is automatically negative. Any formal system that purports to deal with important decisions and, indeed, with the future of the organization is immediately suspect. To the line organization, it represents both a threat to and an encroachment on existing management prerogatives. To many, it will appear as yet another needless staff activity.

The proposed system will be evaluated by comparing the benefits to the costs—although this evaluation may be formal or informal, conscious or unconscious, rational or emotional. The perceived "costs" will include concerns such as

Does it threaten my stature and power base?
How much of my present freedom will I lose?
Will the time it will require from the organization be worth it, particularly when compared with alternate uses of critical management time?
Will it disrupt the existing culture and management style?

The potential "benefits" will be examined in terms of questions such as

How will it benefit me?
How will it benefit the organization?
How will it contribute to the solution of any real problem that we have now?
How can I measure the results?

Unless some significant clearly perceived benefit exists, the net trade-off between these cost and benefit questions will likely be negative.

In some cases, a "repairing the roof syndrome" may exist; that is, when it's raining you can't repair the roof, and when it's not raining you don't need to. When an organization has severe operating problems, it is difficult to invest the management time necessary to introduce a strategic planning system, even if it is agreed that it would be useful. When an organization is performing well, it may not appreciate the need to make such an investment.

Finally, for some organizations, a future may not exist that is both acceptable to all concerned and feasible to achieve. In such cases, a process of realistically characterizing the situation and openly probing the alternatives could be viewed by at least some of the management as a process to be avoided. Resistance can therefore be expected to any system that would deal openly with issues that are perceived by the participants as sensitive.

The foregoing considerations can represent substantial initial resistance to the establishment of a formal planning system.

THE BASIC APPROACH

The only way in the long run to overcome the substantial resistance described is for the planning system to contribute sufficient visible benefit to the organization to make the effort and investment in the system worthwhile.

The issue then becomes one of planning substance: How good is the planning itself? Can it add real value to an organization? Can it demonstrate benefits in a specific time and place?

These questions, however, raise an apparent dilemma. How can a planning system add real value to an organization where the general manager and his or her management team know the business far better than anyone else? From what perspective realistically can a general manager, and particularly a competent and successful general manager, be told how to run his or her business better?

The answer does not lie in the planner's becoming so immersed in the activities of the organization that he or she can then formulate his or her own opinions of the future, which may or may not be at odds with those of the general manager. The only possible value being created here is whatever value is associated with that of a second opinion (which may not be wanted). This approach does not lend itself to replication throughout a large organization and has the undesirable aspect of actually competing with or second-guessing the general manager.

The most useful answer to this apparent dilemma is often achieved by directing attention to strategic decisions. The making of proper strategic decisions is critically important to the future of the organization and is often most difficult. At the same time, the need for these decisions is often unrecognized, and the nature of these decisions is not well understood. By contributing technology, language, and structure to the process of making strategic decisions, strategic planning can make a distinct contribution that is useful to both the general manager and his or her organization.

As used here, strategic decisions are management decisions that have to do with the organization's reason for being, its goals, and the basic courses of actions to achieve its goals. Other types of management decisions can be classified as structural decisions (related to how the resources should be organized) and operational decisions (related to "doing the job").

As it works out, strategic decisions are very different in their basic nature from structural decisions and operational decisions.

Superficially, strategic decisions differ by being infrequent and nonrepetitive. In terms of numbers of decisions, structural and operational decisions probably constitute more than 99 percent of all management decisions. And, although repetition characterizes structural and operational decisions, the typical general manager rarely encounters the same strategic problem more than once. This infrequency suggests that the general manager is not necessarily subjected to an automatic learning process that would develop his or her skill in making strategic decisions.

But a more fundamental difference exists in terms of the mechanism for initiating these decisions. Problems in the structure of the organization—in terms of work flow, procedures, or reporting relationships—quickly become obvious and tend to force structural decisions to be made. Similarly, problems in the operational aspects of the organization—in terms of bookings, purchasing, hiring, production, shipping, scheduling, and so on—become immediately apparent to all concerned. Again, the problems will force operational decisions to be made.

In this respect strategic decisions are different. No natural or automatic mechanism exists in the organization to force a strategic decision. The need for a strategic decision may not be evident. Indeed, the symptoms of strategic difficulties are often interpreted as relating to structural or operational problems. The net result: Strategic problems don't necessarily force strategic decisions.

Strategic decisions are complicated further by the fact that they are difficult to make. For organizations who compete for survival, the strategic decisions need to be made in the context of the competition and have to do with winning or losing. In these cases, the information on which to base the strategic decision is always inadequate. What the major competitor is thinking, what his or her intentions are, and how he or she will react to your actions are all necessarily unknown. The strategic decision must always be made in the absence of complete information. If the general manager waits for "more data" and "more studies," he or she will simply not make needed strategic decisions in a timely fashion.

Yet, despite all these difficulties in making strategic decisions, proper strategy is critical to success. An old military maxim says that, with a sound strategy, some tactical errors can usually be tolerated and the activity will still be successful. But, if the underlying strategy is faulty, no amount of operational effort can overcome this disadvantage. An organization with a faulty strategy faces a difficult future indeed.

So, if we bring together these characteristics of strategic decisions (i.e., they are not forced, they are difficult, and they are critically important), we have an area of management that is not easily or automatically done well. In fact business history and military history are replete with examples of monumental strategic errors. It has been estimated that perhaps one third of the businesses in the United States are today operating with inappropriate strategy.

We therefore have a high-leverage area. Modest improvements in the quality of strategic decisions can make large differences in operational performance. It is in this area that planning can probably make the greatest contribution to an organization.

These considerations then lead to what some believe is the first basic principle of strategic planning and that is

> *Formal planning in an organization*
> *should focus on strategic decisions.*

To be useful to the organization, however, these strategic decisions must be translated into specific actions by the organization. The benefits from improved strategy can be accrued only from the results of such implementing actions. To complete the planning task, therefore, formal planning activities should facilitate the translation of the strategic decisions into parameters relevant to the subsequent management of the organization and the measurement of its performance. A second principle, complementing the first, then becomes

> *The operational activities of an organ-*
> *ization should derive directly from*
> *the strategic decisions.*

This means that the formal planning in an organization should produce outputs that express the strategy in operational terms from which specific actions can be taken.

These two principles represent an approach to planning in an organization that, it is believed, has a high potential for contributing value to the organization.

DEVELOPING THE STRATEGY

In applying the two principles cited, we have found it necessary to better understand the subject of strategy. We have identified a conceptual model for strategic decisions, defined the required dimensions of strategic decisions, and introduced vocabulary to permit more precise communications about strategy. In general, the better the concept of strategy is developed, the better the strategic decisions can be.

In developing strategy, the beginning point is to identify and define the strategic elements of the organization. The working definition of what constitutes a strategic element differs from organization to organization. It is useful to consider that each strategic element must have an underlying justification for its existence or a "reason for being"; that is, it must provide something of value to serve some need external to the organization. If the strategic element is then defined in terms of this basic output and the external need served, the factors that relate to its viability can then be identified. By adding consideration of both direct and indirect competitive efforts to serve the defined external need, a very fundamental characterization of the element can be established. From this fundamental characterization, the strategy for the element can be derived as a function of the differences from the major competitors and the changes taking place in the relevant external factors.

For a business organization, a strategic element would normally consist of a particular set of services or group of products serving a particular market segment. With only rare exceptions, an organization will have more than one strategic element. Because strategic elements are defined in terms of an external need, they need not—and usually do not—correspond directly to the organization's structure.

What is important is that each strategic element requires a distinct strategy. This strategy should be delineated in terms of where to compete (with what products, in what markets), how to compete (with what performance, at what price) and when to compete (the timing issues). It should also include the results to be achieved in this competition. A good strategy should take advantage of relative strengths, minimize the effects of relative weaknesses, and create a new condition of competitive balance in which it is difficult for the competitor to counter.

Not only is strategy needed for each strategic element, strategy is also needed at levels above the strategic element. In the case of a military situation, for example, the distinction can readily be made between the strategy for a particular battle (the strategic element) and the higher levels of strategy needed for the overall conduct of the war.

Note that the nature of these higher levels of strategy for an organization differs from the nature of the strategies for a strategic element. The strategy for an element has to do with winning or losing a competition in the external world. The essence of the higher strategy is to integrate the actions of the constituent strategic elements in such a way that a coordinated approach to the achievement of the organization's overall goals results.

As part of the higher strategy, available resources are allocated among the several elements consistent with their strategies, and each element then assumes a particular role in the overall plan. The higher strategies can also be considered as providing whatever reconciliation is needed between the performance goals of the organization and the performance expected from the existing set of strategic elements. It would include, therefore, whatever new initiatives or new investments are needed. It would also establish priorities and relative emphasis among the various element strategies.

Together, the strategies for the strategic elements and the higher strategies constitute the key high-leverage strategic decisions on which the future of the organization will depend.

TRANSLATING THE STRATEGY

The strategic planning task does not end with the development of the strategies. The strategies must then be translated into parameters relevant to the management of the organization and the measurement of its performance. The important principle here is that, once the strategies have been developed, the organization's activities and investments should flow from the strategies. The strategies become the source of all direction and the framework for all actions. They are in effect the sources of everyone's marching orders.

The resources required by the organization can be derived directly from the statements of strategy. In the business case, the statement of strategy determines the capital additions required, R&D programs required, marketing required, and pricing investments needed. Similarly, the strategy signals what actions and results are required from each of the functional areas of the organization. In the business case again, the strategy determines the outputs needed from manufacturing, marketing, engineering, purchasing, and so on.

All these requirements and activities can then be brought together and expressed quantitatively. In business, the future aspects of the strategy can be represented numerically in conventional financial P&L, balance sheet, and cash flow formats. Also, the strategy usually involves key events that are not directly evident from the numerical representation. Such strategically important events can be treated as "milestones." Examples of milestones include the date of new product introductions, date for installation of new equipment, date of a pricing change, and so on. The financial representation then, together with the milestones, portray how the strategy is expected to evolve in a given time period.

Note that, after the basic strategies have been developed, translated into operational parameters, and represented in financial format and associated milestones, we have a written strategic plan. When properly developed, this strategic plan becomes managements' most basic document.

From a strategic plan, shorter-term operational plans (e.g., one-year plans) can be derived. Such operational plans should always be developed in the context of and consistent with the basic strategies. The operational plan and its associated budgets should be viewed as representing an effective continuing implementation of the strategic plan and as providing a scoresheet for progress during the next time period. Note that with this approach, budgets, programs, and priorities are not established independently; rather, they are determined by the strategy.

To complete the overall system for managing an organization, a control system is required. The operational plans and associated budgets provide the link between the strategic plans and the monitoring and feedback functions of the control system. Also from the strategic plan, a variety of specialized and functional plans can be readily derived. Such plans can include facility plans, capital addition plans, cash and financial plans, personnel requirements, marketing plans, R&D plans, and management development plans. In effect all such plans are representations of the strategy as viewed from a particular specialized dimension.

INSTITUTIONALIZING THE SYSTEM

The previous two sections have presented considerations relative to developing a single strategic plan. We now turn our attention to the additional considerations involved when we attempt to institutionalize this process, namely, that of establishing a strategic planning system for developing strategic and operational plans throughout the organization on a regular basis. The five conditions following must be satisfied if the system is to be effective and gain acceptance. These are of sufficient importance that they may be considered "imperatives."

First, strategic planning must be "mainstream" to the management activities of the organization. It should be viewed as the fundamental activity of the organization from which its other activities derive. If strategic planning is viewed as an off-line or staff activity that occasionally issues reports or makes recommendations, it is not likely to be useful. Or, if strategic planning is viewed as "forms to be filled out for headquarters" and is not used directly by the organization for its own benefit, the system is not realizing its potential.

The second imperative is that the actual strategic plan must be developed by the line organization that will subsequently be responsible for its implementation. Unless this organization develops the plan and feels a sense of ownership, no commitment to its implementation can be expected.

The corollary to this statement relates to the proper role of the planning staff specialist. This person should be the force within the organization dedicated to achieving effective strategic planning, the designer of the strategic planning system, the salesperson for strategic planning, and a resource to assist the line management in strategy development and plan preparation. The staff planning function should be small, nonthreatening, and catalytic; line managers should find it worthwhile to talk to the planner.

The third imperative is that the planning system must provide an absolute discipline to force a periodic review of strategy. After a strategic plan has been completed, it is very tempting to assume that the strategies won't need revision for an indefinite period. Our experience indicates that strategies need to be reviewed formally at least once a year. In some cases changes in strategy have been required between the yearly reviews, but, whether or not a change in strategy is needed, the yearly reaffirmation of the strategy has proved to be a worthwhile use of management time. Haphazard or irregular attention to strategic planning cannot yield timely or high-quality strategic decisions.

The fourth imperative is that control must derive directly from the strategic plan. The operational plan should be completely consistent with and in the context of the strategies involved. The control activities should be related directly to this operational plan. Thus, the day-to-day managing of the business relates back to the strategic plan. Indeed, unless this coupling exists, the strategic activities will become irrelevant with time.

The final imperative is that every aspect of the strategic planning process should be kept as simple and as straightforward as possible. The planning system should not ask operations for anything that the operations people don't need for themselves anyway. The documentation required should be straightforward and be kept to a minimum; it should avoid the impression of being bureaucratic.

Strategic issues are inherently complicated; the planning system should assist in achieving proper decisions, not in further complicating the problem.

If strategic planning is based on the two principles presented earlier—that is, focusing on strategic decisions and having the operational activities derive from the strategic decisions—and established as a system consistent with the imperatives discussed earlier, the probability of its being effective will be enhanced greatly. The more effective the system, the better will be its chances for acceptance.

Benefits

An important factor in the acceptance of strategic planning by an organization is the organization's perception of benefits to be realized. It will be useful, therefore, to identify what these benefits really are.

For a strategic planning system based on the principles discussed in the preceding sections, the major benefits can be identified as follows:

1. *Better performance.* To whatever extent improved strategies are developed and implemented, correspondingly better performance can result.
2. *Improved sense of direction.* The explicit strategies developed provide an overall framework and sense of direction for the organization. This can lead to more effective day-to-day decisions and to more focused efforts by the organization.
3. *Increased understanding.* The process can contribute to increased understanding of the business and to improved communications about the business, both within the organization itself and to higher levels of the overall organization. This results in greater confidence in the business both up and down the organization and in more informed support from higher levels.
4. *Earlier warning of problems.* A strategic inconsistency or a weak strategy signals an area to be watched. Often problems can be caught at the strategic element level long before a loss situation develops for the organization.
5. *More effective decentralization.* In effect, the system provides a scheme for delegation in a diversified organization. By establishing agreed-upon strategies and implementational plans, decentralization of structural and operating decisions can usefully be achieved.

Acceptance of strategic planning by an organization will depend on these benefits being credible and being important. These benefits, however, are not equally important to all levels in the organization or to all organizations.

For example, the fifth benefit—more effective decentralization—might be particularly important to the chief executive of a rapidly growing, highly diversified organization who is becoming increasingly concerned with his or her management problem. On the other hand, none of the benefits might be of interest to the chief executive of a highly successful small business with only a few related strategic elements. That C.E.O. could conceivably view the first three benefits enumerated as not needed (he or she "is already there") and the last two benefits as not relevant.

Thus, the difficulty of gaining acceptance will differ from organization to organization, in part as a function of the perceived importance of the benefits. Even under circumstances most favorable to strategic planning, however, a distinct selling effort on behalf of the planning system will be required.

ACCEPTANCE

In the first section of this chapter, the factors that predispose the typical organization against the introduction of a planning system were presented. In the preceding section, the benefits that could be expected from a soundly designed strategic planning system were listed. These benefits, although very significant, may take several years to realize. The initial problem of acceptance, therefore, is to be able to realize the longer-term benefits in the face of the existence of immediate negative factors.

The initial impetus to introduce strategic planning into an organization must come from a decision by the organization's chief executive. This initial impetus must have sufficient momentum to override the negative factors until the benefits are seen clearly. In practice this requires determination on the part of management to stay with the process for several years. During this period the support of the organization's chief executive is critical. Without this support, establishment of a planning system is not possible.

When planning is first introduced in an organization, the management team must learn the language and mechanics of the planning system as well as deal with the substantive issues of the particular plan being developed. Fortunately, after a few planning cycles, familiarization with the system is gained, and the planning efforts can then be directed almost entirely to the substantive issues of the plan. When this point is reached, the efficiency of plan preparation, as well as the quality of the plan, improves dramatically.

It has been our experience that with time—perhaps two to three years—those involved in the planning process will usually see the benefits of this activity. Even after the planning system has gained initial acceptance in an organization, however, continued acceptance and viability are not automatic.

Basically, ongoing viability of the planning system requires the continual realization and recognition of the benefits contributed by the system. Practically, this means that with time more and more members of management must become convinced of the value of strategic planning to the organization. If the planning system continues to gain support throughout the organization, its effectiveness will increase, and it will increasingly become mainstream with respect to how the organization is managed. If the planning system fails to gain support, it will flounder and eventually be discontinued.

The difference between the planning system's continuing to gain support throughout the organization and losing support in the organization may not be large. Even with a well-designed and soundly based system, factors are ever present in any organization that resist continued acceptance of such a system. These can include resistance to the discipline that the planning system necessarily imposes, resistance to investing the time required by planning in view of already busy schedules, and resistance to working on long-term strategic issues in view of pressing short-term problems.

To deal with these ever-present forces requires continuing positive support from the chief executive and other key line managers. The support required includes participating actively in the process, giving high priority to planning, and being recognized as a strong planning advocate. The more extensively this broad support to planning extends from the chief executive to other managers in the organization, the greater the probability that the planning system will continue to be accepted.

CHANGE AND FLEXIBILITY

In the early period of our strategic planning system, we had concerns that after several cycles the planning system would become routine and lose its then high level of interest and subsequently its importance. Now that we are in our ninth annual planning cycle, we can say that such has not been our experience.

A number of dynamics exist that keep strategic planning from becoming routine. First, factors external to each strategic element continually change. These include technological, social, political, economic, governmental, and environmental factors as well as continual changes in customers, competitors, and suppliers. These changes often trigger changes in strategy. Sometimes more profound change is required, such as a change in the basic concept of the business, which requires redefining the strategic element. These changes in turn trigger the process of rethinking the higher strategies of the organization.

In an environment of change, the ability to adapt and evolve is critical to survival. In the planning system described, the key to flexible response is to change the strategy whenever conditions so require. Indeed if the strategies are not changed to correspond to changed conditions, the planning system will produce organizational rigidity rather than the desired ability to cope flexibly with change. The annual review of the strategy, the twice-annual planning meetings, and the general understanding that strategies should be changed whenever necessary all contribute to the needed strategic flexibility.

Probably the most common criticism of formal planning systems is that they stifle innovation and creativity. In most fundamental terms, the planning system described here produces a set of strategic decisions from which the activities of the organization derive. Nothing inherent in these principles speaks either for or against innovation; the planning system itself is neutral. Presumably, any set of strategies could be chosen, including strategies that would dedicate the organization to the process of innovation.

What can impact on innovation, however, are the values and goals that are superimposed onto the planning framework. For example, either explicitly or implicitly, every organization establishes priorities and values among such goals as consistency of growth, higher but more erratic growth, stability of work force, tolerance for risk, and the degree to which earnings are protected at the expense of other activities during a market downturn. The planning system itself can tolerate widely different sets of priorities and management cultures. Indeed, the existence of a planning system is likely to force resolution of the priorities among the organization's goals.

CONCLUDING REMARKS

In the preceding sections, the principles of the specific approach to strategic planning used by EG&G have been presented along with the major considerations that seem to be necessary for the planning system to be effective. The system is characterized by developing an explicit strategy for the organization and then using this strategy as the basis for the operational management.

For an organization to accept a planning system of this type, the major argument can be summarized as follows:

1. In any organization factors exist to resist the introduction of a formal planning system.
2. In the long run, the only way to overcome such resistance is for the planning system to contribute real and significant benefit to the organization.
3. To make such a contribution, planning should focus on improving strategic decisions and in helping to translate these strategies into specific actions by the organization.
4. The benefits from such strategic planning may take several years to develop to the point where the benefits are generally recognized.
5. In terms of gaining acceptance, the initial problem is to continue the planning process in the face of the factors resisting its introduction long enough to realize the benefits. During this period, the support of the organization's chief executive is critical.
6. Experience indicates that most of the people involved in the planning system will come to recognize its benefits before the initial period is over.
7. After the planning system has gained initial acceptance, however, ongoing acceptance is not automatic. A set of factors (different from those resisting initial acceptance) is present in any organization that tends to resist continuing these activities.
8. To overcome these ongoing factors, continuing support from the chief executive and all other key line managers is needed in the form of their giving high priority to planning and participating actively in the process. Such active management support, together with the continuing recognition of significant benefits from the planning system, are the keys to ongoing system acceptance.

The planning system described here, although very simple in concept, requires significant management effort and skill for it to be implemented effectively and for it to be accepted generally by the organization. The results obtainable from the system appear to justify such an effort.

12

Strategic Planning as a Tool for Adaptation and Integration

INTRODUCTION

This chapter* describes Borg-Warner's strategic management system, how it relates to planning, and some of the results that have been achieved with it. It also describes how the system is being used and the planning that supports it as a tool for both integration and adaptation.

Among the characteristics of Borg-Warner's strategic management system that we like best is its adaptability. This is a characteristic that is necessary to any management system that hopes to succeed. A corporate management system has to fit the corporate culture and have the ability to evolve with that culture in a complementary way. The planning system that underlies it should be an agent for change, guiding and often prodding the corporate culture, but always remaining in easy earshot so that reciprocal communication is loud and clear.

Borg-Warner is a multinational, multiindustry company. Its operations are decentralized as relatively autonomous divisions. These operating divisions are formed into six major groups in which there is some compatibility of markets or technology, or both. The heads of these groups report to the president and chief operating officer who in turn reports to the chairman and chief executive officer.

---

*This chapter is prepared by Donald Collier, Senior Vice President, Corporate Strategy, Borg-Warner Corporation.

The staff officers responsible for key functions, including corporate strategy, also report to the C.E.O.

The Policy & Planning Committee, which is the senior management committee of the company, consists of the three senior staff officers, the president, and one group head on a two-year rotating basis and is chaired by the C.E.O. It is responsible for allocating the resources of the corporation. Each of the key resources—money, technology, and people—is represented on the Policy & Planning Committee by one of the members.

Theodore Levitt of the Harvard Business School, in an article in *Fortune* in December 1978 about the "science of management," said, "There is only one way to manage anything, and that is to keep it simple."[1] Well, most readers will surely agree with that.

STEPS IN PLANNING PROCESS

First we intend to describe the seven major steps in our strategic management system and show how they simplify the job of managing the corporation. Each of these steps repeats each cycle of our planning system and are, of course, iterative as they are being carried out. The first step is initiated by the senior corporate managers. Those are the individuals on the Policy & Planning Committee who, with the approval of the board of directors, set the goals of the corporation. These goals typically include less cyclicality, higher margins, quality of earnings, and a desire for excellence, financially and nonfinancially. Following the goal setting the corporate managers must develop a method, or strategy, to achieve these goals. Borg-Warner's agreed-on method of reaching its current goals is spelled out in the corporate "strategy statement" that was adopted in 1976. This will be renewed later in this chapter.

The next step is taken by the division managers, with help from the group managers and with agreement by corporate managers, whose task is to decide exactly what are the businesses in which they are engaged. That is, they must separate the overall business into units that can be sorted out and analyzed. For example, What is the market this business serves? What are the products we serve these markets with? Who are our competitors in that market?

This breakdown must be made in a very precise way. It must be made objectively and with as little emotion as possible to develop the best possible strategy to compete in each market. It also has to be made in terms of a team of people (or a potential team) who will be responsible for carrying out the strategy and to whom the company can allocate resources. For our purposes, we call these teams (or potential teams) strategic business units (S.B.U.s).

The third step involves the managers of each of the strategic business units who must now analyze the current position of their units. Their purpose is to develop cost-effective strategies to compete in their markets and thereby achieve goals that are compatible with the overall corporate goals. They must enumerate the results they expect from these strategies in terms of cost (i.e., capital, people, and technology and in terms of the dollar return expected. And it must of course be delineated how soon these results can be anticipated. The company expects this to be done by the line managers, not the planners.

The fourth step involves the group managers who must question and refine the strategies developed by their S.B.U. managers and their translation into costs and expected returns. Group managers can bring to this assignment their familiarity with the markets, with their competitors, and with their own S.B.U. managers. They should have the objectivity of being at least one step removed from the advocates of each strategy. And, of course, they also bring their own experience in dealing with similar business strategies when they ran their own divisions.

The fifth step is the allocation process. This is the job of the corporate managers who divide up Borg-Warner's pool of resources among all the strategic business units in the corporation. Obviously, they must do this very selectively, if the corporation is to achieve the best possible performance. They have to be objective and they have to be hard-nosed. Success here depends, in a major way, on how well the group managers did their job in step four: questioning, reviewing, and refining the strategies of their S.B.U.s. If the total of the S.B.U. recommendations adds up to more than the available resources, the corporate managers have to go back to the groups and ask them to revise some of the S.B.U. strategies.

The sixth step, undertaken by the S.B.U. managers (who in many cases are the division managers) and watched by the group managers or the division managers, now must carry out those plans and make the agreed-on strategy "happen." This calls for singleness of purpose once the plan has been developed and agreed on and the ability to stick to it despite the obstacles that are bound to arise. At the same time, it requires judgment and flexibility and the ability to take advantage of some unanticipated opportunity or to deal with an unexpected adversity. This step requires some system to monitor the "actual" against the "planned" results, so that the managers involved know where they are going and can correct their courses as needed so that corporate managers can keep track of those goals set in step five.

Finally, in step seven, the corporate managers, acting on the recommendation of the group managers and with the approval of the board of directors, reward managers at the group, division, and S.B.U. levels through compensation programs. Simply put, this strategic management system is a straightforward, organized approach to managing a large and complex company. It is a system that uses the best brains at all levels of management to determine what must be done to grow and prosper and to communicate the decisions to all concerned.

EARLY EXPERIENCES WITH PLANNING

How did the company arrive at the goals of step one and the corporate strategy for achieving them? Planning is not a new activity at Borg-Warner. Even long-range planning—if five years can be considered long range—has been done since the early 1960s. This planning, however, was conducted from an operational rather than from a strategic standpoint. Except for major acquisitions, our planning was a bottom–up exercise with growth as the main objective. The corporate five-year plan became essentially an add up of the division plans, always after taking the appropriate discounts, at both the group and the corporate level, to offset overoptimism of the division managers, particularly as they related to forecasts of income.

As can be imagined, this kind of bottom–up operational planning, which asks the question, How can I do more of what I am now doing, but do it better?, was not effective in generating a good corporate strategy. It led to requests for capital that added up to more than the funds available to an increasing level of debt, and to an allocation procedure that tended to equalize the pain of those asking for capital rather than to achieve corporate optimization. Moreover, until the brakes were put on at the end of the 1960s, it led to some rather uncoordinated diversification.

Corporate strategy for the early 1970s was, first, to concentrate resources on the major businesses in which the firm was engaged, then to improve asset management, and, finally, to look for new areas of opportunity that were compatible with the firm's ongoing businesses. For a while we had some improvement in results. In addition to sales growth, there were year-to-year increases in returns as we did a better job of managing the assets than in the past.

But the recession of 1974 and 1975 brought severe declines in some of the firm's major markets, causing the debt–equity ratio to get much too high and profits to nose dive. There were obvious critical issues we had to resolve quickly and firmly. An examination of our position in the industries in which Borg-Warner competed showed a history of cyclical below-average returns, with no strong upward trends in any of them. We found that our debt–equity problem developed because we had not been selective enough in picking the businesses we were trying to expand. We knew that we had set our operating return goal too low to allow for the inflation rate, and we had not set targets specific enough and flexible enough for our operating units to follow. Exhibit 12-1 outlines the dismal result. All during this period (1964–1974) we had lagged the median of the 500, and, although we had accelerated the decline by switching to LIFO accounting in 1974, it was clear that our results were not acceptable. Bolder action was called for.

Strategic planning was appropriate to the times because it asked first, Do we want to be in that business at all?, before asking, How do we do it better? In addition, strategic planning began to focus management's attention on markets, on their growth, and on our share in them rather than on product, which had been our traditional inside-out focus. Strategic planning also gave us a basis to determine the attractiveness of the various businesses that we were in. At the same time, we picked out a dozen or so major issues that our managers thought were the most critical and had to be addressed immediately. We called them "strategic issues" and set up procedures to get top management involved sufficiently so that intelligent decisions could be made on allocating resources to them. This top management involvement in solving strategic issues has become an integral part of our system.

EXHIBIT 12-1

Return on Equity, 1964–1974

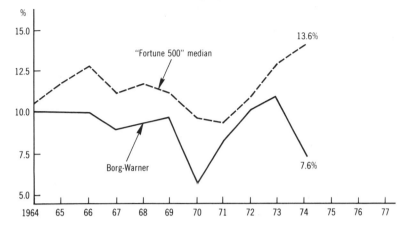

MODELS FOR STRATEGIC SCENARIOS

In 1975 we used computer-assisted financial modeling for the first time to explore alternatives for improving the company's performance. These models allowed us to conduct a number of "What if?" studies. Four of these studies will be discussed here because they became the basis for the strategy that we have followed since 1975.

Case one, "business as usual," was our estimate of what would happen during the period from 1975 through 1979, if we allowed past performance and current trends to simply continue without change, into the future. It showed that our margins and our return on equity would remain well below the average of U.S. industry during the period, that our debt–equity ratio would continue to be too high, and that our interest coverage would be too low to meet the level required for top bond ratings. Finally, it showed that we would operate at a negative cash flow for the five-year period. Clearly, following the "business as usual" formula was a totally unacceptable solution.

Case two was a projection of the five-year plans submitted by the business groups in 1975 for the period through 1979. Now, although the consolidated projections of sales by our divisions were reasonably accurate, our experience showed that their profit projections were invariably too optimistic, frequently by a factor of two, when compared later with the actual results. Although this case projected better results than did Case one, our margins and return on equity still were not likely to reach the average of U.S. industry. Our debt–equity ratio and interest coverage still would not meet our goals by the end of the period in 1979. But there was one positive aspect of Case two: The company would operate with a positive cumulative cash flow. This looked better, but it still wasn't good enough, especially considering our past experience with division profit forecasts.

For the first time, then, we tried a top–down exercise. This model, Case three, we called "honing" the operating efficiency of our businesses. It asked the question, What could be done if we could make reasonable improvements in each of the key operating ratios of our business? The ratios in question were cost of sales to sales; selling, general and administrative expense to sales; investing turns; and days sales of receivables. These ratios for the preceding ten years were studied carefully. Then, taking into account the current and anticipated conditions, we set ourselves specific goals that seemed reasonable. Our objective was to improve the operating ratios by the end of the period in 1979 compared with the goals set by the operating people in Case two. The result here was a marked improvement.

For example, we assumed that we could improve the cost of sales to sales ratio over Case two, the business group projections, by one fourth of a point per year starting in 1976. In a similar way, we assumed that we could improve selling, general, and administrative expense to sales. Our goal at the end of the planning period here would be two points lower. Moving down to inventory turns, we felt that over the period we could increase them by nine tenths of a point. Days sales in receivables in Case two were satisfactory, so we left them unchanged. The other factors in this model were essentially unchanged from Case two, except that we assumed a more realistic and liberal dividend policy of 40 percent of the previous year's earnings.

The results from Case three, then, amounted to this: First, both the margins and the return on equity would be well above the average of U.S. industry by the end of the period. Second, our debt–equity ratio and interest coverage would be well beyond our targets. Third, the cash flow surplus would be about double the level of that of Case two. There was only one cloud on the horizon—the margin on sales still would not reach the level of what we call "companies of excellence," with pretax earnings in the 15–20 percent range. We aspired to that level.

Case four, "being the best company in each of the businesses we are now in," employed the same sales projections as in Case two but used the operating ratios of the best public company we could find, representative of each of the seven major business groupings we had at that time. We applied the operating ratios from each of these companies to the sales of our corresponding business groupings and then consolidated these into an overall Borg-Warner model. Interestingly enough, this case came up with operating income ratios to sales, return on net operating assets, debt–equity, and interest coverage ratios and cumulative cash flows that were essentially the same as those in Case three. Yet in neither case did we reach the operating margins on sales we would really like to have.

This final modeling exercise told us a number of things: first, the operating ratio improvement goals we had set for ourselves were reasonable and attainable. We knew that there were real companies out there in very similar businesses that were achieving performances like these.

Second, we learned that our operating asset management was in pretty good shape but that we needed to concentrate on improving our operating margins.

Third, achievement of these operating ratio goals would help us to reach our short-range goals of beating the *Fortune* median in return on equity and would give us more cash flow to invest in further improvements.

Fourth, we knew that such a performance would be equal to being the leader in each of the major fields in which we were operating but that this still would not be good enough to let us reach our ultimate long-term goals.

And, fifth, to become a real company of excellence, it would not be enough to concentrate only on present businesses. We would have to initiate a positive program to improve Borg-Warner's business mix.

So now it was time to go back to the heads of our business groups, show them what we had learned, and ask them to take part in a similar—and presumably binding—exercise.

DEVELOPMENT OF DYNAMIC BUSINESS STRATEGIES

Using corporate Case three as a model, they were to analyze their own individual businesses and tell us what they thought would be reasonable 1979 targets for those same key operating ratios. It took time and some lively discussions, but, when the group figures came in and were consolidated into a corporate model, the results gave us a corporate performance that was slightly better than the Case three top–down model. At that point, we announced publicly that Borg-Warner's goal for 1979 was to beat the "Fortune 500" median return on equity. In this way, we confirmed to our operating managers that we were deadly serious about meeting the efficiency targets that this exercise had defined.

This exercise established a new corporate strategy for Borg-Warner that differed very significantly from the one we had been following since 1970. First, by setting and adhering to specific, quantified operating ratio targets for our present businesses, we changed the priority from "growth" to "return on investment" for the period 1975 through 1979. Second, we established a long-range strategy of equal priority: using the cash flow resulting from the first strategy to improve the business mix of the corporation, in contrast to the earlier strategy of exploring new opportunities only in areas compatible with our existing businesses and only with capital left over after we had satisfied that required by our existing businesses for all practical purposes, that was zero.

With this as our foundation, we then refined our planning system and our corporate strategy, so we could effectively carry out this basic two-part strategy established in 1975. First, we adopted a strategic business unit approach to analyzing and planning our businesses, so we could decide realistically on the relative strategic promise of each part of the corporate whole, based on its business strength and the attractiveness of its served market. This allowed us to allocate resources—capital, people, and technology—in a way that would move us in the direction of improving our business mix internally. Second, after this strategic business unit breakdown, we refined the corporate strategy statement to spell out specifically the way we planned to reach our short- and long-range strategic objectives.

Let us review that strategy:

1. To improve the performance, with emphasis on margins, of our present businesses, by setting and adhering to specific target operating ratios for each area of our business.
2. To select, by means of SBU analysis, those portions of our present businesses that appeared to have better-than-average performance potentials and to give them priority on resources.
3. To plant seeds for future high-performance businesses by technology generation or acquisition in areas of future promise.
4. To make a few major acquisitions of businesses that would improve the Borg-Warner business mix.

The first two parts of this strategy are oriented toward integration, that is, how to improve the performance of the company as it now exists, with particular emphasis on returns. Parts three and four are oriented toward adaptation; that is, how to change the nature of our business to achieve the longer-range goals of the corporation. In particular, how to bring new businesses into the corporate portfolio to improve the business mix of the corporation. The relative emphasis among these various parts of the strategy is shifting with time. Prior to 1979, the major emphasis had been on steps one and two. Beyond 1979 we will be placing increasing emphasis on steps two, three, and four to accelerate the growth and improve the business mix of the corporation in order to achieve our longer-term goals.

RESULTS THIS FAR

In following the strategy, the first step, is the "honing goal" program, our major vehicle by which to improve the efficiency of present businesses, to meet the short-term goal of beating the "Fortune 500" median in return on equity.

Exhibit 12-2 shows the progress toward that goal from when it was established in 1975 until 1978. It is, of course, a moving target. However, we announced then publicly that we intended to beat the "Fortune 500" median return on equity by the end of 1979, the end of the integrative strategic stage.

Step two attempts to emphasize a better guidance of our allocation policy to the individual parts of our business, favoring those with the greatest promise and holding back on the growth of those with less promise. Thus, through more explicit strategic prioritizing the intent is to improve the business mix internally. In 1978 we made separate allocations to 115 strategic business units. The criterion was return on net assets during, or shortly after, the planning period. Those we believed would exceed the corporate average received the capital they asked for; those we believed would not received only enough capital to stay efficient but not to grow. Starting in 1979, we have broadened the criterion to bring cost-effective growth potential up to an equal priority to returns in making our allocation decisions.

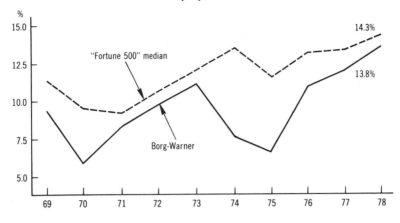

EXHIBIT 12-2

Return on Equity, 1969–1978

Step three, "to plant seeds," is a very long-range program. We estimate that, by using an internal "venturing" procedure on a reasonable number of new business start-ups, it should take about fifteen years before this program can have a significant positive effect on Borg-Warner overall. Financial models cover this period to help guide the program. There are established screening criteria for new ventures at various milestones in their careers. Top management is given a quantitative feel for the cost and returns and a timetable on the program, so that they can enter this program choice decision with their eyes open. Three ventures are now in being. In addition, quantitative goals have been set for each major operating group for new business start-ups in the next five years.

Step four, "acquisitions," was partially implemented in 1978 when Baker Industries was acquired. We had defined and studied strategic issues impacting our business health. To be designated a strategic issue, an item must have a large impact on the total corporate performance and/or make a significant change in the business mix of the corporation. Before being studied, the issues are documented as to their current status; the questions that concern management about them are articulated; the people charged with studying the issues and making a presentation to the Policy & Planning Committee are selected; and a date for the presentation is set. After the presentation, which is accompanied by a written report, the Policy & Planning Committee issues a written response to the presenter of the issue, with detailed recommendations and assigned responsibilities for executing the recommendations. Implementation of the recommendations is tested by the president at his quarterly operations reviews, and a determination is made as to whether the action regarding the issue is on track. This procedure is continued until the issue is implemented fully in the agreed-upon manner or it is returned to the Policy & Planning Committee for another presentation and a shift in strategy.

As can be seen, this facet of our system also follows the steps of the strategic management system outlined earlier—as the implementation of the strategic issue is put in the management objectives of the persons to whom responsibility was assigned. Most of these strategic issues dealt with specific business issues, for example, our worldwide strategy for automatic transmissions or the best route to take in expanding our plastics business. However, a significant number dealt with broader corporate questions. One, for example, was how to reduce the cyclicality of Borg-Warner. This, in turn, led to a study of what was felt to provide the right proportion of service versus manufacturing in our overall business mix.

Many service businesses tend to be relatively steady or contracyclical to capital goods businesses, the latter being the bulk of Borg-Warners operations. The study told us that about a third of our income from service businesses would be about the optimum. Further, it was felt that it would be desirable that these businesses should be less capital intensive than our present Financial Services Group, whose major business is dealer inventory financing—floor planning. Baker Industries, which specializes in protective and courier services, met these criteria. By acquiring it, we raised the potential percentage of our income from service businesses from 10 to about 20 percent—so we were about half way to our goal in this area, as a result of implementing step four in the strategy.

SCORE CARD TO DATE

Examining the score card to date on what has been accomplished on step 1, to improve the return on present businesses, we recall that the road map for this step was Case three of our financial models—honing the operating efficiency of the businesses. This gave us a five-year model to which to aspire in our corporate performance from 1975 onwards. It is probably asking too much to expect any financial model to predict accurately year by year. On the other hand, it ought to be a fairly good predictor of cumulative performance over five years. On that basis, it is working as follows:

1. The trends are in line. It has been a continuous improvement in returns each year as shown in Exhibit 12-2. Undoubtedly, these have at times been helped by the improving economy, but there is more to it than that.

2. Cumulative sales, over a five-year span from 1975 onwards has been 100.4 percent of those predicted by the model. This is more confirmation of our experience that sales forecasts by operating managers tend to be fairly accurate.

3. Cumulative operating income actually came to 92.6 percent of our model—not bad, considering the ambitious level of that goal.

4. Cumulative operating investment needed to reach the target sales turned out to be only 89.6 percent of the model. This confirms that Borg-Warner's asset management is in good shape.

And, finally, for the bottom line, the average pretax return on net operating assets during the five-year period exceeded the model by 3.2 percent. This really gratifying return on net assets performance is, of course, the result of line operating managers' participating in setting their own goals and then vigorously implementing these. It should be pointed out that the cumulative cash flow, when corrected for items such as the Baker acquisition, fell 37 percent below the model. However, all this shortfall occurred in 1979 due mainly to the ballooning effect of inflation on the company's working capital requirements.

Comparing the expected performance for the five-year period from 1975 onwards, first with Case one, "business as usual," the returns on assets results are 32 percent better. Comparing it with case 2, "the business group projections," the performance is 22 percent better. And, as indicated, prior to 1975, the company never did as well as those projections by the groups. And, finally, comparing it with the actual return on assets for the base year 1975, which admittedly was a poor one, the five-year average is almost the double.

So what the planning system did was to show Borg-Warner's operating managers what goals were possible to reach and how to reach them; they did the rest.

NOTES

[1]Levitt, Theodore, A Heretical View of Management "Science", *Fortune*, Vol. 98, No. 12, December 18, 1978, p. 50.

13

Planning as a Vehicle for Strategic Redirection in a Matrix Structure

INTRODUCTION

This chapter* is designed to illustrate the linkage among strategy, organizational structure, and the process of strategic planning using Dow-Corning Corporation as an example. The evolution of this company's strategic situation is described, and changes in the organizational structure and the planning system to accommodate changing needs are identified. Certainly no one type of organizational structure or one approach to strategic planning is inherently superior. But it is vitally important to effective strategic planning to have close compatibility among the planning system, the organizational structure, and the strategic situation of the organization. That kind of compatibility is present at Dow-Corning.

Next, the subject of strategic redirection is addressed, again using Dow-Corning as the example. The implementation of a material strategic redirection is a severe test of any planning and management system. But there are some unique characteristics of the matrix organization with regard to changing direction. Finally, some conclusions based on the experience described here are proposed.

---

*This chapter is prepared by Robert Springmier, Director of Corporate Planning, Dow-Corning Corporation.

EVOLUTION OF STRATEGY

Dow-Corning Corporation was formed in 1943 as a wholly owned joint venture of The Dow Chemical Company and Corning Glass Works. Research programs at Corning had resulted in a new class of synthetic materials called silicones. These materials were part organic and part inorganic, resulting in a unique combination of properties not found in other materials. Corning management had little experience in chemical manufacturing and approached Dow to work with them in commercializing these new materials. The result was the formation of Dow-Corning Corporation located in Midland, Michigan, near the Dow headquarters.

Although records do not show any explicit statement of strategy for the early years, there was clear understanding on the part of all concerned what that strategy was. Dow-Corning was to develop a superior position in organosilicon technology and commercialize that technology as rapidly as possible by making and selling silicones. Because of the complexities of their manufacturing process, silicones were more costly to make than were common organic materials. Although the cost difference could be reduced as silicone production volume grew, there was no expectation that the difference could be eliminated. Therefore silicone growth would have to come through developing a variety of products that could be substituted for organics in applications for which the unique benefits justified the additional costs.

The company was able to implement this strategy very successfully over the years. Sales had reached about $6 million in 1950 and grew about 20 percent per year through the decade of the 1950s. The rate of growth has slowed somewhat since those early years but remains at about 15 percent per year to the present time. Worldwide sales in 1978 were about $500 million.

Over the years, the basic strategy of the company changed very little. Although there was some diversification into synergistic product lines, a high percentage of sales remain in silicones. However, as the company became larger and more complex, the problems of effectively communicating and implementing corporate strategy throughout the organization became more difficult. In the early 1970s the executive committee of the company went through a structured appraisal of corporate strategy. They first agreed on what the implied strategy of the company had been in the past. They then examined the elements of past strategy carefully to see what changes were in order. The result was the first explicit and inclusive corporate strategy statement that could be communicated throughout the organization. This strategy formulation process has since been repeated for major organizational groups within the organization. Resulting strategy statements are reviewed systematically at least once a year.

As corporate strategy evolved from the implied to the explicit, the organizational structure also changed to accommodate changing needs. In the early years, the company operated in a very simple functional organization. The manager of each major function reported directly to the president, whose intuitive leadership and entrepreneurial spirit were largely responsible for the company's early success. He was involved in every major decision and ensured personally that the activities of the various functions were coordinated properly. However, the early success of this organizational style eventually led to its downfall.

Silicones, it was found, could be made in many forms—fluids, resins, sealants, rubbers, and so on. Their unique combination of properties also led them to a wide variety of applications. The strategy was to exploit all viable applications for silicones, and before long the company was selling products to virtually every industry in the United States and other industrially developed countries. Silicone products were also being tailor made for individual applications. This great diversity of market and product scope put a great strain on the simple functional organization. Inevitably coordination among groups slipped. The right hand did not always know what the left was up to.

STRATEGY AND MANAGEMENT STRUCTURE

Divisionalization

In 1962, Dow-Corning moved to a divisional organization in which the operating divisions were defined on a product basis (see Exhibit 13-1). The operating divisions were profit centers assigned responsibility for both short-term profitability and long-term growth of their product lines. The line functions such

EXHIBIT 13-1

The Divisionalized Organization

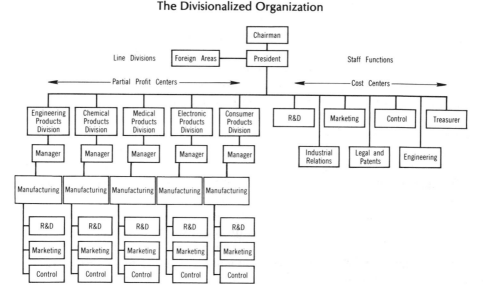

as Manufacturing, Marketing, and Product Development were broken down into product-oriented units and these units reported to the operating divisions. Some staff functions such as Finance, Industrial Relations, and Basic Research remained corporate in scope, but these involved relatively few people compared with the operating divisions. An international division handled activities outside the United States.

This structure improved interfunctional coordination dramatically within the divisions. It allowed profit responsibility to be delegated down into the organization and provided a framework in which each function could identify with profit objectives. It also established healthy competition among the various profit centers. Because each product group tended to be associated with its own group of customers, this structure also provided sharper focus on adapting our activities to the needs of a particular customer environment. Although there were some obvious benefits, it would soon become clear that the divisionalized structure as it existed between 1962 and 1967 would not be appropriate for Dow-Corning's emerging strategic situation.

Whereas interfunctional coordination within divisions improved, coordination between the divisions and corporate staff groups deteriorated. This was a serious problem because the various product groups remained highly interrelated. Many groups shared common technology, and it was not cost effective to have each division supporting its own basic research group. Products in all divisions were made from common intermediates, and it was inefficient to allow each division to build a separate basic intermediates plant. Likewise, there were substantial opportunities for improving both efficiency and effectiveness by sharing some marketing capabilities. But the divisionalized structure, with its heavy emphasis on line discipline, made the management of shared resources very difficult.

Matrix Structure

It soon became clear that our product–market scope was—and would—likely remain extremely diverse, whereas our existing capabilities were highly interrelated. The appropriate organizational structure for such a strategic situation appeared to be a product–functional matrix (see Exhibit 13-2). If managed properly, this structure could combine the advantages of both the functional and divisional structures while avoiding their weaknesses. Dow-Corning instituted such a matrix structure in 1968.

In this matrix, the product groups are called "businesses" and bear some similarity to the product groupings of the former divisions. Each business is a profit center, and each has a full-time manager who is responsible for both short-term profitability and long-term strategic effectiveness of his or her product line. The functions are cost centers, and their managers are charged with functional professionalism and efficiency. Likewise each function has a full-time manager. The business managers and the functional managers are at the same managerial level in the organization.

EXHIBIT 13-2

The Advent of the Matrix or Grid Concept

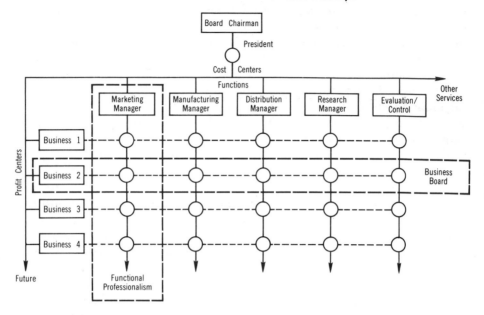

Functions, for the most part, are structured to accommodate major product lines. For example, within the Marketing function separate departments are assigned the responsibility of marketing each business's products. Marketing department managers have dual relationships, reporting both to the director of the marketing function and to the business manager for their product line. The same holds true for the other key functions, that is, Manufacturing, R&D, and Finance. Through dual reporting, we have been able to achieve interfunctional coordination toward profit and growth objectives without sacrificing functional professionalism and efficiency.

To integrate management of our overseas activities, we have added another dimension to the business–functional matrix (see Exhibit 13-3). The matrix is fully operational in the United States, where about half our worldwide sales are made. It is important to point out that the business and functional managers in the United States also have worldwide responsibility for their product line or their function. A similar matrix has recently been established in Europe. Although the European business and functional managers report to the manager of the European area, they also report to their worldwide counterpart located in the United States. The other non-U.S. areas—Canada, Latin America, and Pacific—are developing their own matrix structures as they become larger and more complex.

EXHIBIT 13-3

The Multidimensional Organization

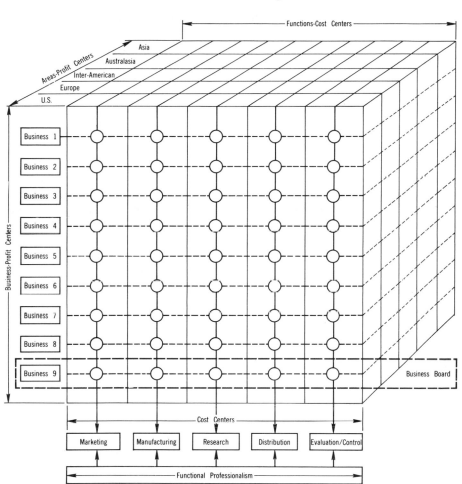

PLANNING'S EVOLUTION

Just as Dow-Corning's organizational structure has been shaped by past strategy, so has its approach to strategic planning followed the evolution of the organization. In the early years of the functional organization, profit planning was done by the chief financial officer and was considered a forecast rather than a commitment. As the company grew, functional managers became more involved in revenue and expense forecasting, but there was little use of planning and budgeting as a method of delegating authority and responsibility down into the organization. The president was the only profit center manager, and he remained involved in all important decisions.

With the introduction of the divisional organization, the profit center concept was expanded dramatically. Division managers were clearly responsible for profit. Thus their one-year plans and, to a lesser extent, their five-year plans were viewed as commitments. These managers were then expected to initiate the action necessary to produce at least the one-year profit specified in their plan. To live with their commitments, it was necessary for the division managers to become personally involved in preparing the plan. A corporate planning manager was named, and a planning system was developed in which plans were proposed by the operating divisions for review by corporate management.

The emphasis during this period was focused almost exclusively on integrative planning. The lack of interfunctional coordination in the previous organization spotlighted the need for better integrative planning. Considerable time and effort, however, were needed to develop integrative planning capabilities. The operating people were not experienced in planning, and information systems had not been designed with planning needs in mind. While considerable progress was made in planning capabilities during this period, there was little attempt to link these plans to the external environment. The planning cycle began with sales forecasts that were primarily projections of past trends. There were no guidelines that required sales forecasts to consider external opportunities coupled with strategic programs to capitalize on those opportunities.

Not only did the matrix organization change the planning roles but it also changed the relative emphasis of various planning activities. Whereas past emphasis was primarily on integrative planning, more emphasis was now placed on adaptive planning. In the past, the main concern was to avoid conflict; now more emphasis was being placed on identifying and reconciling conflict as early as possible.

By 1974, Dow-Corning's planning process identified three planning horizons: a ten-year horizon for corporate sales and capital investment forecasts, a five-year horizon for area and business profit plans, and a one-year horizon for detailed cost center budgets. Three distinct phases were identified in the planning process: an objective-setting phase in which each business and each area establish key five-year performance objectives and specific one-year goals, a programming phase in which resources necessary to meet these objectives and goals are allocated to both operational and strategic programs, and a budgeting phase in which programs are translated into detailed cost center budgets for the following year. Review by the Executive Committee, the top decision-making group in the company, is required before proceeding from one phase to the next. This not only forces reconciliation between the various elements of the matrix organization but ensures that proposals are acceptable at the corporate level before proceeding to more detailed work.

In brief, the planning roles of key elements of the organization are as follows:

1. The functions establish key functional standards of performance and uniform planning assumptions, advise businesses on alternative functional programs, and prepare detailed cost center budgets for approved programs.

2. The businesses assess external opportunities and internal capabilities for their product line, develop five-year objectives and strategies consistent with opportunities and capabilities, and propose specific programs to implement strategies.

3. The areas assess social, political, and economic factors in their countries, develop one-year sales and profit targets for their area, reconcile strategic proposals of businesses with short-term profit goals, and develop operational plans for the next year.

4. The corporate Executive Committee reviews and approves proposals by functions, businesses, and areas to ensure that they represent acceptable performance, acceptable probability of success, and a satisfactory allocation of resources.

5. The Planning Department develops, documents, and operates the planning system, provides resources for analysis of the external environment, and analyzes planning proposals from businesses, areas, and functions and makes recommendations concerning these proposals to the Executive Committee.

No attempt is made to explain the complex information flows and organizational interrelationships of this planning system, but several observations about this system are relevant:

1. The complexity of our planning system is a reflection of our organizational complexity; the matrix organization, in turn, has proven to be most appropriate for managing a very diverse yet highly interrelated line of products.

2. The planning, budgeting, and control systems are closely coupled.

3. The planning sequence starts with general guidelines from the top followed by proposals from within the organization from which corporate management chooses which proposals will be funded and which will not.

The planning system at Dow-Corning appears to be compatible with the current and foreseeable needs of the corporation. It has been designed carefully to fit the company's history, strategy, organizational structure, management systems, and management style. It is also consistent with the established principles and practices for strategic planning systems in general. Yet, when the need arose for strategic redirection at Dow-Corning, the system did not address this need automatically. Substantial top management attention over a considerable period of time was required to accomplish the desired end.

STRATEGIC CHALLENGES

As has been noted, the traditional growth strategy of Dow-Corning has always been to develop new applications for silicones primarily by technological innovation. Because silicones are more costly than are more common organic materials, they seldom replace another material completely. Instead they are substituted in only the most demanding applications. The result is a market scope comprised of a very large number of relatively small applications. This situation, coupled with our willingness to design a new product for each new application, led to a very large number of relatively small-volume products.

Throughout our history, our portfolio of strategic activities reflected our approach to growth. Research, product development, and market development effort was spread over a very large number of relatively small projects. We wanted to pursue every possible application for silicones, but the list of possibilities was virtually endless. This approach to growth was really just a continuation of what had been successful in the past, and it persisted through all the changes in organizational structure and planning systems.

In the early 1970s, Dow-Corning's top management became concerned that this approach would not be as successful in the future as it had been in the past. There were several reasons for this concern. In the 1950s and 1960s we had been especially successful developing new silicone applications in the defense/aerospace industries, but it was clear these industries would provide less growth potential in the future. In consumer and industrial applications, the most significant limitation to wider use of silicones was their high cost. But, to minimize costs, we needed highly automated, continuous production processes making high-volume products. Also, increasing government regulation and competitive pressure were greatly increasing the costs of introducing a new product. It now required higher sales volume for a new product to pay back its development cost.

For these and other reasons, top management concluded that Dow-Corning must move to concentrate its product scope into fewer higher-volume products. This would have to be done over time by continual pressure to eliminate marginal products and by a restructuring of our strategic portfolio into fewer, more ambitious programs. A real change in strategic direction was considered essential if we were to maintain our competitive position and realize our full potential for future growth.

Interestingly, the perception of a need for strategic change was not widely held within the organization. The strategic plans being developed through the planning system looked much like they always had. Although there was a realization that growth seemed to be slipping and competitive pressures seemed to be increasing, there was a widespread belief that more of the same old medicine would cure these symptoms. Motivation and optimism about the future were high.

Although the Executive Committee, the top decision-making group in the company, was anxious to get on with restructuring the strategic portfolio, they realized that attitudes had to change too. We had to become much more selective about which potential opportunities we pursued. We had to demand more and better information about market need before committing R&D effort. We had to be willing to take a larger risk if we expected a larger payoff. Therefore, they decided not to restructure the strategic portfolio by executive fiat. Instead, they chose the more difficult route of building a perception of need within the organization and encouraging middle management to initiate the restructuring. The strategic changes would be made through the planning system operating in a normal mode.

The Executive Committee approached this problem from a number of directions. First, the point was made repeatedly throughout the organization that strategic redirection was needed. Any time top executives gave talks to meetings, this point was made. No specific new course was suggested, but there was great emphasis on the need for more concentration of strategic effort in a business environment that was more competitive and more demanding. While the message sounded somewhat vague, it began to force home the idea that change was necessary.

In view of the highly optimistic sales and profit growth forecasts, the strategic programs of the business were subjected to increasingly more critical review. Throughout the planning process, the Executive Committee challenged the businesses' growth forecasts and demanded considerably more external evidence and documentation. The message was received quickly, and soon the businesses began to question the potential of some of their own pet programs.

The R&D function had to play a pivotal role in strategic redirection. Although not all strategic spending is located in R&D, the activities of this function are the driving force for strategic change at Dow-Corning. The vice president for R&D as a member of the Executive Committee was quick to recognize the need for strategic change. However, he was also sensitive to the problems of unilateral action in a matrix organization. He was determined to protect the matrix relationship of his department heads and use it to advantage in reallocating effort.

He started by establishing functional guidelines describing how allocation decisions for R&D effort would be made. He worked hard to gain acceptance of these guidelines not only in his own function but among business managers as well. He then began systematically evaluating proposals relative to the guidelines as a regular part of the functional planning process. While there was still room for negotiation in determining the final program portfolio, the guidelines showed clearly the direction in which he wanted to move. Soon he was able to get program proposals from the businesses moving in the direction he wanted without specifically directing how programs would be changed.

During this period the Executive Committee also established a more aggressive opportunity identification activity. This activity was organized as a separate business and was charged with seeking opportunities that exploited existing Dow-Corning capabilities but fell outside the scope of the existing businesses. This group was given the responsibility of managing major strategic programs that fell outside existing businesses, and soon they had substantial programs taking us in entirely new directions.

Finally, the Executive Committee as a group became more directly involved in the process of allocating strategic resources. Previously, they allocated resources to function and to business and then relied on the matrix to determine allocation to specific projects. Now they began reviewing a selected list of programs quarterly. Although the total list of programs was too large for the Executive Committee to review every one, they became better informed about the major programs. They now review funding of major programs as a part of the planning process and are contributing directly to reshaping the portfolio.

Although it has taken several years, we are now satisfied that the strategic redirection we needed is being accomplished. Whereas our sales have doubled in the last five years, we have about 25 percent fewer products in the line. We have a higher concentration of strategic effort in major programs, and we believe that they are well defined, well managed, and realistic.

We have healthy competition for strategic resources, a good understanding of how resources are allocated, and a feeling of participation in the process. Some of our new programs have required that we acquire capabilities from the outside—both experienced people and entire companies. Although this is very unusual for Dow-Corning, it has been accomplished with a minimum of disruption. In summary, we are pleased with our progress.

CONCLUSIONS

Some concluding observations based on the experience described are now presented.

1. The matrix organization is uniquely suited to managing a group of activities that is extremely diverse and highly interrelated. However, this structure is complex, difficult to administer, and psychologically demanding. The matrix should probably be used only in situations in which a more conventional structure either cannot fulfill future needs or is in irreconcilable current difficulty.

2. The matrix must have strong, centrally controlled support systems. This structure requires that vast amounts of information be passed among the various elements of the organization. It also involves complex interrelationships among various elements of the organization. Well-defined corporate systems are required to be sure these things are done in an appropriate and uniform way. The planning system is a prime example of such a support system.

3. Planning in a matrix organization works best when management is responding to proposals developed within the organization. The complexities of the organization require considerable communication, dialogue, and reconciliation of differences for a strategic proposal to develop the kind of support you want it to have. It is difficult to fit a top–down initiative into a matrix structure.

4. It is not likely that a major strategic redirection will be proposed from within a matrix. The internal pressure is overwhelming to continue with any course of action that has developed substantial momentum. Top management must, therefore, recognize its responsibility to initiate important changes in strategic direction. The planning system should help management to exercise this responsibility.

5. The implementation of a major strategic change is more complex in a matrix organization than in a more traditional structure. This not only requires that initiatives from the top be translated into specific programs within the organization. It also requires that these revised programs be reconciled with, and integrated into, all plans down through the organization. This reconciliation process requires careful attention and considerable patience on the part of top management.

6. The strategic planning sytem should provide the basic vehicle for implementation of strategic redirection. However, this is likely to provide a severe test not only for the planning system but also for the management system of which it is a part. Top management will be sorely tempted to bypass both the planning system and the matrix and initiate new strategic programs directly. But with flexible and innovative approaches this temptation can be overcome. By sticking with the basic principles of matrix management, the result can be not only better strategic programs but better commitment throughout the organization to make them succeed.

section four

Conclusion

chapter fourteen: Where do we go from here: Implementation Challenges for the 1980s.

14

Where Do We Go from Here: Implementation Challenges for the 1980s

INTRODUCTION*

When discussing with executives what they see today as their major strategic challenges, as contrasted to those of a few years ago, one invariably is struck by the increased emphasis on the environment. Concern, to some extent, seems to be connected with the perception among managers that the environment seems to be becoming increasingly turbulent, complex, and interdependent. Further, it seems to be a widely shared opinion that the firm's strategic planning processes should be adapted to this evolving environmental situation in such ways that specific help can be offered to management to better cope with these challenges. If not able to prove its usefulness in such turbulent circumstances, formal strategic planning as we know it is dead.

Throughout this book we have seen indications of how strategic planning might look in the future. It serves little purpose to repeat these discussions. It is, however, appropriate to synthesize what might be some major aspects of a likely overall view of the shape of planning to come. In doing this, we shall emphasize some prospective major environmental trends that may suggest ways in which strategic planning may enable the corporation to interact successfully with such trends. Through planning, the firm can impact its own evolution with, it is hoped, more control. Above all, we shall look at some specific aspects of the design and

---

*This chapter is prepared by Peter Lorange, The Wharton School, University of Pennsylvania.

implementation of strategic planning processes that particularly seem to require strengthening under such expected circumstances.

Taken together, these aspects of design and implementation lead us to a concept of more dynamically evolving strategic planning. The task of being able to manage this process explicitly will probably become increasingly important for the corporation that intends to succeed in the future.

If one adopts a passive attitude toward the increasingly complex and frequently hostile environmental trends, the conclusions drawn might lead to the belief that one's own organization has a small chance at survival. But such passive observations of the environment imply acceptance that there is next to nothing that can be done about these trends—an unacceptable outlook to many corporations. As with most other living systems, a healthy corporation typically reflects a strong drive toward continuity, self-renewal, and survival. It is within such a context that we discuss planning's roles.

To protect its future, the firm must be prepared increasingly to respond actively to those developments in its environment that might create new opportunities and/or lessen potential negative impacts. Our major premise in this chapter is that a corporation's strategic planning system can in fact enable more effective interaction with the environment. We claim that properly designed strategic planning can help to create new viable alternatives, facilitate choices with respect to what seem to be more preferable developments in the environment, and assist in making this future happen. As Eric Trist has stated,[1]

> In fact, there is no such thing as the future, only futures. Which of the possibilities will be realized depends not a little on the choices we make—which in turn depend on our values—and also on our taking an active rather than a passive role. The paradox is that under conditions of uncertainty one has to make choices, and then endeavor actively to make these choices happen rather than leave things alone in the hope that they will arrange themselves for the best.

Of the many potential aspects for design and implementation of a corporation's planning system, we focus on four broad issues that we believe merit particular attention:

1. the redefinition of business
2. the emergence of an overall consistent strategic system
3. the positions to take vis-à-vis emerging external constraints
4. the handling of internal constraints

The following pages contain brief discussions of each of these issues. When these arguments are taken together, we shall see how a dynamically evolving strategic process concept emerges.

THE REDEFINITION OF BUSINESS

A major step in the progress of effective strategic planning has been the increased understanding of how to define a business. Particularly, the realities of the environment are now reflected better in our definition. Increasingly, the inadequacies of the business unit definition being dictated by past relations and political considerations within the firm are being acknowledged. The development of a set of "building blocks" for the firm that truly reflect the environment that the firm's businesses face is a major prerequisite for good planning.[2]

Rapid changes in the environment suggest that the definition of businesses should be reviewed frequently, so that the relevance of the business definitions can be maintained. It seems to be an increasingly important aspect of planning for the future to facilitate such a reassessment. This task is already being done in planning today. But it is done typically on an ad hoc basis and occurs frequently as the result of intervention from outside sources such as consultants. With an ability to undertake a more continuous redefinition of one's businesses, it seems appropriate to include that as an integral part of "normal" ongoing planning activities.

On the other hand, more continuous redefinition of businesses might lead to other difficulties and challenges, for instance, with another environmental trend. One such trend has to do with the development of the organization's acceptance of its tasks and the institutionalization of its roles. It seems to become increasingly difficult to reorganize in many of today's societies due to, among other things, the inability to relocate people with ease, to close down plants, to fire employees, or to change people's jobs. Legislation that restricts flexibility in job tasks is indeed growing. Moreover, acceptance among employees of rapid changes, job rotations, and moving of families is diminishing. These constraints obviously affect management's ability to reorganize a company to better reflect emerging business environments. We have a dilemma: On the one hand, there is a need for more rapid business redefinition; on the other hand, there is less opportunity for reorganization.

Planning should be able to point toward a way to approach this issue. One possibility is through increased use of dual organizational structures and strategic structures, as this will reflect the need to redefine the businesses and develop an operating structure that might remain more stable. The critical "linking pin" between the two coexisting structures becomes the planning process.

Although various "matrix structures" have been around for some time, evolutionary factors will probably cause the strategic structure to become more tailored within the company so as to reflect particular businesses. For instance, a typical project organization might be most appropriate for coping with a start-up business. But, as the business develops, it may become more advantageous for the business to integrate increasingly into the existing organization through a more full-fledged matrix structure. Then, as the business matures further, a more functional, efficiency-driven organization might become more appropriate. Thus, within the "umbrella" of the operating structure, one should find different types of "quasi-matrix" strategic organizations, overlaying the operating structure, and some evolving more rapidly than others.[3]

The rate of change in technology, impacting both the product life cycle as well as the environment, will probably increasingly become a distinguishing factor among the planning processes in different companies. With a relatively short life cycle and rapid environmental change in general, one will probably see a close overlay of the strategic and operating structures with the result that executives will have responsibility within both structures. On the other hand, with relatively more stable environments coupled with longer product life cycles, one might expect executives to be assigned responsibilities to tasks within the operating or the strategic modes on a more unilateral basis.

We may increasingly see a call for a different type of attitude among the executives, in terms of flexibility, willingness to maintain a sense of continuing education, development, and so on. We shall discuss this later in the chapter as part of the internal constraint issues. Also, this type of dual structure—in part evolving rapidly, in part remaining stable—calls for management support systems of a different degree of sophistication. For instance, more flexible management information systems, tailor-made incentives, a well-developed control system, and so on will have to be implemented. We shall discuss these issues in the next section.

THE EMERGENCE OF AN OVERALL
CONSISTENT STRATEGIC SYSTEM

With the pressures for a strategic management approach as a vehicle for adapting to environmental opportunities and threats, it is becoming important to see planning in a broader context for at least two reasons. First, it seems increasingly necessary to make use of a broad, relatively all-encompassing set of strategic processes to develop an overall "tool" to facilitate the organization's ability to adapt as necessary. For this task, corporate management needs a set of tools with which to impact the organization through indirect pressures and stimuli. In this way management can attempt to instill behaviors within the parts of the organization that may encourage a tailor-made coping with the environmental realities that each of its businesses faces. Global, sweeping management system responses, on the other hand, are likely to become less and less effective. Consequently, a multifaceted strategic system—where a tailor-made planning process for each of a firm's businesses can be reinforced by effects from the control system, management incentives, and so on—might increasingly be called for.[4]

Second, the various processes and systems within the company that have evolved over time and have been created as responses to particular pressures and needs might increasingly have unintended counterbalancing effects on each other. For instance, whereas the planning process might attempt to facilitate a more open, adaptive, long-term perspective within the businesses, the control system might act as a constraint through its emphasis on short-term performance. With the inevitably increasing abundance and complexity of formalized systems and processes within the modern corporation, the likelihood of dysfunctional counteractive effects might increase. Again, an overall coordinated viewpoint of the various systems that can be seen to constitute the strategic processes seems called for.

Which major management systems constitute such a strategic process? In addition to the planning process more narrowly defined, these might be listed as follows:

1. the control processes (more broadly labeled "strategic control" and "operating control")
2. the management information systems
3. managerial incentives
4. organizational climate, that is, style and autonomy associated with organizational forms within the broader organization itself
5. managing the strategic process

Let us discuss each of these in more detail, with the emphasis on how to see them as aspects of an overall emerging strategic system. Let us also finally discuss how this requires the systems to be managed in a coordinated fashion so as to prove effective.

The Control Processes

The control system may be the most obvious candidate for coordination with the planning system, not only so as to avoid acting contrary to plans but so as to reinforce the strategic behavior intended for each business.[5] This means that performance will need to be measured not solely along the more traditional dimensions such as profits, costs, and return on investment, all of which tend to reinforce relatively short-term performance optimization. There will be a definite need to coordinate short-term measures with strategic performance measures, such as changes in market share, changes in growth, changes in critical environmental assumptions, and so on. Performance will have to be interpreted as having two sides, that is, as having a long-term versus a short-term trade-off. The issue is *not* whether one makes a high profit per se but rather, whether the short-term performance component (high profits) is achieved with an accompanying strategic component that is reasonable and in line with a firm's intentions. A first requirement to the control process appears to be the development of multidimensional performance criteria for measuring both strategic and operating performance. But how can such measures be operationalized (i.e., being both relatively objective and relevant)? How can we develop ways of reconciling long-term and short-term performance measures so that they can be interpreted together? Who should administer this measurement process? The controller? The planner and the controller together? If so, how should the tasks be divided?

The strategic control process will also have to be tailored to the particular strategy of each business. One can therefore expect a stronger role for line management close to a particular business strategy to develop the strategic aspects of the control process. This would complement the more standardized corporatewide control procedures administered by the controller's office. This does not mean that the controller's role will disappear. It merely means that the controller needs to cooperate with the custodians of the other strategic systems so as to make sure that the control system can be tailored as discussed.

How can such a practical interaction develop between the line and the controller? Can the planner play a role relatively similar to that of the corporate planner when it comes to strategic control (i.e., a catalyst), while still maintaining an effective job in his or her more classical management control tasks? When it comes to the tailoring the control process to each business, this seems in particular to require a different trade-off between the strategic control and the management control balance in each instance. How should this be done in practice?

Management Information Systems

The management information systems will also need to be coordinated with the rest of the strategic processes in a careful and consistent manner.[6] With the advent of strategic control, coupled with the need to frequently redefine what constitutes the strategic business element dimension, a flexible management information system is necessary to avoid chaos. Thus, the information must be available in such a way so as to allow businesses to be redefined and data recut, reassembled, and so on.

The requirement to the design of the management information system calls for more careful attention to definitions; ability to aggregate and disaggregate among product lines, business elements, and business families; and attention to recreating historical trends for newly defined businesses so as to have comparability over time. Can this be done? How can we ensure management information system capabilities do not become bottlenecks in strategic management?

Another aspect of the role of the management information system will be to provide more meaningful data displays so that the system can evolve into a "decision support system." How can this facilitate the interactive communication process that planning is? Can time in review meetings be spent more effectively? Can line managers "expand" their cognitive limitations to deal with several interacting variables, as seems to become the case when control tasks are involved?

Managerial Incentives

Management incentives systems will also have to be coordinated carefully with the rest of the strategic processes, so as to reinforce the kinds of strategic behaviors that are being sought. Partly, this aim might be achieved by developing performance measures that more appropriately reflect an individual's contribution to both strategic and operating success. Without such "personal control yardsticks" highlighting the contribution of each individual manager relative to some explicit strategy-driven expectations, it is difficult to see how an incentives process might reinforce desired strategic behavior.[7]

Such an individual yardstick of control must of course be consistent with the overall strategic and operating control system typically deriving its information from these institutionalized systems. Particularly, it seems critical that individual control should focus on the trade-off between strategic performance and operating performance, so as to lessen a manager's typical ambivalence in these respects. Under today's circumstances, pursuance of operating goals counts more heavily. Lack of strategic performance, on the other hand, can often be tolerated as long as operating expectations are being met. To operationalize these issues, how do we create "personal control yardsticks" that are tied to the overall control processes? How can the strategic versus operating trade-off be handled?

Another aspect of incentives deals with the form of the incentives package itself, which now includes bonuses, salary increases, and other mechanisms that might be relatively less important due to taxes, level of affluence, and so on. Other factors such as those tied to job promotions, job rotations, degree of autonomy, job redefinition, and so on should become an increasing part of the process. How can the concept of a more flexible incentives package be introduced?

With the slowing of growth in many companies, management is often restricted in its use of promotions as an incentive. As the hierarchical organizational pyramid fills up, care should be taken not to "stagger" the organizational pyramid with extensive new layers of managers, thereby creating inefficiencies and bureaucracy. Here, particularly, the effects of creating more meaningful jobs through "opening up" the strategic structure dimension might play a role, assigning managers to strategic task forces, creating responsibilities for strategy fulfillment in addition to operating jobs, and so on. The incentive system should probably increasingly be seen in such a light. The overall challenge and meaningfulness of managerial jobs will likely become an incentive. This again fundamentally calls for an opening up of the strategic processes (i.e., a more participative strategic involvement than has been in the past). To operationalize incentive effects of these kinds, explicit cooperation must exist among the function managing the incentives, those dealing with job assignments, and the corporate planners. How can this be done?

Organizational Climate

Let us now touch briefly on the style and autonomy within parts of the organization. As was noted, it seems important that the organizational form be tailored within the company as it relates to the strategic dimension, so that autonomy can be provided where necessary to pursue new growth and new business development. One should not be "drowned" by mature, existing, well-established styles and procedures in such instances. Thus, organizational design should become more flexible and be tailored to the particular business needs at hand. However, the operating dimension will typically remain quite stable. The issue of providing strategic autonomy while creating unambiguous links with the operating structure will become increasingly important. Organizational flexibility should not mean organizational chaos. How can we develop an organizational climate that permits the flexibility necessary for change? What can be done to evolve an organization's understanding that strategic flexibility will have to be achieved in parallel with operating stability? Which are the implications in terms of systematized learning activities? How can the evolution of organizational climate become more consistent with the needs of the strategic reality?

Managing the Strategic Process

At least two major questions will probably become increasingly articulated when describing the task of managing the strategic processes. These will probably be a growing part of the jobs of the strategic process custodian of the future (we shall not call that person the planner even though it may very well be that planners will become the administrators of the overall system).[8]

First, the effectiveness of the strategic system will depend to a large extent on how well the system is able to meet the needs of the various businesses in terms of supporting their strategies. This means that the strategic system must increasingly maintain the capability of allowing for tailoring within the company. As such, overall global systems will become less and less useful. This will happen unless capabilities can be developed within the overall system to address the needs of each business, while of course maintaining some overall coordination and consistency. Has such a process already started? If so, what factors are we using in our tailoring?

Another potentially critical management issue deals with the evolution of the strategic system over time. Given that the needs of businesses will change, it seems increasingly important that the strategic processes are managed so that such needs can be maintained over time. Otherwise, they may become less and less relevant. With the evolutionary pressures on the strategic processes, the overall consistency among the elements of the process also needs careful tending. Evolution as well as maintenance of consistency seem to be increasingly important management tasks. Are we modifying and updating our processes sufficiently today?

Who might be expected to manage the emerging strategic system? Who picks up this job, be it the existing controller, the planner, or someone else, is not all that relevant. The issue is that some form of closer overall organizational linkage seems to be required among the custodians of the present subsystems or elements in the strategic process. To achieve this, it will probably become increasingly common that a senior staff officer will be responsible for control, planning, management information systems, incentives, and organizational issues. Unless such close organizational linkage is attained, it seems unlikely that the strategic process can emerge sufficiently free of inconsistencies and fragments that will allow it to become a tool that can be managed explicitly.

A second requirement in this process of managing the strategic systems is the close relationship that needs to be developed among the strategic tasks. The strategic processes can be developed and evolved so as to reinforce the strategies that senior management intends to pursue only if the staff custodians of the processes have exceedingly strong insights into these strategic thrusts. Thus, the staff's task of managing the processes will probably evolve as part of senior management's task. The staff executive will have to work closely with senior line management. How is the role of the planner evolving as of today relative to senior line management? How does it evolve relative to other staffs such as the controller, the management information system function, personnel?

ENVIRONMENTAL CONSTRAINTS

We have seen the importance of the environment as impacting the strategic planning task, and we have determined how a realistic assessment of the environment provides the focal point for the articulation of strategy and the attempts to implement it. For instance, we raised the issue of strengthening the planning process so as to be better able to pursue business opportunities and/or avoid the threats. This calls for taking environmental considerations into account with respect to such diverse issues as better understanding of shifts in the marketplace, of emergence of new products from technological developments, of impacts of economic factors and cycles on one's business, and of anticipation and counteraction of competitive moves. This section discusses challenges to the strengthening of the planning system.

A number of analytical efforts have been made to capture what seems to be the thrust of key environmental trends, both from disciplinary points of view, such as political, economic, demographic, and ecologic, as well as from a cross-disciplinary standpoint, such as scenario analyses, futurism, and so on.[9] Although discussions of such trends might be highly interesting on their own, our purpose is to examine potential impacts on planning.

In this connection, let us consider five major environmental trends to see what types of changes in planning tasks these might call for:

1. scarcity
2. politics
3. attitudes
4. power shifts
5. technology

These five environmental issues do not, of course, represent an exhaustive listing. While they may not even be the most important ones, they still seem significant and quite uncontroversial.

Scarcity

One environmental trend seems to be a rising shortage of natural resources, such as energy, food, metals, water, or clean air. The shortage in physical terms will, of course, mean a relatively stronger increase in de facto costs of the raw materials. Presumably, we can expect this trend to continue. To anticipate its consequences is to be able to cope.

At least two basic attempts should be made to strengthen planning efforts accordingly. First is setting priorities that emphasize businesses that can make efficient use of the scarce resources and developing businesses that are not exposed too negatively to the increased de facto prices of raw materials with an ultimate deterioration of profits. Facilitating these choices may call for a sharper business unit segmentation, a more explicit assessment of the overall portfolio patterns of the firm, and changes in overall risk exposure due to acceleration of such scarcity trends.

Second is spotting supply deficiencies and seeking out alternative sources to fill such shortfalls. Technological scanning of new raw material-saving developments should be undertaken. In total, the planning process might help the corporation to deal with scarcity by creating alternative responses to shortages.

Politics

Let us now turn to environmental changes related to the evolving world wide political situation. As always, economic conditions are changing rapidly, with growth in some countries and stagnation in others. Similarly, political conditions are changing, some countries becoming less stable, others more so. Legal and attitudinal trends change vis-à-vis various businesses, typically according to an irregular global pattern. In total, the overabundance of changes in the international order might call for particular strategic planning process responses for planning to remain effective.

What consequences might these types of factors have for the design of effective planning systems? Development of procedures that would permit realism with respect to essential emerging environmental issues (i.e., a strengthened corporate intelligence service) might provide impetus for developing a consistent approach for handling these issues. Unless an overall realistic picture regarding environmental constraints is developed, the danger of sequential atetntion to such issues exists, and a strategy of "giving in" versus "picking a fight" on the wrong issues may emerge. Does the planning process assess the priorities of issues accurately?

A second, related requirement calls for the gathering of information regarding positions of one's supporters and one's adversaries. While such information typically cannot be gathered by direct interaction with the various interested parties alone, it might still be possible to improve one's insights regarding others' positions through systematic analysis and interpretation of these efforts over time. To what extent do present planning approaches incorporate such key external stakeholder analysis? In general, what seems to be called for is a more effective interaction between the firm and the major constituents in its environment: the government, labor unions, consumer activists, and so on. To what extent does one's planning process facilitate this?

Attitudes

Let us now turn to a third evolutionary issue in the environment, namely, effects from changing values among consumers, unions, political constituencies, and so on. One attitudinal issue relates to the importance of growth. Increasingly, it seems that growth per se is being challenged and that no-growth situations are becoming accepted as the norm. Further, the traditional authority of organizations to expect strong individual performance and job commitment is under question. How does planning respond to such attitudinal trends to remain useful and effective?

An undifferentiated view that no-growth is normal and acceptable might, of course, strain a firm's ability to provide for its own self-renewal and evolution. It might increase the likelihood of a corporation's eventual demise. Thus, it seems particularly important that the planning process provide some counterbalancing pressure for self-renewal, say, by stimulating segmented growth opportunities within the firm. How does the planning process create such a felt responsibility and pressure for self-renewal within segments of a company? How can a business family that is basically quite mature be helped to pursue potential growth opportunities that might still exist?

It is also important that management feel a sense of "ownership" of the strategic direction of their firm. Otherwise, the authority of senior management might increasingly come under attack, and indifference rather than commitment might become widespread. Planning must provide some "rules" and set some "binding" agreement between senior management and management throughout the organization. The planning process should provide each manager with the "protection" needed to bring out and discuss differing views on strategic direction. In line with this, the role of meaningful feedback by senior management might become increasingly critical. In practice, however, to what extent do our planning processes seem to foster added organizational commitment and strategic understanding?

Power Shifts

A fourth environmental trend deals with changing roles of institutions in society. Interests are changing; pressures on the corporation from outside interest groups are consequently in flux. Strategic planning might be able to make these types of environmental constraints more explicit as part of the planning process. This in turn might engender more in-depth analysis and monitoring of these factors. To what extent, however, are such environmental interest group factors being assessed relative to our own strategies? When is it necessary to monitor such factors and how is it done?

Another requirement for handling emerging environmental constraints seems to be an increased emphasis on corporate portfolio flexibility, for instance, preserving the ability to reassess the priority of certain businesses and/or geographic areas relative to others. This permits deemphasizing highly exposed and visible businesses and areas and developing businesses and areas that are less volatile. Thus, it seems critical to develop a selected approach of interacting with and responding to interest groups to preserve and modify a set of mutually acceptable business strategies, coupled with an overall portfolio view. This would also facilitate provisions for selective challenges of critical environmental issues relative to business as well as provide indications of when to deemphasize a business and/or a country instead. The planning system should help to highlight "where to fight and where to give." To what extent, however, do present planning approaches provide a vehicle for consistent overall assessments regarding the dealing with outside interest groups or within the context of our business strategy–portfolio strategy tasks?

Technology

A final environmental issue deals with the evolving role of science and technology. We can, of course, expect technology to develop at the same or at a higher rate as in the past so that the product life-cycle concept of providing evolutionary pressure on strategic positions will continue to play a key role. Business segmentation may more routinely have to be redefined, driven by changes in the know-hows we are depending on. This is in addition to the traditional product–market considerations per se. It is, in this respect, critically important to develop know-hows that are tailored to a particular business so as to create a realistic climate of specialization and competition advantage.

A consequence of the planning system will be an increasing need to see one's know-how pool as *the* strategic resource, which may have to be "allocated" more in a portfolio mode throughout the company. Strategic planning should increasingly be expected to facilitate the transfer of know-hows within the company in a way analogous with the transfer of funds in today's typical planning processes. How can this be done in practice? What procedural moves will be called for? What will be some of the human constraints? What aspects of know-hows might be transferable from a mature, cash cow business setting to a new-business, start-up setting?

These are examples of ways in which the strategic planning process might increasingly serve as a tool in interacting with and responding to environmental trends. We can expect the planning process to increasingly help the firm to create its own future, not passively accept environmental developments. We can certainly conclude that there seems to be increasing demands on strategic planning to play an active role in improving the integration of the environment and the firm's decision-making path.

INTERNAL CONSTRAINTS

Let us now turn to a fourth set of issues that will likely shape the requirements of strategic planning, namely, how to cope with emerging constraints that might be expected to develop within the firm itself and might affect planning. The challenge here will be to come up with a planning approach that allows management to at least ameliorate dysfunctional effects from such internal constraints that might develop. Some of the issues raised here have been touched upon already; nevertheless, it is useful to make an overall summary of these issues. Emerging internal constraints and handicaps created by the organization itself may increasingly become barriers to effective strategic management. It is indeed puzzling that such self-inflicted handicaps are frequently so dominant.[10]

Flexibility in Organization Style

The first set of issues deals with the need to develop an organizational style that is sufficiently flexible so as to allow the organization to adapt to new opportunities yet maintain a sense of operating stability and continuity. In this sense, it seems important that organization members get on-the-job experience as well as training in working as teams. What is the role of career planning? How should people be sensitized to issues such as communication, listening, and small-group behavior, for example? Basic training on the job as well as through course preparation in being better able to work in ad hoc cross-functional task situations seems essential.

Similarly, avoidance of building up of overly strong "functional kingdoms" (i.e., organizational units that do not communicate easily with each other) seems to be a problem. We want to develop strong functional levels of specialized competences, but responsibility has to exceed strict authority. How is this done?

How should the planning system be structured to maintain organizational flexibility and be willing to take responsibility beyond a narrow functional authority? At least two design issues might be relevant. First, it seems important to have a relatively large number of members of the organization work on task force teams. Such teams are typically created to carry out strategic programs. Memberships on these teams might well be in addition to the ongoing operational job. How should the selection of a larger group of executives to take part in planning tasks be carried out in practice? How can the "best" people be taken away from operations? How do we avoid having the same people do everything? The strategic program will be faced with the issue of control (i.e., monitoring of progress, etc.). Further, managerial incentives might be based on program fulfillment performance in addition to ordinary operating performance. Thus, a de facto "two-hat" responsibility and sensitivity might be created. What steps might be taken to institutionalize such dual responsibility?

A related design issue deals with the formulation of the strategic programs themselves. It seems important that, when such programs are being formulated, they should be "owned" by teams of executives, typically from various functions, so as to allow for maintenance of cross-functional creativity. Further reinforcement comes when a division or a business is presenting its plans. Major strategic programs might then allow the program to do the presentation, thereby giving a larger number of managers exposure to the top management, and vice versa. However, functional presentations should be deemphasized. In total, in development, presentation, and execution of strategic programs, strict functional involvement should be avoided and the cross-functional nature of these tasks should be emphasized. Such measures and others might contribute to more flexible behavior among a relatively large group of managers.

Executive Obsolescence

A second group of internal constraint issues relates to the danger of obsolescence among executives and the work force as a whole. Given the rapid environmental challenges projected, the capability for continuous accumulation of new knowledge and experiences within the firm and its businesses seems essential. Lack of relevant skills could become a true barrier. In fact, the human resources might increasingly be seen as depletable. What active measures, if any, can be initiated to counteract this depletion?

How can the planning process play a meaningful role in this respect? Should the planning process be seen as a learning process? This would probably imply that a plan should be interpreted as a basis for improvement, not as a "final" document to be accepted without additional consideration of improvements throughout the year. How can such attitudes be established more broadly throughout the company?

With the advent of more meaningful control processes and management incentive procedures, it might be more realistic to take advantage of the learning aspects of planning, to systematize experiences when unable to meet plans. A control attitude should, however, be avoided. How can a balance between learning and overly restricted control be reached? The planning process might, to some extent, be a self-adjusting process whereby the plan is seen as a standard and the control system feeds in information for continuous improvement of this standard. In this way, the planning process can be a true learning process.

Organizational linkages within the firm must be tailored in such a way that the learning can take place. If one group of executives develops the plans and another group of executives is concerned primarily with the control aspects, but there is little or no organizational linkage between the two groups, the learning procedure will be less effective. How can we develop meaningful organizational linkages so that information is interpreted in strategic *and* operating terms by the same executives?

An example might illustrate this dilemma. In one company management control is by worldwide country organizations. Some countries are in the process of being built up; other countries' markets are more mature. Having a control process based on each country makes it difficult to follow the strategic development of each business on a worldwide basis. As a consequence, country considerations leading toward short-term actions to improve country performance make it more difficult to develop new businesses and might even accelerate the obsolescence of certain businesses. By not seeing performance both in terms of shifts in strategic positions of one's worldwide businesses as well as in terms of changes in countries' operating performances, the performance picture is skewed.

Given that human capabilities and skills might increasingly be seen as *the* most important strategic resource and that it may become increasingly expensive and time consuming to assemble resource teams around a particular business that possesses the necessary competences and professionalism, to what extent should we attempt to generate new business opportunities around an executive team that is in charge of a business approaching maturity and might be phased out relatively soon? Can executive competence be equated with funds, that is, seen as a relative liquid resource? A competent management team could be used to search for a new business and create a new business opportunity around their executive skills, though this, of course, breaks with tradition. The advantage of seeing human competences as a transferable strategic resource seems to be that time and expenses in assembling a scarce resource might be cut down; the danger, however, might be that thinking could become unrealistic, even wishful, in terms of creating business opportunities for an existing organizational team.

One example of making the human resources more transferable involves the mining division of one company that was being scaled down while a mining engineering business of another was being developed. This provided a vehicle for maintaining a high level of competent mining engineers. Predictably, however, a major problem seems to be that good skills in mining to not necessarily transform that easily into good operational skills in mining engineering.

Segmented and Sequential Thinking: Parochialism

A third source of internal constraints has to do with an emergence of sequential thinking and parochialism within the firm. One example might be greater executive loyalty toward a particular plant location or country organization than to the overall company. The effect might jeopardize the ability for the company as a whole to develop portfolio strategies. How can the planning process cope with a potentially reduced acceptance of the need for flexibility and a portfolio approach? How should the planning process be designed to meet such challenges?

The corporate executive office will probably have to play a major role in strengthening the planning process to deal with portfolio acceptability issues. First, in reviewing business plans, a portfolio point of view must be followed strictly. Second, feedback to an individual business might be seen increasingly within a portfolio context (i.e., not as feedback that is inherently "right" or "wrong" but that makes sense as part of the fit of the particular business within the corporation). Third, corporate management might be increasingly aware of the dangers of ad hoc involvement in problem solving throughout the company. The overall portfolio interdependency issue might be lessened, which, in turn, might lead to behavior among businesses calling for adjustment in their business strategies and modification of their resource requirements and their intended creation of discretionary resources for the portfolio in such a way that these issues become decided on unilaterally, disregarding the dysfunctional and disturbing effects on the portfolio as a whole.

In total, it seems that corporate management will face a major burden in terms of developing a portfolio style for the company. It seems to be, to a large extent, a matter of developing a way of managing, an attitude, that reinforces the portfolio point of view. If the corporate management allows itself to assume the role of firefighter, then line management will not be able to adhere to the portfolio discipline within the various businesses. The question of how to develop a portfolio discipline is of course critical. What other measures are there to pursue this?

Values, Style, Tradition

To what extent do a company's style, traditions, and values become barriers to adapting to new business opportunities? On the one hand, the internal culture and style of a company can be a major asset in making strategies become implementable because of the ease of communication and of understanding issues given that everyone is coming from more or less the same background. A planning process based on a highly unique style, say, on strong technological tradition and success, might be tailored differently from a planning process within a company that has a more diverse set of styles to consider. The formality of the process, in particular, might be less when the style within the company is strong. However, style and values might cloud the true developments in the environment. Wishful thinking, commitment to particular technological approaches, sunken interests, and so on could handicap the redefinition of businesses, modification of objectives and strategic programs, and the development of new businesses. Particularly, it might become difficult to rechannel strategic resources and to make new priorities. This would be true even for a company that is relatively narrow in its overall portfolio, which is frequently the case when a high sense of common technological style is apparent.

Power as a Constraint

The issue of power within an organization does, of course, become critical in strategic resource allocation. If the power structure is so decentralized that it is difficult or impossible to carry out portfolio reallocation, the CEO is more or less unable to shift the direction of the portfolio. Instead, each element receives more or less the same resources it has received in the past or typically generates for itself. Within business families, too, power situations could prevent the development of new business. When functional executives are exceedingly strong and well established, they can make it very difficult to develop a meaningful strategic program.

The question of power seems to be a true issue in terms of effective planning. Unless the CEO is entrenched well enough to have the power to carry out a portfolio strategy, this form of planning will be seriously limited. Lack of power might be due to the fact that the CEO has a relatively short time left in office. Weak performance of the company over a relatively long period of time or particular decisions that have turned out badly may have undermined the CEO's power. Or top management is such that the CEO faces a large number of strong executives, not a coalition, and thus must handle the portfolio strategy on his or her own.

It seems highly important to have a group of executives at the top of the organization who can work together to develop a portfolio strategy. The same can probably be said for each of the business families and the businesses themselves. Strategy development and implementation require cooperation.

In total, we see that internal constraints due to (1) lack of flexibility, (2) lack of relevant competences, (3) loyalties to sectors within the company, (4) traditions and style, and (5) power balances can seriously jeopardize the corporation's ability to pursue opportunistic and active strategies. Modifications in the planning process to counteract such measures are therefore probably critical. Do we do a good job in seeing the planning system as a vehicle to break down internal barriers? A particular difficulty relates to the fact that we are dealing primarily with attitudinal changes, style issues, and learning issues that might require a particularly strong will, patience, and consistent behavior and commitment on the part of top management.

CONCLUDING REMARKS

In this chapter, we have seen aspects of what might become the shape of strategic planning in the future. Throughout we have seen that major challenges to planning are likely to stem from rapid environmental changes, discontinuities, crises, and other turbulent conditions. To remain useful, therefore, the planning process must show a strengthened ability to help management cope with developing strategies and implement their strategic decisions in such emerging environments. An internally driven planning process will in all likelihood become even more dysfunctional in the future.

Developments in the planning process that might be visible ten years hence stem from four areas. Some of the issues seem to point toward relatively explicit and straightforward modifications of our planning approaches; others constitute real challenges.

First, is the need to develop a strategic structure that lends itself to frequent redefinition of the strategic business entities yet allows for a workable linking with a more stable operational structure.

Second, is the need to tailor not only the planning process to the emerging needs of the various businesses but also to tailor all the strategic subsystems to the same businesses. We should also be able to maintain consistency among the various systems and processes for the purpose of evolving these in a coordinated manner. What we are seeing, in fact, is the emergence of an overall, integrated strategic system. We may find the terms "planning systems" and "planning processes" used less in the future.

Third, is the need to monitor the environmental constraints, through sharpened environmental scanning, through sharpened strategic control, through accepting the values of a broader set of interest groups in one's development work.

Fourth, is the need to develop a strategic style within the company that allows for dismantling such internal constraints as lack of flexibility and lack of effective competence building. The challenge to strategic planning over the next decade will certainly not be exclusively within the developments in processes and systems. Rather, the challenge facing our executives to modify their styles to make use of the emerging strategic process tools is particularly critical. Powerful planning approaches that are becoming available have already shown their usefulness and power. The challenge to excel through strategic management has certainly never been greater.

NOTES

[1]Eric Trist, "The Environment and System—Response Capability," *Futures*, (April 1980), p. 114.

[2]Derek F. Abell, *Defining the Business: The Starting Point of Strategic Planning* (Englewood Cliffs, N.J.: Prentice-Hall, 1980).

[3]Henry Mintzberg, *The Structuring of Organizations* (Englewood Cliffs, N.J.: Prentice-Hall, 1979).

[4]Carter F. Bales, Donald J. Gogel, and James S. Henry, "The Environment for Business in the 1980s," *The McKinsey Quarterly*, (Winter 1980), pp. 2–21, and Donald McLagan and Christopher Caton, "The 1980s: A Strategic Planner's Dilemma," in *U.S. Long-Term Review* (Lexington, Mass.: Data Resources, Inc., Spring 1980).

[5]Peter Lorange, *Corporate Planning: An Executive Viewpoint* (Englewood Cliffs, N.J.: Prentice-Hall, 1980).

[6]See, for example, Peter G. W. Keen and Michael S. Scott-Morton, *Decision Support Systems: An Organizational Perspective* (Reading, Mass.: Addison-Wesley, 1978).

[7]See, for example, Peter Lorange, *Corporate Planning: An Executive Viewpoint, op. cit.*

[8]Charles W. Hofer and Dan E. Schendel, eds., *Strategic Management* (Boston: Little, Brown, 1979); George A. Steiner, *Strategic Planning: What Every Manager Must Know* (New York: Free Press, 1979); and Peter Lorange, *Corporate Planning: An Executive Viewpoint, op. cit.*

[9]See, for example, Herman Kahn, Leon C. Martel, and William Brown, *The Next 200 Years* (New York: Morrow, 1976); Donald Schon, *Beyond the Stable State* (New York: Basic Books, 1971); Jan Tinbergen, *Rio: Reshaping the International Order* (New York: Dutton, 1976); American Assembly of Collegiate Schools of Business and the European Foundation for Management Development, *Management in the 21st Century* (Harrison, N.Y.: Arden House, 1979); Donella H. Meadows et al., *The Limits to Growth* (New York: Universe Books, 1972); E. P. Schumacher, *Small Is Beautiful* (London: Blond and Briggs, 1973); Peter Hall, *Europe 2000* (London: Gerald Duckworth & Co., 1977); or, for a critical discussion of "futurology" and the undifferentiated assumption of limits to growth, see Seymour M. Lipset, "Futurology," *Across the Board*, Vol. XVII Nos. 3 & 4 (March–April 1980), pp. 17–26 and pp. 28–37.

[10]See, for example, Duane S. Elgin and Robert A. Bushnell, "The Limits to Complexity: Are Bureaucracies Becoming Unmanageable?" *The Futurist*, (December 1977).

Indexes